THE PALACE DIARIES

The True Story of
Life at the Palace
by Prince Charles' Secretary

'*The lights come on. I blink and realise I am alone in Charles's private quarters at Sandringham. The last thing I remember was watching a film at his side. It was magical. Then it dawned on me. I - a mere Royal secretary - must have dozed off on the sofa next to his Royal Gorgeousness. I'm in disgrace. How did that happen? My inner nanny - the stern sensible voice in my head - answers the question. You fell asleep through a combination of the following: Charles's ultra-stiff gin and tonic and tiredness stemming from your insatiable demands the previous night on one of the Royal chefs.*'

THE PALACE DIARIES
Charles, Camilla & Me

Born in 1964, Sarah Goodall was raised in rural Shropshire. In 1988 she was employed as a Lady Clerk at St James's Palace. In 1999, the year before she left the Palace, she was appointed a Member of the Royal Victorian Order. She lives in London.

She has allowed the distinguished writer Nicholas Monson to interpret her astonishing true story in a frank and lively manner. Is it her fault she falls in love with HRH the Prince of Wales? Think Bridget Jones and Sex in the City, and throw in Royal intrigue set amongst the backdrop of Royal Palaces and the upper levels of British Society.

Nicholas Monson was born in 1955. Author of *The Nouveaux Pauvres*, a book about the turning fortunes of British Royalty and the Upper Classes. He has written for *Tatler* and *Harpers & Queen*, *Vogue Homme*, and many British newspapers, including the *Sunday Telegraph* and the *Daily Mail*. He lives in London.

As the inheritor of an ancient barony, Nicholas, the future 12th Lord Monson, is unfazed by the grandeur of the Royal family, an attitude which gives his prose a fizzing irreverence. He writes about Her Majesty the Queen, assorted Princes, Dukes and Duchesses with affection as if he is one of them which, as a direct descendant of King Edward 1st, actually he is. Camilla is his cousin via their mutual ancestor Sir Thomas Monson of South Carlton, Lincolnshire, where his family still live.

Nicholas is also half-American. One direct relative is General Roy Stone, a hero of the American Civil War. Another is Colonel William Alexander Powell, the author, international journalist and documentary film-maker for Samuel Goldwyn.

Sarah Goodall
& *Nicholas Monson*

THE PALACE DIARIES

The True Story of
Life at the Palace
by Prince Charles' Secretary

Dynasty
Press

First published in the United States in 2008 by
DYNASTY PRESS LIMITED
36 Ravensdon Street
London SE11 4AR
United Kingdom

ISBN: 978-0-9553507-1-9

A catalogue record for this book is
available from the Library of Congress

Typeset in Times New Roman
Printed & bound in Canada

This book is primarily an account based on the
life, experiences and recollections of Sarah Goodall
while employed by HRH the Prince of Wales.
In some cases, names of people, places, dates, sequences or
the details of events have been changed for literary
purposes and to protect the privacy of others.

*To my mother, and those friends at
the Palace who helped me through the
darker days (you know who you are)*

The book has been a huge success in Europe, selling over 100,000 copies. Translations from English include German, Dutch, French, Italian, Swedish, Finnish and Romanian. Rights have also now been sold to Russia, Latvia and Estonia. The British BBC have produced it as a talking book. The film rights have been bought.

Acknowledgements

The Palace Diaries was written during a difficult time for both authors and would not have happened without the support of a score of people. For their generous financial and moral support, the authors thank Amanda Harling, Christopher Stewart-Moore, John Brennan, Rupert Lewin, Nanzee Soin, John Wellington and Isabelle Gillard. For their time and their generosity in sharing their Royal knowledge, the authors thank Susan Clark, Christopher Wilson, Adam Helliker and Lady Colin Campbell. For his assistance on pay roll calculations, the authors thank Martin Levin, and for his help in Paris, Anthony Peto. For their diligence in the editing process, the authors thank Ailsa Bathgate, Deborah Warner and Charlotte Pike. For his patience and advice, the authors thank their agent Peter Cox. For their hospitality, friendship and many kindnesses in South Africa, where the book was completed, the authors thank Charles and Lilian Loys Ellis, Stephen Morris, Ronel Openshaw, Noel and Beth Hunt, Karen Durney, Lawrence McDowell, Richard Procter-Sims and Albert, who looked after us so well.

Contents

Forgive and Forget

November 2005

His Royal Highness the Prince of Wales, wearing a rather becoming Nehru jacket, is greeting me right now. I curtsey. He asks what I want to drink. As if he needs to ask. It is always the same. He proceeds to pour me an extremely stiff gin and tonic and hands it to me. I gaze into his radiant blue eyes . . .

Suddenly, I am jolted. Damn. I always love that dream.

Right now, our illustrious Prince is being fêted in New York. As for me, well, I am sitting on the top deck of the No. 9 bus in London. It is six o'clock and already dark. As we chunter up Piccadilly, I turn my head and spot the distant glimmering lights of St James's Palace through the gloom of Green Park. Or are my eyes deceiving me? The thought of the Palace still evokes in me an emotional tremor.

A passenger gets up, leaving his evening paper on the seat. How jolly considerate. I pick it up and glance at the news. It is full of stuff about my former boss, the Prince of Wales, and his wife of six months, the Duchess of Cornwall, and their trip to the United States. This tour is supposed to be about promoting Britain's interests. Oh really? Kindly pull the other one. No, this tour is Charles and Camilla's big charm offensive to win American hearts. It has all been carefully orchestrated. Moreover, they are taking the advice of the most skillful spin doctors, who are no doubt twisting the arms of compliant journalists.

I never worked directly in the media department of the Palace but, all the same, even I can say that it is probably too much to expect the USA to embrace Camilla when the memory of Princess Diana remains so vivid.

Devotion to the memory of Diana, particularly in the States, still borders on the religious. While many in Britain now have a more balanced view, for others elsewhere it seems she continues to walk on water – a martyred saint, no less, whose life and happiness was destroyed by Charles's adultery with *"the rottweiler"*, Diana's pet name for Camilla.

Besides having to overcome the stigma of being the 'other woman', Camilla has the additional obstacle of competing with Diana in the glamour stakes. It is, of course, unjust to judge people on looks but that is the cruel world for you.

I look at the photographs of the outfits Camilla has been parading in. Not a bad effort, girl, I think. But what did the American press have to say about it, I wonder? Oh dear. 'Frump Tower', I read, was the headline splashed across the *New York Post.* The public relations team supporting the Palace evidently has its work cut out.

Still, at least the tone of the coverage here in Britain is a great deal more sympathetic to Camilla than it was before the couple married in April. There was hardly a kind word written or spoken about her. I myself vented spleen, which, astonishingly, became a lead article in a Sunday newspaper.

I shared the front page with His Holiness, the Pope no less, who had died the day before. 'CAMILLA HAD ME FIRED AS CHARLES'S SECRETARY!' the headline screamed.

Yes, I certainly got a lot off my chest that day. I imagine it would have quite spoiled the Royal breakfast. But since then, I have been thinking hard and, yes, possibly I was too harsh on Camilla, but at that time my sentiments synchronised with the mood of the nation.

You may rightly ask: why would anyone care about what I, Sarah Goodall, a forty-year-old unknown woman, have to say about the Royal relationship? What authority do I have to comment? And why on earth should my opinions and my story be front-page news? How did it all come about?

In late March, a fortnight before the wedding of Charles and Camilla, I had been having dinner with friends. One of the other guests was a newspaper Editor. When he heard that I had worked at St James's Palace for twelve and a half years, and that Camilla had played a role in my downfall, his eyes lit up. Days later, I was interviewed at length and paid a handsome fee. Some thought I was betraying the Prince of Wales. When you have no capital and a tiny income, it is frankly difficult to summon sufficient pride to turn down such an opportunity. I was barely solvent. All the same, I never expected that my story would be trailed on the front page and that my interview would cause such a sensation.

What I said about Camilla was tough and, like I say, I have since moderated my views. I have to accept that I also played a rôle in my own downfall. Yes, I am far from perfect. I also feel sorry for Camilla in as much as those who continue to adore Diana feel compelled to hate Camilla. But Diana herself was never the saint or victim of popular myth, at least that is what I contend.

And I can say that from personal experience. I do not for a second doubt Diana's outstanding qualities. I think it wonderful that she used her glamour to great effect for charity. On occasion, I was close at hand when she was warm and kind. But I also saw her other side and feel it can be honestly said that the sainted Princess could be at times deceitful, manipulative and pitiless towards those who stood in her way or those she chose to discard.

Also, if having affairs when one is married is something to be seriously condemned, then as many rotten eggs should be flung at the memory of Diana as at the persons of Charles and Camilla. And I am not just talking about Diana's affair with the dashing Army officer James Hewitt. To be frank, she was a passionate woman. If you think Captain Hewitt was the only stallion in her stable, then you are in for a surprise.

When I read a few years ago that the ancient Treason Act had been abolished, I remember thinking that all of Diana's former lovers must be breathing a collective sigh of relief. If it had ever been acted upon, there would have been a lot of lopped heads at the Tower of London, I can tell you. I am not saying Diana was promiscuous or a tart; I am saying she was liberated and had a very healthy sexual appetite. There is nothing wrong with that. I have quite an appetite myself. But it is wrong to condemn other people – in Diana's case, her husband Prince Charles – for what you do yourself. Princesses in glass palaces should not throw stones.

Others who were close to Diana say she was mentally disturbed, probably as a result of her parents' divorce. Some maintain she had a 'paranoid schizophrenic disorder', others a 'narcissistic disorder'. They have the backing of some qualified psychologists, so such claims are not to be airily dismissed. For the ordinary person like me, therefore, the question is: was she a fruitcake, or was she at times just a spoilt bitch determined to get her own way? I think all of us can be a bit loopy at times but was the Princess more so than the average? All I can say is that she behaved, on occasion, quite appallingly towards Prince Charles, driving him to despair at times. She could also suddenly turn on her devoted friends and her staff. So I suspect it was a bit of both.

The tough question is whether Camilla was responsible for the end of the Royal marriage. I really don't think so. To my mind, Diana loved the *idea* of being the wife of Prince Charles. Why? Because she adored the idea of being the Princess of Wales. But loving the status of being a Princess is not the same as loving the Prince who is your husband, is it? Frankly, I don't believe Diana ever actually loved Prince Charles. If she had, she would have behaved in an entirely different way. Had she truly been a loyal and adoring wife (and behaved like one), he would have grown to love her fully and been devoted to her. I cannot imagine he would ever have sought happiness in the arms of Camilla or indeed any other woman. I have observed him at close quarters for years and that, I believe, gives me the authority to make such a statement.

Whatever other people might think, Prince Charles and Camilla are a genuine love match. As the No. 9 trundles on, in my mind's eye I raise a glass of champagne. 'Forgive and forget, and good luck to the both of you, Your Royal Highnesses!'

Later that night, back at my studio flat in South Kensington, I review some last changes to the final draft of my memoirs as written by Nicholas Monson. *Voilà*! we have finished. Watch out world!

This story about my life during my twelve and a half years in Royal service is a personal and emotional account. I have attempted to be completely frank, and I still blush on re-reading various passages. But if you are not prepared to tell it like it is, then it's hardly worth telling the story, is it?

I still adore my former employer Prince Charles and, in spite of insinuations I have since heard and read elsewhere, nothing like *that* (and you know precisely what I mean) happened between us.

I have now got over what happened between Camilla and me. Whatever else she might be, Camilla is loyal and loving, making her the ideal support for a sensitive, thoughtful and well-intentioned future King.

So, what is my motivation to write this? First answer: I hope to make some much-needed money. Is that such a sin? The second: my story of twelve years inside the Royal Household is one, I hope, you will greatly enjoy.

As you will see, I hugely enjoyed it myself . . .

1

Flying to the Moon

Early May 1988

My story starts in a dowdy two-bedroom flat in Fulham. At 30
Buer Road off the New Kings Road, near Putney Bridge, to
be precise. Buer Road is an uninspiring row of Edwardian
terraced houses aesthetically relieved by its avenue of pretty
trees. I share the flat with the divine Kate, whom I quite by
chance met through a friend. I am twenty-four and working as
a secretary for Phillips, a smart auction house in the West
End. I could have been a qualified chartered surveyor by now,
but I ran away from my studies at the Royal Agricultural
College in Cirencester.

It is Sunday evening. I am mooching about, reflecting on
anxieties typical of a young girl about town: my boyfriend,
Merlin (aaargh!), weight issues and, most importantly, the
next party.

Opposite me is the house of Princess Margaret's son, the
dishy Viscount Linley, trendy furniture designer. I can't help
myself and tweak my curtains. I make out his silhouette and
that of his sexy blonde companion, Susannah Constantine.
Who would have thought then that Susannah would shoot to

television fame as Trinny Woodall's 'other half ', clothes critics to the nation?

Frankly, the glimpses I have caught of David and Susannah through their windows, cavorting, smooching and other stuff I shouldn't divulge, make me jealous. God, are they cool or what? I see him in the morning, the smooth young Viscount in his smart black hatchback with the number plates HMO. What does HMO mean, I wonder? Her Majesty's Offspring? Perhaps just High Maintenance Offspring? Sigh. Some girls have all the luck.

So here I am. The washing machine is quietly chugging in the background while George Michael and Wham! serenade me in the foreground. I am leafing through a glossy magazine, applying a new and daring shade of crimson nail polish and demolishing a bottle of chilled Chardonnay when the phone rings. It is Mummy ringing from far and distant rural Shropshire, where yours truly lived her innocent childhood years. Mummy requires her weekly update from her harumscarum only daughter and will predictably find something to fret about, as mothers do.

I deftly parry the questions about Merlin, then Mummy asks if I have heard the rumours circulating on her cocktail-party circuit about Prince Charles and Princess Diana.

'What rumours?' I ask.

'Their troubles,' she pronounces in a Delphic tone.

'What troubles, Mummy?' There is a pause.

'Troubles,' she repeats. Clearly, I am not to be trusted with any further disclosures. What does she think I am? The hotline for a newspaper diary? There is silence again.

'How long have they been married, Mummy?'

'About seven years. What's that got to do with it?'

'Everything! I hear everyone has "trouble" after seven years of marriage.'

Mummy ignores my cynicism, unbecoming in one so young. 'It's probably just a passing thing,' she sighs.

What does she mean 'passing thing'? Are they rowing, having affairs, or what? Mummy can be so maddening at times.

'Still, as the future King and Queen, I do hope they work things out,' she pronounces.

'I daresay there are a few women out there who don't,' I retort cheekily. 'He is gorgeous. I don't care if he does have big ears . . .'

Mummy cuts in. 'Sarah, stop dreaming. You have as much chance of having any contact with the Prince of Wales as, well, flying to the moon.'

Why is it that my mother has the ability sometimes to make me feel six years old? She then changes the subject to something boringly prosaic.

'Darling, do you *have* to leave Phillips? Phillips is such a, well, prestigious place to work.'

'Money, Mummy. They pay a pittance. They expect everyone who works for them to have a private income. I just can't survive on the wages they pay.' I sense her despondency.

'But what will you do?'

I roll my eyes in exasperation. 'Phillips is not the only employer in town. I have signed up with an employment agency . . . what's it called? . . . Bernadette of Bond Street . . Yes, I know, it does sound like a West End call girl. And yes, I am sure I am not being lured into the white-slave trade . . . Mummy, stop it! Bernadette is sweet . . . What sort of job? Oh, a boring one, no doubt. I'll probably end up slaving for some dull executive in some grim tower block in the City, but at least I will be earning wages I can live on.'

'Well, I did tell you not to give up the land-management course,' she pronounces.

I roll my eyes again. 'Yes, Mummy, I know it's my fault.'

I reflect wistfully on my sudden departure from Cirencester. My reason: silly rows with my former boyfriend, Andy. To marry or not to marry was the question, and becoming a farmer's wife just then was not the answer. But Andy, darling Andy, so charming and oh so eligible, the younger son, if you please, of a wonderful Earl, a shining star in the House of Lords. Cripes. Had I played it differently, I might now be his daughter-in-law!

All those rows! What on earth were they all about? So stupid in hindsight. Just why did I give up my degree course and flee to London? Was it all worth it for Merlin? Ah, yes, Merlin Hutchings, gentleman lawyer of Piccadilly with a red sports car and swish studio flat in Cheyne Walk. But honestly, what girl could have resisted a fling with Merlin? And I'd always wanted a boyfriend in London.

My inner nanny reprimands me. You should have resisted. It is this fling with Merlin that has cost you Andy. My inner nanny is right. And I must admit it: right now, I would prefer to be with Andy.

'Darling, are you there?' Mummy disturbs my reverie. We continue chatting, then I head to bed.

The next day, I take the bus to Phillips, which, for those of you who don't know, is not quite in the same class as Sotheby's or Christie's but is still a bastion of gentility, as well as an efficient clearing house of ancestral artefacts; a favoured emporium which enables the English gentry to meet their obligations to the Inland Revenue.

I get off the bus at Green Park and trudge up New Bond Street. At the top, I turn onto Blenheim Street, where before me is the dirty-cream-coloured 1930s home of my employers. I enter the building through the navy-blue doors to be greeted, as always, by the cheery cockney porter. I pass by the little office of Paul Gillan, who scrupulously monitors everyone to make sure we are in on time. And time here is early in my book – 8.30! If we were a City trading organisation, I would understand, but we are a team of connoisseurs, expert in assessing the value of old artefacts. Why do we have to be at our place of work when civilised people are only just finishing their breakfast? Why?

The time rule applies to everyone from directors downwards. It even applies to my ex-boyfriend Andy's sister, who, as the daughter of an Earl, is a Lady in her own right. You would have thought they might make an indulgent concession for members of the aristocracy, but no. If you fail to make it in by 8.30, you are in for the high jump, whoever you are!

But that is the only drawback. The best bit of the work is the Green Room sale that takes place once a month. I have been tipping everyone off about it. It is basically a sale of the cheap stuff we receive that has no great financial value. Half of my friends have now furnished their flats and houses through the Green Room sale. Last week, for example, my friend Druscilla bought two chests of drawers, a woven Persian carpet, a bookcase, two prints of Highland stags and a Chesterfield leather sofa. Cost? £270. Not bad, eh?

Yes, Phillips is a lovely place to work, I sigh. But I have to face facts. I can't afford the luxury of working here all my life. The offer to take me off secretarial duties and train me as a cataloguer is tempting but with no accompanying offer of a salary hike, my darling bosses are missing the point. Who can survive on a take-home wage of £154 a week? That covers just adequately my basics: bus fares; rent and share of rates; telephone bills; electricity, water and gas; food and drink. What about clothes, shoes, make-up, toiletries and the occasional night out? I can't continually beg from my mother and father.

At lunchtime, I slip out to the employment agency to see what they have to offer me.

'Ah, there you are,' says Bernadette, the handsome, middle-aged brunette who appears to have taken a kindly interest in my future. 'I was hoping you might drop in. I have put you up for something that might interest you. I sent them your details some time ago and they have just rung up to say they would like to see you – today, if possible.'

'Will they pay well?' I ask hopefully.

'Better than what you are getting now.'

'How much better?'

'About £1,000 a year better.'

'So, after tax, what would my weekly wage be then?'

Bernadette does some calculations on the back of an envelope. '£169.92 a week.'

Yes, that is a definite improvement. Hey, I will be able to afford to buy the odd pair of tights. I reflect gloomily that the only way forward in life is to be an ambitious career woman. I should enter the City of London. Who knows, one day I could conquer the citadels of finance! So here I am about to say I want a job in something like banking, where I could earn a wage with which I could buy more than the occasional dress, but I can't help but be curious. After all, this employer has asked to see me. I should at least find out who he is.

'So what is this job, then?'

Bernadette looks me in the eye. 'It's a job at St James's Palace. It's secretarial work for His Royal Highness, the Prince of Wales. Would you be interested?'

Interested? Is Bernadette kidding me or what?

Ten minutes later, I am striding down old Bond Street. To hell with Phillips – I'll take an extra half-hour and say it was a doctor's appointment. Crossing over Piccadilly, with the magnificent Ritz Hotel to the right of me, I continue my journey down St James's Street, past Berry Brothers, the wine merchants, and then the great gentleman's clubs – White's, Brooks's and Boodle's – all of them converted from eighteenth-century townhouses that were once the London homes of assorted earls, marquises and dukes.

At the bottom of the street, I arrive at the Tudor gates of the great sprawling Royal palace. Two tall, dashing guardsmen in full dress uniform with rifles at the ready stare fixedly ahead in their sentry boxes beneath the clock tower. Beyond them, next to the entrance, is a police barrier. Bernadette is amazing – the scary police officer already knows my name! PC Scary then issues me with a visitor's pass and I cross the cobbled Colour Court, before taking my first tentative steps into the inner portals.

The entrance hall is cool and flagged with stones that shine with a wonderful centuries-old patina. A receptionist asks me to wait in the Chinese Room and I enter a beautiful room decorated wall to wall with delicate illustrations of a romantic China of the past – stooped, bearded peasants pulling carts along scenic winding roads in picturesque countryside.

Chocolate-box fantasy or an honest depiction of a bygone age, I ask myself? The beautifully carved furniture is, I note, Chinese Chippendale. The year at Phillips has not been entirely wasted, I reflect.

I sit marvelling at the splendour for about ten minutes until the receptionist pops her head round the door to tell me to go upstairs for the interview. Oh my God! Am I nervous or what? I step upstairs, passing a fabulous large painting of the coronation of George VI, father of our own dear Queen Elizabeth, on the way.

I am suddenly seized by a panicky thought: what if the Prince of Wales interviews me himself? God, if he is in the room at all, I swear I'll faint. That would be awful. Then perhaps not, I muse. Not if I aim my swoon in his direction. Imagine the scene: the concerned Prince cradling *moi*, the fainting would-be secretary in those powerful arms. So strong from swinging polo mallets, he lifts me effortlessly and carries me to a nearby *chaise longue*.

'Quick, someone!' he cries out. 'Get the smelling salts!'

Stop it, Sarah. Get a grip. Pull yourself together.

I enter the office. My face, I hope, is now a model of cool composure. I am ushered to a chair. To avoid gazing at my prospective interrogators and fainting, I inspect my surroundings. The walls are a dirty buttery cream – not been painted for a good six years, I would venture. On them hang some indifferently framed oil paintings – and they could do with a good clean, too, I think to myself. The compositions are of Venice, it appears, sometime in the eighteenth century – gondoliers on canals against the stunning backdrop of beautiful palaces. I gulp. They are all by Canaletto. I remember that Sotheby's sold a Canaletto the week before for

£5 million! I count three in the room, then remember seeing Venetian scenes in the passage outside. Crumbs, a fire sale of these daubs here could feed Africa for a month.

I look down. An Aubusson carpet perhaps would be a fitting counterpoint to the splendid collection of old Masters. Instead, I find a dirty-brown wall-to-wall fitted carpet that should be bundled into a skip, if you ask me. Then I notice the filing system.

Filing system? It is all I can do not to laugh. No smart array of metal or wooden filing cabinets, rather a series of cardboard boxes stacked side by side and on top of each other. At a Royal palace?

There is a cough and I look up. I redden. I do hope they didn't think I was being rude. Oh stupid, stupid Sarah! Facing me is a panel of three – two men and one woman. They introduce themselves.

The first is Commander Richard Aylard. He is the Temporary Assistant Private Secretary to the Prince of Wales, which means, he tells me, that he helps to ensure the smooth running of the Prince's busy office. Next, there is a lovely swarthy Foreign Office official, seconded Deputy Private Secretary David Wright, whom I find myself rather fancying. And finally, there is sweet and lovely Jenny Denman, whose job title I don't take in at that point as all my thoughts are focused on dreamy David.

Oh dear, no Prince of Wales. Sigh, but what could I expect? He is probably too busy running his charity, or denouncing an ugly building, or perhaps sorting out the 'troubles' to which my mother mysteriously referred.

Then come the questions. What experience do I have? How fast is my typing speed? Can I take dictation? Am I a team player? Would I enjoy working at the Palace? Some kind of joke question, surely? David Wright is smiling at me and it makes me feel wonderfully confident. Then there is silence and he whispers to his colleagues. They confer like contestants in some television quiz show.

I look away, pretending to take an avid academic interest again in one of the Canalettos, hopefully looking as if my own family possessed one or two rather similar.

'Sarah,' he says, staring at me sternly, 'your agency sent us your details a week ago. As you can imagine, we have very stringent security procedures here. I hope you don't mind, but we have been checking you out. We check out *everyone*. We know pretty much everything about you.'

I find myself reddening. Oh my God. Will I now be arrested for my unpaid parking tickets? Presumably they know I was nearly expelled from school for that lark in the dormitory that went horribly wrong. I feel abject. This is too awful. I am about to burst into tears.

'Congratulations!' he says, startling me. 'Would you like to start work in, say, two weeks' time?'

I nearly faint. Get a grip, Sarah. Try to be cool. I fail. 'Er, yes!' I splutter. Damn the money, I will *starve* to work at the Palace!

Dreamy David continues his friendly banter. 'I must say, you look very Christmassy in your red top and green skirt.' My God, what an embarrassing combination! I look like an elf! Are they desperate, I wonder, or is it possible that I really am the Royal material they are looking for? I just can't believe it!

I leave the Palace not walking but floating, wafting gently on a cotton-wool cloud pulled with silken cords by handsome liveried footmen on the ground below. The drizzle of rain around me is actually glorious sunshine. The cars before me in St James's Street are a procession of gilded carriages. I wear not a silly green skirt and red top but a fabulous flowing ballgown. The Alice band on my head is a glittering diamond-studded tiara.

I gaze giddily at the dashing guardsmen in their scrummy scarlet tunics and think of the Foreign Office charmers I have just met – suave men called Private Secretaries who don't do secretarial duties at all. I look around the cobbled court of this beautiful palace filled with ancient treasures and replete with mysterious traditions. Oh my God! This is *my* world now. And for ever. For these magical moments, I am as much a princess as any princess in the Royal Household.

Late May 1988

It has been a busy two weeks, what with working my notice at Phillips. And it was so sweet of them to throw me such a nice leaving party. I ended up getting quite tiddly. Talk about the hangover from hell the next morning! Good thing it was the weekend.

Merlin and I have agreed to split up. Frankly, the passion was fizzling out and I can't help thinking about Andy – first, it was just occasionally; now, he invades my thoughts the whole time. Two years we went out together, then I blew it. And worse, he has got a girlfriend in Cirencester with the same name as me! I have never met her, and I hate her. Two years is a long time to go out with someone; well, it is when you are only twenty-four.

Oh, and Mummy obviously thought I was joking when I told her of my new job: 'April the first was six weeks ago, darling.' It took me another minute to convince her it was the truth. She was quite bowled over, as were my two darling brothers. Sweetly, she said she would speak to Daddy about helping with the rent. The Palace may pay me £16 a week more than Phillips did, but that is hardly enough to propel me into comfortable solvency, is it?

So here I am, about to walk into the Palace again. When, I wonder, will I meet my employer, His Royal Highness? This morning? This afternoon? How do I address him? Do I curtsey every time he passes? Will I be able to stop myself fainting when he looks at me?

I pass by a nodding policeman at the entrance and butterflies dance madly in my stomach. Naturally, I have ditched the red-and-green outfit for something more in keeping with my elevated status, all black and very chic. I can hardly meet the Prince of Wales looking like an elf, can I? I shall appease American Express later. The police officer waves me through the door and the receptionist hands me a pass indicating that I have 'official' clearance, no less. From now on, I can enter the Palace without a by-your-leave. The keys to the Palace are mine!

Next I am taken to an office where I am asked by a sombre-looking fellow to sign the Official Secrets Act. Isn't this something just for spies? I suddenly feel inflated with a sense of huge importance. No more a humble would-be cataloguer for an auction house. Oh no, I am a critical cog in the Palace Establishment. Then a rogue thought slips to the front of my mind. I wonder what would happen if I just said, 'No! I won't sign the Official Secrets Act!' Has anyone done that before?

I catch the eye of Mr Sombre as he pushes forward the form. No, I bet they haven't. I scribble my name. Goodbye, my frivolous freedoms! Hello, my grave obligations to the Crown of the United Kingdom and its far-flung dominions! I am now a paid-up, utterly loyal soldier of the Palace, a Miss Moneypenny, ready to serve my master, the Prince of Wales and future handsome King of England.

Will a confidence ever pass my lips now? Never. Not ever. Bribes will not induce me nor torture ever break me. My loyalty to the Crown is total. I will lay down my life for the Prince before I ever spill even a sliver of a confidential bean. The nation's secrets are secure with me. Oh yes. And that is official.

Having been asked to sign the Official Secrets Act, I then speculate that the tasks I shall be charged with are of a pretty heavy nature. I shall be dealing, no doubt, with highly sensitive material, stuff that could bring down governments. My countenance now is one of a fitting severity. I wonder if the Prince will have an adjoining office where I shall be called in to take minutes of his critical dealings with ministers of government?

'Fan mail, Sarah,' says Mr Sombre. 'That's what you will be dealing with.'

I try not to look astonished. I have to sign the Official Secrets Act for fan mail? Then quickly I realise that it is code, an amusing Foreign office metaphor for something altogether more serious. I smile with complicity.

'Fan mail,' I repeat, with a slight arch to one of my eyebrows.

He looks at me oddly. 'Yes, fan mail, Sarah. His Royal Highness gets stacks of it. About a hundred letters a day. It wouldn't be proper just to bin them. Your task is to reply to them.'

'All of them?'

'Yes, Sarah, all of them. In fact, we have a great sack here that needs to be dealt with ASAP.'

'All part of my secretarial duties, I suppose,' I say breezily.

'No, Sarah, fan mail is your *sole* duty. Fan mail is your domain.'

I nod in humble acquiescence. Well, a girl has got to start somewhere.

'Oh, and one more thing, Sarah. In the outside world, you would rightly be called a secretary, but here in the Palace you are a Lady Clerk.'

A Lady Clerk, eh? Sarah Goodall, Lady Clerk. Mmmm. Like it? I love it! Just wait till those snotty debutantes coming to Druscilla's drinks tonight hear that I am a 'Lady Clerk at the Palace'. They won't be snubbing *me* any more! Oh no.

'I have asked one of the staff to come and show you to your office and then introduce you to the other Lady Clerks.'

Other Lady Clerks? 'Er, how many Lady Clerks are there?' I ask hesitantly.

Mr Sombre frowns in a puzzled way. 'Good question.' He starts counting with his fingers. 'Twelve, I think. Yes, twelve.'

A tall blonde with high cheekbones enters. She is wearing a Prussian-blue designer dress. She is slim, elegant and gorgeous.

'Meet Geraldine,' he says.

Geraldine smiles at me, fixing me with her cornflower blue eyes. At this very moment, I again feel like the new girl on my first day at school, frightened and alone. She is the Head Girl, confident, beautiful, protective and kind. I have a crush on her immediately.

Geraldine takes me through to a large stateroom with a

gray marble fireplace above which hangs a gilt-framed portrait of King Edward VIII, uncle of Queen Elizabeth and son of George V.

In each corner stands an oak kneehole Edwardian desk. The girls sitting behind three of them give me wan smiles and I smile back, trying hard to look quietly acquiescent and unpresumptuous, as new girls should.

'Meet the others,' says Geraldine, taking me through to the two adjoining rooms where the other Lady Clerks are positioned like symmetrical sentinels. I raise my hand and give all of them a shy girly wave – signalling, I hope, a non-challenging appropriate demureness that they will see as becomingly humble. Geraldine then whisks me down the corridor through to the kitchen where we make a cup of instant coffee and delve into the office biscuit selection. Biscuits, especially ones with chocolate on them, are one of my terrible weaknesses.

'The three State Rooms where we Lady Clerks work were originally three inter-connecting drawing rooms. In fact, they were the rooms where Edward VIII wooed Wallis Simpson,' she explains.

Wow. I know all about that affair. Who doesn't? Here was the King who had it all, then lost it for the love of an unsuitable woman. It was one thing for a King to have a fling with a divorcée, but it was quite another to insist on marrying her. Consequence: he had to give up his throne and abdicate. All for Wallis. She must have been some woman.

'Actually, it was Wallis who seduced him rather than the other way round, but clever women like Wallis always leave the men thinking that the reverse is true,' Geraldine adds with a knowing wink.

I have in my mind a picture of the thin, elegant and gamine Wallis, then this transforms into a vision of the three State Rooms with the desks removed and elegant Regency furniture in their place. I see the dapper King and his *soignée* mistress exchanging decorous repartee straight out of a play from Noel Coward. They both hold cocktails in one hand and exotic Turkish cigarettes in the other, while tall tail-coated footmen stare blankly ahead. Their courting ritual is full of dipped eyelashes, soothing metaphors and hammering hearts. How utterly romantic.

'You know how she got him hooked?' Geraldine breaks into my reverie.

I shake my head.

She leans forward and whispers, 'BJs!'

I smile knowingly. She takes a sip of coffee.

'And she first did it here. Imagine, the first officially recorded BJ in Britain, here in St James's Palace.'

She laughs and I laugh, too. But what on earth is Geraldine talking about, I wonder nervously? What is a BJ? Come on, Sarah, think! Geraldine is the Head Girl here and you are exposing yourself as an ignoramous. I focus my mind. American woman introduces an English King to a BJ.

Was it an early form of hamburger, I wonder? Was the King, perhaps, a foodie? So she got him hooked on hamburgers. I smile back knowingly. Geraldine is peering at me closely.

'You don't know what I am talking about, do you?'

I smile nervously. God, I am an idiot. I am so parochial, I feel like crying. She puts me out of my misery. Leaning forward again, Geraldine brings her lips close to my ear. I smell her perfume: Chanel No. 5.

'Blow job.'

I find myself blushing.

'Yes,' continues Geraldine, pulling back. 'The women at Court referred to it as Wallis's "oriental practices". Apparently, she learnt her boudoir skills from the courtesans in a Shanghai brothel. At least that is what the Foreign Office told the Prime Minister at the time. But it could have been part of a smear campaign against Wallis. Who knows? The British ladies felt they couldn't and certainly wouldn't compete on such a base level with an accomplished seductress. It wasn't for the likes of them to take up outlandish erotic skills. So they dismissed her as a common tart, as if their scorn alone would make her disappear.'

'Big, big mistake. They should have learned from Wallis is what I say. Just think – the Abdication Crisis could have been averted!'

Geraldine wiggles her finger and a beautiful diamond engagement ring catches the light. 'You won't learn that in the history books.'

Five minutes later, I am still flushed. Just to think, I have been given an entirely new take on the Abdication Crisis: namely, the failure of the ladies of the English Court to embrace the blow job in their erotic repertoire.

Perhaps, like me, they preferred to believe fellatio was just a character from Shakespeare. I wonder what my history master would make of Geraldine's interesting and probably unarguable thesis. And how, possibly, would David Starkey, Antonia Fraser or Simon Schama answer her?

Geraldine now tells me about the job of fan-mail correspondent, a post she herself once held. 'As you will learn from the fan-mail postbag, the Royal Family has a profound effect on people,' she says. 'If you are British, it is bred into you. I have even seen staunch republican Labour politicians get weak-kneed in front of royalty.

'In moments of crisis or deep reflection, many people who in less cynical times were called loyal subjects want to reach out to a member of the Royal Family who appeals to them, such as our employer, His Royal Highness, the Prince of Wales. Think along the lines of Roman Catholics who often pray to their preferred saints as well as to God.'

'Your task here might sound trivial, but it isn't. Your letters acknowledge the relationship of the Royal Family with the people, which is why everyone gets a response. Your reply will be neutral and dignified; always transmitting respect. An acknowledgement letter bearing the printed St James's Palace address ensures that the connection continues. And – this is important – you reply even if the respondent is insulting. In every daily postbag, you will get your fair share of insults and brickbats.'

'Lecture over,' she says. 'Let's go to your desk.'

Geraldine is now sitting by my side at my desk. The putative auctioneer in me speculates how much this kneehole desk would fetch. I reckon £80 tops. But then again, there is the St James's Palace provenance. Who could put a price on the snob premium? You could probably multiply that figure by six at least.

I get a surprise when I see what is sitting on the desk – a computer! Frankly, I am expecting a quill and inkpot, or possibly an old Adler typewriter. That, at least, would be in keeping with the cardboard filing system that continues around the perimeter of the office, covering the depressing brown carpet that spreads around us like a tide of sludge.

Geraldine opens a programme on my computer and a letter appears on the screen. The glories, I soon learn, of the utterly obscure DW4 system!

'The template for your responses,' she declares.

Geraldine then explains the fan-mail drill. First, I have to sift through every postbag and separate the personal from the fan mail.

'They are easy to pick out,' she says. 'Letters that are written in elegant ink and posted in an expensive envelope invariably tend to be from his friends.'

'So, should I take these letters to Prince Charles personally?' I ask.

'No, Sarah. You take them to Commander Aylard. Then he will make a judgement on presenting them to HRH.'

I look flummoxed.

'Sorry, Geraldine, but who is HRH and where is he in the chain of command?'

Geraldine smiles at me sweetly. 'Sarah, HRH stands for His Royal Highness. It is the name we all give him, though sometimes we refer to him also as "The Boss".'

'Oh,' I say. 'HRH it is, then.'

Inside, I am curled into a knot of embarrassment. How can you be so *stupid*, Sarah? I have an internal Punch and Judy show going on where the embarrassed Judy is whacking the ignorant Punch. No more Prince Charles or the Prince of Wales, Sarah, he is now and forever simply 'HRH' or 'The Boss'.

I learn there are three standard responses to letters he receives where the writer is not known to HRH personally.

1. To the warm and affectionate. Thank you for your letter addressed to the Prince of Wales. His Royal Highness is deeply touched by your expressions of warmth and support. He has asked me to send you his best wishes.

2. *To those in need of help*. Thank you for your letter, drawing this matter to the Prince of Wales's attention. His Royal Highness has instructed me to pass it to the relevant office to look into it further. While he cannot become involved, he wishes to thank you for the trouble you took to write to him. He has asked me to send you his best wishes.

3. *To the insulting*. Thank you for your letter addressed to the Prince of Wales. His Royal Highness has noted its contents with interest. He has asked me to send you his best wishes.

While I am taking all this in, Geraldine suddenly looks at her watch. 'I think we should break for lunch, don't you?' she says. 'Follow me!' So I do.

We sweep out into the street. The sun is shining and I am oh so happy!

'Where are we off to?' I ask.

'BP,' Geraldine replies crisply.

We swing right onto the Mall as I struggle hard to contain my surprise. Why on earth are we having lunch at BP? BP, as everyone knows, stands for British Petroleum, one of the largest oil companies in the world with petrol stations everywhere. I am not a dummy – I realise that BP does not just sell petrol at its petrol stations but sandwiches as well. All the same, a petrol station is the last place I would expect Lady Clerks to dine. Palace customs are certainly strange, I think to myself as we cross over by Buckingham Palace.

Around us are scores of smiling tourists, snapping away with their cameras. The handsome guardsmen with their bearskin hats stand erect in their sentry boxes. I look up. The flag is flying at full mast, telling the world that Her Majesty is in residence. Down we now stroll onto Buckingham Palace Road. Still no petrol station in sight.

'Here we are!' says Geraldine, turning to address me. I look at her bewildered. What is she talking about? Where is the petrol station? We are still alongside the walls of the Palace! What is going on?

Geraldine nods to a police officer standing by a door and the next thing I know we are walking *into* Buckingham Palace. Oh my God! So this is what she meant by 'BP'. I can't believe it! My jaw is hanging loosely as I gaze around, completely awestruck.

'Come on, Sarah.' Geraldine urges me on and I follow her upstairs into a large room that has been converted into a canteen, and a pretty grand one at that. Large round tables overlaid with white cotton tablecloths have proper silverware on them – no standard-issue stainless-steel cutlery here.

Geraldine introduces me to Graham, the camp and rather wonderful *maître d'* who is in charge of food in the Royal Officials' canteen. The silver-haired Graham has a bouffant. He wears black trousers and a white open-necked shirt. I choose a plate of delicious-looking beef stew with dumplings that he strongly recommends and then sit down with Geraldine, who introduces me to the other Royal Officials at the table.

'Are there other canteens?' I ask.

'Yes, the Royal Household canteen for the senior bods at the Palace, and the stewards' canteen for footmen and under-butlers. BP is a village, literally. It even has a Post Office and a bar.'

Graham next suggests some jam roly-poly with custard. I

am so pathetic; I just cannot resist. Geraldine is more disciplined, I note. Just a salad and an apple for her. What a glutton I am but, my goodness, the food is delicious.

By twenty past two, we are back at our desks and it is time for me to tackle the intimidating, large gray postbag that is my 'domain'. With trepidation, I begin my task. One thing I soon realise is that Geraldine has not drilled me in the appropriate response to the letters from the loonies! Cripes, there must be about ten of them. Does he get as many as this every day?

I idly wonder if, perhaps, the volume of loony letters HRH receives is in direct relation to the cycle of the moon – so, when the moon is full, the postbag is stuffed with correspondence from crazies, scribbled at the height of the moon's manic influence. Conversely, when the moon wanes, the loony letters are reduced to a trickle. Time will tell.

Loony letters, I soon realise, can be spotted, like the personal ones, from the envelope alone. Rarely new, the envelopes are scruffy and second-hand. HRH is addressed in completely eccentric ways such as 'Charles, Buckingham Palace, England'. How obliging of the Post Office to steer them to me, I think, as I try and make sense of the maniacal and ridiculous content.

Some are simply deranged ramblings from troubled souls, poor things. Other scribes are keen to alert HRH to some impending evil conspiracy involving alternately the Vatican, the Freemasons, the Jews, the Muslims, the Feminists, the Vegetarians, Darth Vader (I kid you not) and even the Environmentalists (such wicked people).

My favourite of the batch, though, is a concerned correspondent who cajoles my employer for failing to lead his subjects in the imminent war against the aliens in our midst.

If he is talking about traffic wardens, I am with him. Should I create an *X-Files* folder, I wonder? Letter three, I decide, fits the unhinged category.

But what am I to do with the personal letters that I have sorted for HRH? I look for Commander Aylard, but he is not in his office. Geraldine is not at her desk either. I explain my predicament to one of the Lady Clerks in my office. She returns a neutral stare. Clearly, my attempts at a charm offensive have hit stony ground.

'So do I give them to HRH myself?' I ask innocently.

The question certainly appears to break the ice. Next thing I know, she makes eye contact with one of the other Lady Clerks and simultaneously they put their hands over their mouths to stifle their giggles. I stand there momentarily amazed. I am suddenly the girl of eleven on her first day of school, being confronted by two bullies. Fighting back the tears, I swing round and head straight to the bathroom. I want to run from the Palace and never come back.

I push open the bathroom door. Thank goodness no one else is in the loo! I pull the door shut, reach for the loo roll, tear off some tissue and dab my eyes, which are glistening with tears. What was so funny about that? I only wanted a straightforward answer. Oh, where are you, sweet Geraldine, my protector? Commander Aylard, why aren't you at your post in my hour of need? I feel so isolated and alone.

Come on, Sarah, buck up, says my inner nanny. You are twenty-four, not eleven. Stop snivelling and hold your head high. You are fearless enough on the hunting field, so why should a couple of office harpies make you dissolve into a puddle? That's better. You will get through this.

I take a deep breath and pull the chain (but since no one

else is there, who am I kidding?). I step out and apply some make-up. No way will those two bitches have the satisfaction of knowing I have been crying. Oh no!

I stroll down the corridor, head held high, and notice Commander Aylard is back at his desk.

'Commander, I have the personal letters for HRH for you.'

'Please, Sarah, call me Richard.'

Well, Commander, you command me to call you Richard, then Richard it is. First name terms, eh? I feel like a Palace insider already and this is only six hours into the job.

'I have followed Geraldine's instructions and I think I can recognise them now immediately.'

'Well done, Sarah, I am delighted that you are getting the hang of things so quickly,' he continues. 'Bring them in.'

'Yes, Richard,' I purr.

I return to my office beaming, scoop up the personal letters and flash my tormentors a confident smile.

'Just back to see Richard,' I say. They look appropriately taken aback. That's shown them.

I walk slowly to Richard's office, savouring the pictures on the wall and the rich historical ambience of this famous ancient Palace. It will take more than the icy demeanour of two unfriendly Lady Clerks to scare me away from this heavenly place of work. I set the personal letters on my Commander's desk. As I am about to turn and leave, Richard then pays me another compliment.

'Excellent, Sarah. I am already starting to think you are a complete natural at this job.'

Carry on like this, Richard, I think, and you'll overtake Dreamy Dave as my Palace crush!

2

New Girl at the Palace

July 1988

It's now my second month in the office and I have made three or four friends here. Phew! My best friend right now is Susannah Perkins, who has been seconded from the Royal Air Force and consequently has the rather fancy title of 'Flight Officer'. I keep imagining her soaring out through the window like Tinkerbell.

The titles here denoting rank in the armed services are understandable, but some of the Court job titles are baffling to anyone who has not mastered 'Palacespeak'. A test for you. What does a Liveryman do at the Palace? Does he paint the Royal livery, perhaps? No. Any guesses? A Liveryman is a porter. He just carries things. What is an Equerry? Sounds like something to do with horses, doesn't it? The Prince's Equerry probably did once arrange the Prince's horses – before the invention of motor cars. Now, in the person of Major Christopher Lavender, he helps arrange the Prince's movements, with Commander Aylard acting as his assistant. In the outside world, he would probably be called a personal assistant or, if one was going to be corporate, he might have the title nowadays of logistics manager.

Here is another: Travelling Yeoman. Does he travel before the Prince, perhaps, alerting the people to the impending Royal visit with the cry of 'yeo!'? No. Any guesses? The Travelling Yeoman's job is to make sure suitcases are dispatched and all returned safely on Royal tours. Sometimes he is given an alternative title of Baggage Master. The Travelling Yeoman or Baggage Master at St James's Palace is the wonderful Sergeant Ron Lewis, who has been with the Prince since the earliest days. We all call him 'Sarge'.

To my way of thinking, it is undoubtedly more exciting to have a quaint job title. How much more romantic and mysterious it is to be a Travelling Yeoman than a suitcase manager, an Equerry than a logistics manager, a Liveryman than a porter, a Lady Clerk than a secretary. Some of the mystique and grandeur of the Royal Family rubs off on even the humblest of Palace staff through these arcane job titles. It inadvertently marks those of us who work here, making us nearly as remote from the world outside the Palace walls as the Royal Family itself.

I am in a state of particular excitement today because Susannah has booked us the tennis court inside the private gardens of Buckingham Palace! I am as thrilled as a child on its first trip to the zoo.

That afternoon, all dressed in our whites, we enter the Palace grounds from Buckingham Palace Road through a door in the wall called Electrician's Gate, between the Royal Mews and the Royal Collection. I hold my breath and try not to let Susannah see how awestruck I am. The sun is glinting through the trees as we walk along a path that follows the edge of the whole garden. We go past a funny wooden bridge over a little lake, where we catch sight of the breathtakingly beautiful pink flamingos, which are marooned there – wings clipped – in the Royal lake.

Then the tennis court comes into view – a hard court slightly in need of repair, with moss and leaves around the edges. Here we are alone, not another soul in sight, and fifty yards from the far edge of the court is Hyde Park Corner – the busiest roundabout in the country! Incredible. I realise that thousands of people experience these gardens at the annual Garden Parties, when the Queen entertains selected worthy citizens for tea, but few have the privilege, like I do at this magical moment, of enjoying them in empty tranquillity. Well, it is tranquil if you ignore the noise of the traffic.

Susannah and I warm up and then swing into an energetic game. I am completely outclassed. Susannah Perkins can not only fly airplanes, she could, if she wanted, compete at Wimbledon. I feel like a novice up against Martina Navratilova. Still, if one has to be humiliated at tennis, I think, what better place than here in the empty gardens of Buckingham Palace?

As I pick up yet another of the balls that I have hit into the net, I suddenly see the distant figure of the Queen's Assistant Private Secretary Sir Robert Fellowes, whom I had met at someone's leaving-drinks party, walking his Labrador. Sir Robert has the complete trust of Her Majesty. But when he gets frustrated, he is known to shout at people, especially down the telephone. It is said he has even shouted at the Princess of Wales! But then, he *is* married to one of her sisters, so I suppose, with her being 'family', that is permissible. He has also shouted at Fergie, the Duchess of York, though, as she is a first cousin of his, she's 'family' too.

Apparently, the Duchess and the Princess are really good friends and they don't really appreciate Sir Robert's verbal blasts. Consequently, they have given him the nickname 'Bobby Bellows'. I wonder if he knows he is called that?

We resume our game as I watch Her Majesty's lampooned Palace coordinator stroll out of sight. Right now, I could do with Sir Robert's vocal chords. When you are at the Hyde Park end of the tennis court, the din of the traffic is so loud that you have to yell the score.

August 1988

It is a warm evening and I am sitting at home in my bra and panties sorting out all the envelopes from abroad that the Prince has received this month. The stamps all have a value for charity and I cut them from their envelopes for silver-haired Alan, a Liveryman who volunteers to donate them. Well, a girl has got to do something with her time when she doesn't have a boyfriend. Better practising *noblesse oblige* than hanging out in wine bars, I think, though not with much conviction.

Feeling a bit bored and curious, I flick back the curtains to see if the strapping young Viscount, first cousin of my employer, HRH, is about. No sign of his smart black convertible VW Beetle. Sigh. He is probably out wooing the curvaceous Miss Constantine at Como Lario or possibly somewhere like Nikita's, the Russian restaurant on Ifield Road. I imagine the two of them sipping fruit-flavoured vodkas and nibbling exotic caviar on blinis with sour cream and chopped egg while gazing lovingly into each other's eyes and murmuring sweet nothings. I let the curtains drop back.

It is my own damned fault, I think, as I wipe away a tear. I have no one to blame but myself. Running off to London to be with Merlin was, of course, going to hurt Andy. No wonder he doesn't want me back. I broke the trust. Idiot, idiot girl that I am. God, I miss him so much.

I gaze at myself in the mirror and pull in my tummy. My boobs aren't bad at all, legs are fine, but there is no disguising the fact that Graham's yummy hot lunches in the Royal officials' canteen are making me pile on the pounds. Not even the strenuous weekly games of tennis with darling Flight Officer Perkins can compensate for this amount of calorie intake. Carry on like this, girl, and you will be as attractive to men as a beached whale. I must, *must*, diet. Simple: copy Geraldine. If she can do it, so can I!

I open up today's newspaper. My goodness, Princess Diana is getting so much publicity these days. She seems to be *everywhere*, except, that is, at her husband's side. Earlier this year, she was at Great Ormond Street looking after Prince Harry, who had just had a hernia operation, while HRH was having a holiday break in Italy. It seems an odd thing to invite the world's press to witness your visit to hospital to see your own sick son. But maybe it is common practice if you are a Royal figure.

Maybe, I ponder, it is also something to do with the fact that the Princess of Wales is so absolutely stunning that the press cannot get enough of her. All the same, you should draw the line somewhere. After all, the press could surely not have pictured her running up the hospital steps without some sort of tip-off beforehand?

The strange thing is that no one in the Palace, at least not in my office, ever discusses anything about HRH's private life. I suppose it is simply seen as uncool. The office line seems to be that we are above that kind of tittle-tattle. Of course, I recognise that I must be loyal to my employers, particularly when mine happen to be the future King and Queen of England. But damn it, loyalty should not preclude me from knowing what is really going on!

One thing in particular niggles me: what, I wonder, is the point of all these newspaper stories about one Mrs Andrew Parker-Bowles, whom it is stressed is HRH's 'close and loyal friend'? Surely we all have close and loyal friends. What on earth is wrong with that? Are they hinting at something else? Hey, what would I know? I have my own problems to deal with.

The phone rings. My God, could this be, by chance, adorable Andy? Might Andy have dumped my namesake? Could he be pining for me right now in Cirencester? I take a deep breath before answering the phone. I must not seem to be desperate. Three rings, four rings, five! I snatch the phone from the receiver. 'Hello,' I drawl in a tone of voice that I trust conveys sophistication and languid momentary boredom. There is silence.

'Hello,' I drawl again.

'Sarah, is that you?'

I recognise the voice and redden. 'Yes, Mummy.'

'Extraordinary. It didn't sound like you at all. I thought I must have got the wrong number. Look, I have spoken to your father about this money thing and he has kindly agreed to give you a cheque to cover your debts. We appreciate you have to look smart the whole time at the Palace, and clothes and shoes do cost a lot of money. More than that, we hate the idea of you fretting over your overdraft when you should be happy and enjoying yourself.'

I start wiping a tear. 'Thank you so much, Mummy.'

'Your father and I also want you to know how proud we are of you.'

I find myself crying.

October 1988

I am sitting quietly at my desk, sifting through HRH's postbag, when in strides Captain Gorgeous in the form of the Honourable Rupert Fairfax. There is a bat squeak of excitement from the assembled Lady Clerks, though they all pretend to be fully focused on their respective tasks. As if.

The Honourable Rupert is the Temporary Private Secretary to HRH. His other title, I am told, is the Assistant Private Secretary for Industrial Affairs. I don't know about the 'industrial' part of his title, but he certainly looks qualified for 'affairs'. Besides being drop-dead gorgeous, he is the unmarried brother of Lord Fairfax (pretty yummy himself), making him *utterly* eligible. None of us Lady Clerks is sure quite what Rupert's duties are but, frankly, none of us cares. So long, that is, as he makes our day dreamy by deigning to make the occasional courtesy call, a visit that invariably leaves us swooning.

Rupert's chief interest, we all know, is polo. Polo is a sport that appears to demand his attention most afternoons, particularly at Smith's Lawn near Windsor. 'Just off to play some chukkas!' he often informs us as he passes by in his indecently sexy white jodhpurs and knee-high leather boots. We all sigh.

Why don't you mount me today rather than a polo pony, I remember once thinking outrageously one hot afternoon, praying Rupert had the gift of telepathy.

Today, Rupert is dressed in a smart blue suit. For the first time in what seems like ages, he looks at me, smiles and says, 'Hi, Sarah!'

Instantly, I pick up on the waves of jealousy emanating from my Lady Clerk colleagues. Normally, this acknowledgement from the office pin-up would have caused me to faint on the spot. But not today. Today, I merely return him a restrained smile.

'Hi, Rupert.'

I dip my head down and return to my task. From the corner of my eye, I can see that he is a tad bemused. Rupert is probably thinking he has greeted me at 'the wrong time of the month' or possibly, knowing the vanity of some men, that I am a lesbian. Fat chance. Wrong on both counts. Rupert bestows his dreamy attentions on another Lady Clerk while I return to the Boss's fan mail and my private inner thoughts.

Today is different from other days at the office. It is my mood, you see. Normally, I am happy, very happy, being in this lovely job. But something happened last night that has greatly affected me. It has quite altered my state of mind and I am not happy now. No, not happy at all. Happy is not the right word for what I feel. Happy is pathetically inadequate. The right word is ECSTATIC!

Last night, I took a call expecting it to be Mummy and, oh my God, it was darling Andy! It took me quite by surprise, as you can imagine.

'Sarah,' he said. 'I miss you so much.'

'And I miss you,' I bleated in reply.

Andy then proceeded to invite me to dinner tonight at L'Oranger on St James's Street, which, as everyone knows, is hugely fashionable and awesomely expensive.

'Honestly, Andy, you don't have to take me there. Why don't you just come over here and we can have a takeaway pizza?'

'Sarah, I absolutely insist.'

So L'Oranger it is. Wow. Before the day is out, I need to find Geraldine for a girly chat – somewhere discreet where she can give me expert advice.

An hour later, I am with her in the kitchen. We are sipping coffee and I am trying hard (and failing) not to pick up the chocolate biscuits on offer. What I have to ask her is not the easiest of subjects to broach. Under such circumstances, it is best, I think, to launch straight in.

'Geraldine, how do you give a blow job?'

For this one and only time, I succeed in making Geraldine lose her composure.

'Did I just hear what I think I heard?' she asks after she has finished spluttering into her cup.

'I understand the basic principles, of course. But I really want to do it so well that the particular man in question will remember it as the best that he has ever had.'

'And because of what I told you about Wallis Simpson and her "oriental practices" you think I am probably the best person round here to give you advice?'

'Yes,' I nod.

'You're right,' she sighs. 'I am.'

She pulls me closer. This is not the kind of conversation we want anyone to overhear.

'The top is the most sensitive. Think of it like an ice cream that you wish to lick from every side. When you go further down, be extra careful of your teeth: *never* touch him with your teeth. Remember, he is very sensitive. otherwise it will be like serating a sausage. He won't like it.'

Geraldine notices an empty wine bottle by the sink. She proceeds to place it on the kitchen counter, then bends her head down. My God, I was expecting advice, not a demonstration!

'Like so.'

I watch with fascination.

'What are you doing, Geraldine?' says a voice from behind.

Oh my God. One of the other Lady Clerks, whom I will call Esther (for reasons which will become obvious!) has walked in!

Geraldine looks up completely unfazed.

'Hi, Esther. I am teaching Sarah the art of a good BJ.'

I go scarlet. Geraldine, how could you? Why didn't you lie? Make something up? I will never live this down!

'Carry on,' smiles Esther.

'Well, actually, I think Sarah understands now, don't you, Sarah?'

What do I say?

'Yes,' I mumble.

Geraldine takes the bottle to the sink, washes it, then hands it to me.

'Have a go then!'

'I can't!'

'Yes, you can, Sarah.'

Oh well, I can't disappoint the Head Girl – even in front of Esther – so down I go.

'Hmm,' says Esther. 'Try stroking simultaneously. Always works for me.'

I nearly faint at the candour. This is like tips from *Cosmopolitan*. But better.

'Bravo!' says Geraldine.

'Star pupil,' smiles Esther.

Well, I am certainly one of the girls now. I might as well be as candid as them.

'I am not sure about the swallowing bit.'

'You have had oysters before?' asks Geraldine.

I nod.

'The first time you had them, you thought them a bit slimy and strange, right? Well, so it is with swallowing. You get used to it and then you like it. And, like oysters, it is nutritiously high in protein. A perfect midday meal.'

The three of us collapse in giggles.

Later on, I take a call from adorable Andy.

'You will have an evening to remember!' he declares. 'We will have champagne and lobster thermidor.'

And afterwards I will have oysters. And, dearest Andy, tonight, you too will have a night to remember. The toast is to you, Wallis Simpson. And Geraldine and Esther.

Early November 1988

It is afternoon in the office and we are all having a wonderful giggle. One of the Lady Clerks called Helen has recently been bringing her wire-haired Jack Russell terrier, Basil, into the office. Helen shrieks out his name so fiercely sometimes, we have renamed her Sybil, after Basil's wife in the classic television series *Fawlty Towers,* starring John Cleese.

For our amusement and Basil's exercise needs, we have taken to dismantling a particular curtain pole, which we place between the doors of the connecting state rooms. Basil is commanded to jump over it, which he does with determined enthusiasm, reducing us to shrieks of laughter while portraits of various sombre monarchs stare down at us. What do they all make of this undignified pandemonium, I wonder?

In the midst of this merriment, an operatic voice greets us with an aria from Verdi's *Rigoletto*. It is the claret-faced Ken Wharfe, the incredibly funny Personal Protection Officer of the Princess of Wales. Dear Ken often comes over to see us these days and we hugely enjoy his visits. But sometimes I wonder why he is not at Princess Diana's side. Perhaps she is getting protection elsewhere, I think naughtily, making poor Ken, in such moments, somewhat redundant. Really, Sarah, this is outrageous. Stop it! It is just that I am starting to feel so liberated that I see sex everywhere. What am I turning into?

'My goodness, girl,' says Ken after he has finished his aria. 'you have more flowers on your desk than Covent Garden Market.'

It is true. Andy has been quite expressive in his affections of late.

'Besides the obvious, what is your secret, Sarah?'

I give Ken a demure smile and carry on with my task. My secret, Ken, is one I share only with Geraldine, Esther and Wallis Simpson.

Another great joy in the office is that Miss Frosty, who was handling the Princess of Wales's fan mail, has left and been replaced with Victoria Mendham. Darling Victoria is, I can report, lovely, pretty and delightful. Since she has joined, she has been nothing but pure joy. Poor Victoria has a slight lisp and I say 'poor' advisedly, because a lisp can be quite an impediment when you have to answer the telephone here. Our standard greeting is a chiming 'The Prince and Princess of Wales's office'. Now say it again with a lisp: 'The Printh and

Printheth of Waleth'th offith!' See what I mean? Or, as Victoria would say, 'Thee what I mean?'

Victoria and I have recently been having hysterics over some of HRH's fan mail, mainly from women in America's hinterland who, for some reason, blatantly proposition him. Perhaps rumours of HRH's 'troubles' are circulating strongly in the Midwest? These letters of proposal always contain a photograph. It is rarely a snap and usually a studio photograph, for which the lady in question has gone to some expense. The huntress for HRH's affections invariably wears an outfit similar to those worn by Diana during her engagement. They even do their hair in a similar style as well. No, girls, I want to say, you have got it wrong! That look is no longer à la mode. It is passé. Get modern! But my telepathic cries go unheeded. Today, I have chosen the following missive as the Love Letter of the Week but, because I must be discreet, I have changed the name and address of the suitor:

> Dear Charles, I do hope that you don't mind me addressing you so. I know what with you being the future King of England that I should address you as Your Royal Highness but I have long sensed that you and I might have an intimate connection. And one day, a happy day, you would be calling me Millie (short for Millicent) and me calling you Charles. I realise this is strange to you but I have long had the feeling that Princess Diana is not the right woman for you. Looking at recent photographs of you, I think I am right, as you look really strained and sad. And you once looked so happy in yourself. Because I feel this strong connection between us, you won't be surprised to know

that I have created a small shrine for you in my back bedroom. I have pictures of you at your school in Scotland, as a naval captain, as a fighter pilot and as a polo player. You really are a fine and worthy successor to your mother, Queen Elizabeth. I spend many happy afternoons in this room gazing at you.

As you will see from the attached photograph, I weigh 120 lbs and stand 5 ft 8 in. tall and I am 31. I take regular exercise and attend church every Sunday. I am also a passionate woman, so you won't be disappointed in that department, if you know what I mean!!!

Todd Shecter and I divorced two years ago, so I know the pain of a break-up. If that ever happens with you and your wife, Princess Diana, you will find me comforting and most understanding. I find prayer helps. Incidentally, I have two children, Sherman and Britney, ages 5 and 3. If you and I ever 'make it', I know Todd won't object if you adopt them. I am sure they will play well with Prince William and Prince Harry and, besides, they will like being a Prince and Princess themselves! They will certainly like having bigger bedrooms and servants and stuff!

If you finish with Princess Diana, then you know who to call!

Yours truly,

Millicent Shecter,

1103 Canyon Drive,

Little Springs, Milwaukee.

Sorry, Millicent from Milwaukee, but you are joining a long queue! This week alone, you are competing against Penny from Nebraska, Cheryl from Idaho, Nancy from Alabama,

Billy Jean from Jacksonville and Cathy from Montana. And, girls, dare I say it, if HRH does ever divorce, you will be facing some stiff home-grown competition. I cannot imagine that the ladies of Britain will let the Royal Prince go without a fight! It happened once with an American. Never again. Oh no! Our boudoir skills are up to speed now. You can rely on us to keep the British end up!

The award, however, for the most enterprising pitch goes to Gemma from Salt Lake City.

> If, Sir, you convert to being a Mormon, you can have
> as many wives as you like! There will be no need for
> any divorce ever!

I am tempted to present this to Commander Aylard but think better of it.

But it is not only droves of American women that HRH sends into a swoon. The Boss has a persistent admirer in Jorge, a bodybuilder from Barcelona in Spain. I have so far received three letters from Jorge. In each, he professes undying admiration for HRH and urges the Boss to employ him as his bodyguard and devoted servant. To demonstrate his credentials for such employment, Jorge attaches to each letter photographs of himself posing virtually nude. My favourite is one of him crouching down and flexing his muscles. His flesh-colored jock strap is most becoming.

Poor Jorge, I think, you are barking up the wrong tree here. If you are seriously seeking Royal work, I want to tell him, you should redirect your efforts to Buckingham Palace, where at least half the male staff are inclined to a conspicuous fondness for the company of other men. They would certainly appreciate your magnificent physique!

One of the problems, I fear, is that the standard letter we send back to these admirers only encourages them. My reply to Millicent is the same as my reply to Billy Jean, Gemma, Jorge, etc.:

> Dear Millicent,
> Thank you so much for your letter.
> His Royal Highness is deeply touched by your expressions of warmth and support. He wishes you all the best.
> Yours sincerely,

Would I be put off by a response like that if I harboured delusional romantic cravings for someone I had never met? If I was Millicent back in Little Springs, Milwaukee, the very idea that HRH might have actually read my letter would make me faint. No wonder so many admirers feel encouraged to continue writing. The standard letter is absolutely proper, but I can see why, in the minds of some, it is construed as a bit of a flirtatious come-on.

I shall await with interest a second letter from Mrs Millicent Shecter enquiring, no doubt, about the prospective bedrooms and special privileges that will be accorded to their future Royal Highnesses Prince Sherman and Princess Britney.

Victoria has it just as bad. Though her postbag for the Princess is about half the size of mine (lucky girl), a lot of the love letters the Princess receives are from gentlemen who make Millicent's overtures seem utterly reasonable. Such suitors generally inform the Princess they have been commanded to have a relationship with her by no less an authority than God. Well, I suppose it is said that the

Almighty moves in mysterious ways. Who are we, mere humble minions at the Palace, to say these love-smitten gentlemen are mistaken?

Mid-November 1988

Today is HRH's 40th birthday. Happy Birthday, Your Royal Highness! The nation salutes you. I can say this with some authority because I have been working here all hours trying to sort out his postbag. You would not believe how many birthday cards HRH has received. Over five thousand. They started coming in three days ago. There are huge sacks of them piled up round my desk. I gaze at them despairingly. How am I going to answer them all? It will take me months. I decide to put the problem to Richard Aylard. He immediately grasps the enormity of the task and makes an executive decision there and then.

'Don't bother to reply to any of them.'

'What, none of them?' I say, somewhat shocked.

'The cards sent to HRH by his friends, of course, have to be replied to, so I suggest you go through them all and separate those from cards from organisations and members of the public. You can hand me the cards from his friends.'

'What do I do with the other cards?'

Richard looks at me and shrugs.

'There is no room here to put up five thousand cards. We don't even have the space to archive them, so there is just one thing for it – bin them.'

Richard is quite right, of course, but somehow it seems so brutal. I have a strong feeling they should be displayed somewhere in public to acknowledge the affection of the people for their future King. Somehow just chucking them straight into the rubbish feels sacrilegious, even if it is, I suppose, the only sensible thing we can do.

So here I sit sorting out the sackfuls of these birthday cards, stacking them into piles of fifty. One in six cards, you will not be surprised to hear, is from a Millicent of the USA, using HRH's birthday as an opportunity to push forward her claim as a future mistress or wife.

Many might condemn these women as shameless hussies, no less. But I for one rather admire their 'Go For It' spirit. Bravo, women of America, bold huntresses of the human heart! Let's face it, you not only won and married our Edward VIII, you later, in the person of Hollywood actress Grace Kelly, snaffled the ultra-eligible Prince Rainier of Monaco.

I also think it seems a pity to chuck out these particular cards because someone clever – a psychologist, historian or anthropologist – might gain some valuable insight into the collective and optimistic yearning of another nation's women to possess the heart of a remote and married Royal prince over 4,000 miles away. What's that all about? Do British women yearn collectively for American dynastic leaders?

Why not? I could hardly imagine a British woman turning down a Mellon, Kennedy, Vanderbilt or Rockefeller or indeed any of those grand people who are part of the 400. Would I pass up such an opportunity? You can bet I wouldn't. So what is the difference between America's natural aristocracy and Europe's nobility? It's all in the title. Everyone loves a Lord; they go mad for Marquesses, dotty over Dukes and they swoon over Princes.

Princes are the tops. It all goes back to childhood when we young girls dreamt of being Sleeping Beauty or Cinderella. We were pretty but vulnerable to a grim fate. Who rescued us?

Not Mr Charming, not Lord Charming (though he might do), but *Prince* Charming! You see the ultimate Alpha Man just has to be a Prince.

Now there are lots of strange people who pass themselves off as Princes, but there is only a handful of proper real ones. You can find them in the Who's Who of grand people, the *Almanach de Gotha*. But for the average girl, the Prince you want to go for is a British Royal one. Step forward Your Royal Gorgeousness, my very own HRH Prince of Wales.

However, the efforts of the Millicents are not entirely in vain, I think, as I tear off the American stamps from the envelopes. More donations for Alan the Liveryman.

Some of the other birthday cards are really touching, notably those from classes of primary-school children around the country. I discreetly put these aside and make an executive decision of my own to reply to them. After all, what's a small effort on my part when you can make twenty children's day by thanking them on Palace notepaper on behalf of their future King?

Another batch of cards are from the two hundred-odd organisations with which HRH has some association, like the Abbeyfield Society, for example, which does fantastic work for the elderly and has an active branch in Shropshire. Being a local girl, I am obviously dead keen on it – I admit I always make sure that any correspondence I spot from the Abbeyfield Society, of which HRH is patron, is dealt with pronto. Another Shropshire charity is the Ironbridge Gorge Museum Trust, of which HRH is also patron – priority response here too!

The majority of the cards, however, are from random members of the public simply wishing HRH hugely well on this momentous milestone. It just goes to show how right Geraldine is. There is a huge spring of natural affection for HRH, which is not reflected in the gallons of ink the media uses to mock or belittle him. I sweep the cards into the refuse bags feeling horribly guilty.

It is not just cards that HRH receives. The office has been sent six huge unsolicited birthday cakes. What are we to do with them? Richard is inspired. We will get the liverymen to deliver them to nearby hospitals. Clever Richard.

So what is HRH doing today? I learn that he is up in Birmingham, where his main charity, the Prince's Trust, is throwing a celebratory lunch for him in the Birmingham tram depot. Is this where the future monarch should be having his 40th birthday lunch? In a tram depot? Is the Princess up there celebrating with him, I wonder?

It is now 4 p.m. and I am thinking about a drinks party I am going to this evening when suddenly Dave Dreamy Wright summons us all into a room. I should imagine that he wants us all to sign some huge birthday card for the Boss. It seems a bit pointless, since I will only have to chuck it in the bin after HRH sees it – if he ever does.

But no, it appears as though he is going to make an announcement. So, here we stand, all the Lady Clerks. What is he going to say? Do we have tomorrow off? Is there to be an office holiday, perhaps, to celebrate our future king's milestone?

'I just wish to tell you that His Royal Highness will be here in about ten minutes. Kindly stop working so we can all be with him to celebrate his birthday!'

I feel the ground falling away from me. The Boss is coming here to spend half an hour with us, his Lady Clerks, on his

40th birthday! Oh my God. If only I had known, I could have gone to the hairdresser! I could have gone out and bought a smart dress for the occasion and those second-hand Russell & Bromley shoes I spotted in the local charity shop. This is too much!

I look around. I can see everyone else is exhibiting the same mix of excitement and anxiety – except, of course, for Geraldine, who looks quite unfazed as per usual. We then trot like a collective herd to the Ladies to sharpen up our appearances. I am dressed much like the others in a pale Laura Ashley skirt and a frilly Princess of Wales collared shirt. I pull out my lipstick and then quickly apply some mascara. We all trot back again.

A large white cake is now carried into the room and placed on the table. Another one! Where do they come from, all these cakes? Am I nervous or what? It is like having to face the Headmaster all over again. I decide to hide behind Geraldine. What is the protocol when meeting HRH? I have never done this before. I have a flash of inspiration. I will take my cue from Richard Aylard, who is standing alongside Geraldine. After all, Richard is the Assistant Private Secretary no less. If he doesn't know what to do, then who does?

There is a mild commotion outside and then in walks HRH. My goodness, he looks so handsome and athletic – much younger than his forty years. He is wearing, *so* appropriately, a single-breasted suit with the Prince of Wales check, which suits his colouring perfectly. But it is his eyes that captivate me. They are deep blue and they twinkle. I stare at him hypnotised. Oh dear. I think I am falling in love. My future King stands just eight feet away. I come over all light-headed. I do hope I don't faint.

My inner nanny cuts in. Don't be a silly girl. Pull yourself together. I study the back of Richard's head intently. Suddenly, Dave Dreamy Wright calls out, 'Happy Birthday, Your Royal Highness!' Everyone then echoes the greeting and I see Richard bowing in front of me. I follow suit and then look around. Oh my God! All the women are curtseying. Of course. I find myself blushing a deeper shade of scarlet.

Oh no! How can I have done this? I nervously glance around, expecting to see some of my Lady Clerk colleagues sniggering at my dreadful *faux pas*. But I realise that I am at the back. No one could have seen me. Phew! I begin to breathe more easily when all of a sudden I am seized by an appalling realisation. Yes, someone could definitely have seen me. *He* was facing me. HRH himself! Oh, the embarrassment of it all!

HRH is by this time talking to Dave Wright and Richard. He proceeds to cut the cake. I get a whiff of it even from the back. It appears the fruit-mix contents have been liberally doused in rum. A few bites of this cake and you would be over the limit.

HRH then steps forward to hand out slices of the intoxicating *gateau* to all of us in the room. Was it shyness or a genuine reluctance that made everyone put up their hands and say, 'No thank you, Your Royal Highness'?

He chats to some of the Lady Clerks, eats some of the cake, and I gaze in awe from behind the safety of Geraldine's back at my future King. Did he notice my appalling mistake? Probably not. And if he did, would he really care? I cannot imagine him taking offence. Indeed, I think he would find it rather funny that a new Lady Clerk was so gauche that she bowed instead of curtsied. In fact, if he did see it, it has probably made his day. I just wish it wasn't me that had been the idiot.

December 1988

We are all in a state of feverish excitement here at the office as today is the Royal Christmas lunch. I had an absolute wardrobe crisis this morning, as you can imagine. Panic stations or what? I think I tried on every outfit I own, slinging them all onto my bed in an absolute frenzy. My God, I have *nothing* to wear, I thought. Then I remembered my job interview.

What was I told? That's right! I remember. Deputy Private Secretary Wright told me how much he liked my outfit. He said it was very 'Christmassy'. Inspiration at last! But where had I put it? I hadn't taken it to the charity shop, had I?

Phew! There it was at the very back of the wardrobe. Sigh. Relax. Yikes, it is not ironed. Panic stations again!

Anyway, here I am, flustered like all the other Lady Clerks. Every available mirror is in use as we re-organise our hair, adjust our dresses and re-apply make-up.

'Do I look all right?'

'Yes, darling. you look fabulous!'

'No, seriously!'

'Seriously, you look super!'

'Oh my God! I have laddered my tights! This is a disaster!'

'Don't worry. I have a spare pair, I think, in my desk!'

Honestly, we are like a coop of flapping chickens! Suddenly, it is announced that the coach has arrived. Oh my God, I am so excited I could be sick! We all bundle out of the front door and across the Stable yard. We all scramble into the coach as excited as children on their way to a birthday party.

The coach takes us sedately through Piccadilly and round Hyde Park before we stop at the Berkeley Hotel in Belgravia. I notice other coaches arriving, too. As we alight, some of my Lady Clerk colleagues start waving to the passengers disembarking from them – all staff from Kensington Palace and Highgrove.

In we walk to the reception, which is very art deco, very 1920s. There must be a hundred of us. I find myself mingling with butlers, under-butlers, gardeners, Valets, chauffeurs – the entire retinue from the two palaces and HRH's beautiful country home in Gloucestershire, which, sigh, I suppose I will never get to see.

The staff at the Berkeley Hotel are all so charming and attentive, welcoming us with ice-cold champagne. Thrown in amongst so many strangers, Victoria and I stick closely together, not letting the other out of our sight. Geraldine, a veteran of the Palace, is admirably cool and confident, gliding with ease through the throng.

Suddenly, there is a discernible hush. I follow everyone's eyes and look to the entrance. Oh my God, it is *him*! This is the second time I have seen HRH, my esteemed boss, in the flesh. My heart starts to beat as hard as it did the first time. In he walks, smartly dressed in a gray flannel suit, fingering his cuff, his distinguished Royal cheeks glowing healthily. All at once, the men bow and we women bend our knees and curtsey. Phew, this time I get it right.

I am embarrassed to admit it, but I have been practising my curtsey in front of the mirror for this very occasion every night since I bowed. Normally, when I am a bit piddled late in the evening, the curtsey is quite extravagant, a kind of theatrical Regency flourish, where I cock my head to one side, my fluttering eyes looking demurely towards the red carpet. In my Royal fantasies, there is always a red carpet.

My other curtsey, i.e. when I am not piddled, is much more restrained and I bob my knees and smile graciously. It is this restrained curtsey with which I now greet His Royal Highness. Ho, hum, it comes but once a year, I think to myself. Next year, who knows? I might try and catch his Royal eye with my Regency curtsey!

Then there is another hush and in walks the Princess of Wales. My goodness, she looks stunning, wearing a navy-blue coatdress with gilt buttons. Sorry, Millicent, you cannot even begin to compete. No wonder the press cannot get enough of her. The assembled company bobs and bows again.

Now we are walking through to the dining room, where we cluster around the seating plan. I am a little sad and disappointed to find that the seat on my right is empty. Oh dear. Perhaps someone in HRH's employment at Highgrove or Kensington Palace is ill. Anyway, I find my place and sit down. The first course is vegetable roulade, and very scrummy it is too. I don't know a single soul at the table, but we all engage in polite banter.

At HRH's request, the theme for this Christmas lunch is Italian, so the second course is pasta with cepes, a tasty exotic strain of mushroom. We are served some delicious red and white Italian wines. The sum total of my knowledge of Italian viticulture extends to Chianti and Frascati. What we are being served right now is anybody's guess.

I glance around and note that the Prince and Princess are at two separate tables. I wonder whether this is a deliberate policy or possibly something to do with their mysterious 'troubles'.

As the main course is taken away and I am talking some polite nonsense to somebody, there is a sudden hush at our table and a voice behind me politely says, 'Excuse me.'

I recognise the voice. Now where have I heard it before? It does have a very familiar ring. I turn round and as the chair right next to me is pulled out I nearly fall off mine in amazement. Oh my God! I cannot believe my eyes. Sarah, is this really happening? His Royal Highness, the Prince of Wales, the Boss, is sitting down next to me and politely greeting those around him.

Come on, Sarah! Take a deep breath. Get a grip, girl. So that is why the seat was empty. He was intending all along to sit next to me at the pudding stage. Oh my God, it is all too much! Just as I am absorbing this extraordinary development, he turns his frame round to me. He looks into my eyes and then opens his mouth.

'Hello, you look strangely familiar. Have we met?'

I gaze back into his oh-so-beautiful blue eyes. I muster all my self-control. This is my moment with my employer and future King. Don't blow it, Sarah!

'Yes,' I squeak. Come on, Sarah, get on with it, girl! 'Your Royal Highness kindly offered me some cake on his birthday.'

I look down, blushing. Sarah! What are you up to, speaking to him like that? Why are you saying *his* birthday as if he is not here?

'So you are a Lady Clerk, then?'

'Yes,' I squeak again, staring at my napkin.

'Do you find the work interesting?'

Of course I find the work interesting, I want to tell him. More than that, I absolutely love it. But I am so overwhelmed that my tongue freezes and is unable to obey the screaming commands of my brain. So I put on a wan smile, glance at him sideways and nod my head.

'Hmm,' he says in contemplation. I look up now. His Royal Magnificence has now turned his attention to our third course, the *panettone*, a rich Italian bread-like cake made with eggs, fruit and butter. I see him picking out the sultanas in a rather testy fashion and pushing them to one side. Sultanas are not HRH's thing, I gather.

But my mind is focused on one thing. After my risible attempt at discourse, will he speak to me again? He now turns his Godlike gaze to a man across the table.

'I say, Chris, those cepes were delicious. Any chance, do you think, of us finding any in the grounds?'

My future King is no longer addressing me but Chris Barber, his chef at Highgrove. Oh my God, he is so close I could actually touch him! Aaargh! I inwardly scream. This is all too much. What would you pay, what would you do, Millicent, to be here in my place? Take a deep breath. Treasure this moment, Sarah. You are sitting next to the future King, here, right now. Look around. Remember this scene. You will be telling your grandchildren about it one day.

Never mind that you completely fluffed it and failed to construct even one coherent sentence. You are here. You are touching the face of God . . . well, not quite, but close enough. Naturally, because you are so pathetic a conversationalist, he won't ever want to sit next to you again. Hardly a Jane Austen, dear, are we? He will probably insist that you are kept as far away as possible, so he never gets lumbered with you again. But, never mind, this is it. The future King of the United Kingdom and Commonwealth is here at the seat on your right.

'So what is the task that Richard has allotted you?'

Am I dreaming? He is addressing me. Actually talking to me again. He has given me another chance. Oh kind and wonderful Prince, I won't fail you now. And I won't fail myself this time either. Keep cool, Sarah.

'I am in charge of your fan mail, Your Royal Highness.'

'Very good. I do hope it is not too tedious for you.'

'Oh no, Your Royal Highness, it is very, very, very, very interesting.'

His Royal Highness is looking at me closely and smiles. Sarah, you idiot. How could you be so stupid and repeat 'very' like that? He probably thinks you are an imbecile.

'Good. Keep up the good work. Oh, and please forgive me, I never asked your name.'

'Sarah,' I gulp. 'Goodall.'

'Well, Sarah, I am delighted to meet you.'

His Royal Handsomeness then turns his attention to someone else. And I sit in a state of rapture. His words echo in my ear. He asked *me* to forgive *him*! For what? He knows my name. He has repeated my name. He said *Sarah*.

My inner nanny cannot take any more of this: Sarah, stop being an idiot. Of course he said your name. It is his job. You are his employee, girl! Get a grip. But my romantic rapture is still in the ascendant.

Suddenly, there is a hush. And up he stands. He starts to speak from here, next to me. My God, it gets better. On his other side, I note, is the man I was speaking to earlier, who works as something or other at Kensington Palace. So I am *the* woman at the side of His Royal Perfection as he addresses the assembled throng. My goodness, my grandchildren will hear this over and over again, whether they like it or not.

I glance round the room. All eyes are on HRH as he speaks – except, I notice, those of his wife, Princess Diana. The Princess is in a far-off table at the other end of the room and she is whispering to one of her table companions and giggling. Surely this is not really quite the right thing to do when your husband is giving a speech? Surely, Your Royal Highness, your little joke can wait at least until your husband has finished speaking? Is this bad form or what?

Her loss, think I. *I* am at his side instead. No disloyalty from me, oh no! I gaze up and quietly glow as he masterfully compliments us all. History in the making, Sarah. This, right now, is what I am experiencing. Not the nation's history or his history, but *my* history.

'You have all done so well this year and I want to thank you so much for that. Keep up the good work!'

I will, I will.

His Magnificence pauses and looks around, even casting a glance at me. This is too much!

'I see a lot of new faces here this year . . .'

Yes, Your Royal Gorgeousness, and you have noted mine!

'Oh my God, how many of you are there now? You seem to be getting bigger and bigger!'

We all roar with appreciative laughter.

'Happy Christmas to you all!'

And happy, *happy* Christmas to you!

HRH sits down again. Then one of his detectives comes up and whispers in his ear. Next thing, he stands up and, giving us all a quiet wave, slips from the room. Sigh. He has left us. Till next year, dear and darling HRH!

From the corner of my eye, I notice that the Princess is also leaving – by a completely different door. How odd. Perhaps this is for security reasons to foil any possible assassination attempt? Or possibly it is for a much more straightforward reason – one that I don't really want to contemplate. How sad. How very sad.

Suddenly, we are all being swept up again. Into the coach we clamber, all gossiping and giggling. Out we get at St James's Palace and moments later we are in the State Rooms. Do we talk about our one-to-one encounters with HRH or the Princess of Wales? Of course we don't. We are Lady Clerks at the Palace, don't you know? And Lady Clerks never stoop to that kind of obvious boasting, do we? Oh no.

We all leave the office rather tipsy. I am in a tearing hurry to get back. I can't wait to pick up the telephone and tell Mummy everything!

3

Food and Weight

January 1989

On Tuesday last week, following the Christmas jollities, I returned home to Buer Road and found it odd that I had difficulty fitting into a dress I had bought just six weeks earlier. How strange. Had the dress mysteriously shrunk or did I pick the wrong size? So I went into the bathroom and weighed myself. Obviously something was wrong with the scales. So I picked them up to adjust the setting. Oh dear. There was nothing wrong with them at all!

No, I won't tell you how much I now weigh. It is too embarrassing. God, was I depressed or what? The next day I discussed my weight issue with Victoria. She said she was also depressed about her weight. What? I would die to be as slim as her. What is she on about? But that's women friends for you, I suppose. We always do everything by consensus, right down to sharing paranoia.

Anyway, we decided to go to a newsagent to find a helpful magazine or two and discovered *Slimmers* and *Slimming*. We bought both and split the cost, which is pathetic, I know, but we were both broke. Victoria took *Slimmers* back on the train to read and I took *Slimming*. We read them cover to cover and then swapped the following evening. Victoria told me she particularly likes the case studies of Before (a hippopotamus) and After (a giraffe).

Well, you have guessed it. By Friday, we started our diet. One of the tricks about going on a diet, I have read, is not to think about food, especially while you are working. You must put it out of your mind. Think about a favourite dress, a party, a boyfriend – sex, even! But don't succumb to the seductive commands of the tummy because, before you know it, you'll be in the kitchen unconsciously nabbing one of those chocolate digestives and piling on the calories. This is sensible down-to-earth advice. Who could question it? But what if part of your job relates to food? You think mine has nothing to do with food? Think again.

Somebody somewhere has recently written in the press that one of HRH's favourite dishes is roast nut cutlet and that the Princess's is watercress soup. Moreover, the Royal couple even have special recipes for each that they instruct their chefs to follow. So all week Victoria and I have been inundated with these damned requests from members of the public to send them the respective recipes.

I have tried both dishes myself. They are absolutely delicious. Unfortunately, my diet plan forbids me from having either of them again, at least for the moment. So you can imagine that, four days into the diet, the hunger pangs Victoria and I feel anyway are painfully exacerbated as we dutifully reply to yet another respondent with letters enclosing the recipes. I torture myself by reading them once again:

RECIPE FOR HRH THE PRINCE OF WALES'S VEGETARIAN NUT ROAST

six to eight servings

INGREDIENTS: 1 tablespoon of virgin olive oil; one-third of a cup of toasted hazelnuts, ground; Two-thirds of a cup of walnuts, ground; Two-thirds of a cup of brazil nuts, ground; 12 oz of tomatoes, blanched, peeled, and chopped; 1 large onion, finely chopped; 2 cloves of garlic, finely chopped; Quarter of lb fresh mushrooms, chopped; Half teaspoon of dried basil; Half teaspoon dried oregano; 1 teaspoon sea salt;1 egg, well beaten

METHOD: Preheat the oven to 220°C. Lightly oil a 2-lb loaf tin or round mould. Line with greaseproof paper. Place the nuts, tomatoes, onion, garlic, mushrooms, basil, oregano, sea salt and egg in a medium-sized bowl. Mix until the ingredients are thoroughly combined. Turn the mixture into the prepared loaf tin, smoothing the surface with the back of a spoon. Place the tin in oven and bake for 30–40 minutes or until roast has shrunk slightly from sides of the tin. Let cool slightly and, with a knife around the edges, turn out to a wooden board or plate. Cut into thick slices and serve with mushroom or onion gravy.

(If, like the Prince of Wales and Mr Carluccio, one likes to go and 'gather' fresh cepes, then these could always replace more conventional mushrooms.)

RECIPE FOR HRH THE PRINCESS OF WALES'S WATERCRESS SOUP

four to six servings

INGREDIENTS:2 oz of butter; 2 oz of flour; 2 pts of chicken stock; 12 oz of watercress (chopped with large stems removed); 1 pt of single cream

METHOD: Heat butter in a saucepan and stir in the flour, stirring for a few minutes. Remove from heat and pour in the chicken stock, whisking hard. Bring to a simmer and add watercress. Return to a simmer, cover and cook over a low heat for 20 minutes. Puree in a blender, return to saucepan and heat, adding the cream. Ladle into bowls.

At lunch, Victoria and I do our usual and head off to the Buckingham Palace canteen. What has Graham got for us today? Oh dear, it is one of the chef's specials: beef stroganoff with mashed potato. Adam was lured into sin with an apple – even I could resist an apple, but beef stroganoff with mashed potato is a diabolic temptation that would make the Heavenly Host salivate.

Victoria and I look at each other. We are not, I repeat, *not* going to be tempted. But, oh God, it doesn't just look delicious, it also smells divine. As they catch the heady and enticing aroma, my nostrils quiver involuntarily. Victoria senses the weakening of my resolve.

'Remember the pledge,' she says firmly.

'The salad, please, Graham,' I say with a sigh.

'But are you sure you don't want the stroganoff?' asks Graham, his camp intonation giving each syllable a theatrical lilt.

'Not today, Graham. I will have the salad, please.'

'Hmm. But you will have the sticky toffee pudding afterwards, won't you? You do like your sticky toffee pudding, don't you? Even more than jam roly-poly. I remember last time we had that on the menu, you had seconds!'

Graham is quite clearly an agent of Satan. Summoning all my self-control, I manage to say, admittedly in the most strangulated voice, 'And afterwards I will have an apple.'

Graham cocks an eyebrow. 'An apple it is, then. The sticky toffee pudding is, I assure you, delicious. Perhaps after the salad, you will change your mind.'

'Graham, kindly stop being sadistic.'

'As madam pleases.'

Victoria and I sit down. I bite into a fresh, wholesome, nutritionally enriching stick of celery. Yuck! 'If that man had his way, he would have me turn into Two Ton Bessie,' I lament.

'It is not just you, Sarah. I am suffering too,' Victoria mournfully replies.

We stare miserably at two officials from Buckingham Palace across the table as they tuck in to the steaming stroganoff. Their expressions show all too clearly that they are tasting heaven.

'I cannot bear this,' says Victoria.

'Me neither.'

Victoria and I push aside our plates, each grab an apple and leave.

With an hour left to kill before we are obliged to return to our desks, we set off to Knightsbridge to see the last of the January sales. Soon, we are peering enviously into fashionable shops, some of which we enter, pretending we are buyers. We wish. On my Palace wage, which has now increased this new calendar year by just £15 a week, it is the charity shops we should be perusing.

While Victoria and I are salivating over a gorgeous crocodile-skin Hermes handbag, a snip at £400, I ask her whether she has ever met 'The Bossette', which is office slang for Princess Diana.

'Just once.'

'What about you? Met the Boss?'

'Just the once.'

We continue ogling the bag until a severe-looking assistant, dressed top to bottom in fascist designer black, comes up and asks 'Can I help you?' in a tone that suggests he knows perfectly well that he can't. We mumble the obligatory 'Just looking', and he swings away, giving us a contemptuous sneer as if to say, 'Dream on, ladies!'

I address Victoria again. 'Funny that our lives are dedicated to their postbags yet the Boss and Bossette remain as remote from us as from the people whose letters we answer.'

'Yes, I suppose that's true.'

'Imagine, we could work for them all our lives and still know no more about either of them than what we read in the newspapers.'

The thought lingers a moment before wafting away. We saunter out of the shop and continue our journey down Sloane Street, peering periodically through shop windows.

'Victoria?'

'Yes?'

'I'm starving.'

'So am I.'

We dive into a sandwich shop.

February 1989

Next time you order game from the Royal kitchens, I tell myself, *do not* assume that the bird or animal will come seal-packed and ready for the oven, as if you are buying it from a supermarket.

The game of which I talk is two 'Windsor' pheasants reared and shot on the Windsor Castle Estate of the Royal Family. Well, I presume that is the case, otherwise they would be called Royal Sandringham pheasants or Royal Highgrove pheasants.

Knowing that Andy likes his game what he calls 'high' and I call pongy, I order the pheasants for collection on Tuesday and when the day arrives I head off to BP to pick them up. I enter the Palace through the side entrance and go through the customary security procedures. I then set off to the door down to the kitchens. But I appear to have gone on autopilot and it is only when I am upstairs in the dining room that I remember what I have come for. No, Sarah, it is not a meal you are after but those pheasants! I turn round to retrace my steps and then I suddenly notice that the door to the front entrance hallway is open. I sneakily put my head round to see what it is like.

Oh my God. Over 100 foot in length and 30 feet wide, it is amazing. Before me are beautifully carved gilt mirrors, precious displays of porcelain, priceless old Masters, marble busts, huge crystal chandeliers and wonderful French eighteenth-century furniture. At the other end are two busty domestics squashed into their white overall dresses pushing their old-fashioned Hoovers backwards and forwards over the lush red Wilton carpet. I take a breath. I shut my eyes.

Right now, I imagine there is an orchestra playing Strauss's *'The Blue Danube'* and that I am waltzing round the room in a flowing silk ballgown. In my arms is my tail-coated handsome and adoring Prince, my darling Andy. Round and round we go without a care in the world. Problems of meeting rent demands, paying utility bills, affording a decent hairdresser, etc., all the tedious anxieties which bedevil me on a daily basis have flown like an exorcised bat from the French windows before me. I am now a princess, held in the arms of the man of my dreams in this fabulous palace. I am no longer on earth but in heaven. 'Tra, la, la, la, lah! lah-lah! lah-lah! Tra, la, la, la, lah! lah-lah! lah-lah!'

Suddenly, I hear a cough. My dream fragments. Behind me is a young and rather dashing livery-clad Footman. I give him an embarrassed grin and mutter something like 'just looking' before heading swiftly back down the stairs to the basement.

While above is all opulence, grace and splendour, the world below, I discover, is like the bowels of a huge oceangoing cruiser. The walls are painted battleship gray and there are pipes and ducts and silver cladding everywhere. I go down a corridor searching for clues. There are closed doors marked with strange titles like 'Master of the Clockworks', 'Keeper of the Mirrors' and 'Privy Purse Entrance'. I feel I have gone back two hundred years in time.

In this unfamiliar and strange new world, I feel like Alice, lost in a surreal stretch of Wonderland. I expect a liveried rabbit to appear any moment with a pocket watch.

Eventually, I do find a Liveryman purposefully striding down the corridor. He directs me back down the corridor to the kitchens. Was it the bad light or did he look unnaturally pale? Has he lived here all his life, I wonder? Has he ever been upstairs even? Has he seen the sunlight?

I enter the kitchen. It is huge and painted an off-white. A doorway into a larder has no door but thin strips of seven-foot plastic through which I can see some harassed-looking kitchen staff fetching and carrying the victuals for the evening's meals.

I am shocked at how utilitarian the whole place is, with huge ovens and massive metal sinks. I was expecting some magic in the kitchens somehow, to reflect the glory of the rooms upstairs, or I anticipated at least a homely warm feel, with jars of olive oil, racks of spices and the tempting smell of baking. The few chefs before me don't even have those lovely white chef hats you see in old movies. How disappointing.

I introduce myself to one of the chefs. He is clueless about my pheasants. Oh dear. I try another. So is he. Panic stations! I strike lucky with the third chef. He goes through the strip-plastic doorway and eventually emerges with my Royal wildfowl. I can't believe my eyes. My pheasants have been neither gutted nor plucked! If it wasn't for their limp posture, you might well have thought they were just asleep and were ready, on awakening, to fly away.

'What am I supposed to do with these?' I bleat.

'Sorry?' he says.

'I can hardly put them in the oven like this, can I?' I wail.

'No, madam, that would not be advisable.'

'Well, why aren't they plucked?' I wail again.

'Presumably, because madam did not order them plucked.'

'You have to *ask* to have them plucked?'

'Yes, madam. It is £1 extra.'

One pound! I would pay twenty right now for them to be plucked. I look at the chef with a pleading and winsome expression. Right now, Mr Chef, you see before you a maiden in frightful distress. Surely, you will come to my rescue?

'Sorry, madam, in normal circumstances I would do it myself, but it's impossible for any of us this evening. State Banquet upstairs. And, as you can see, we are understaffed.

There is a nasty bug going round. Half the kitchen staff are laid up.'

I suppose Her Majesty and her guests do take priority, I unhappily concede as I lug the beautifully plummaged fowls up the stairs out of BP and down the Mall to my car, ignoring the odd looks from passers-by.

The following day at lunchtime, I trudge round various butchers in St James's, Victoria and Knightsbridge ready to pay any price to have the creatures prepared for the oven. And every butcher turns me down.

'Sorry, madam, we would happily do it, but it is not allowed any longer.'

'What do you mean, not allowed?'

'New law. You need a special gaming license.'

'And you don't have one?'

'No, madam.'

'Does *anyone* have a gaming license?' I ask despairingly at the fifth butchers.

'No one *we* know in London, madam.'

That night, I ring Andy to explain my predicament.

'Don't worry. I will pluck them myself when I get down. Love plucking pheasants,' he says and I almost believe him.

Not even a dedicated countryman like Andy can actually *like* plucking pheasants, even special Royal Windsor pheasants. Sigh. What a gentleman my Andy is.

On his instructions, I hang them both from the banisters, so they look like two murderous convicts of the bird world left on the gibbet as an ominous warning to other criminally inclined fowl.

Oh dear. I return on Thursday, completely forgetting that I have left the central heating on. Consequence: the flavoursome process of degeneration has accelerated alarmingly. The smell suggests they have been hanging for twenty-four days, not twenty-four hours. After opening all the windows to dispel the fumes, I shove the birds into the freezer.

Andy arrives on Friday with a huge bouquet of flowers. My heart is all his anyway, but the extravagant gesture makes me dissolve into a puddle. Not having seen Andy for a week, plucking was hardly the first thing on my mind; something else rhyming with it was, though.

Coming out of the bedroom much later that night, I suddenly remember the pheasants. Aaargh! I rush to the freezer and pull them out. They are in a state of frozen rigour mortis, hard enough to be used as offensive weapons. Had I not been so happy with adorable Andy, I think I would have cried.

So here I am the following morning with Andy, gutting and plucking these goddamn chilled pheasants, with feathers all over the floor and the kitchen work surface. As the feathers fly and the entrails of the fowls are torn out, I feel I am performing some ghoulish voodoo ceremony. This is just not civilised; it's medieval. I work at a palace. What are we doing? This is Fulham, not Haiti. And I am not a Priestess of the Black Arts. I am a Lady Clerk!

'This is fun,' says Andy cheerfully.

I give him an odd look. Yeah, like a day out in an abattoir is fun. But then, with the task completed, Andy and I set about preparing the meal.

'Ever told you about a great family recipe?' asks Andy.

'Not now, Andy.'

'No, really. It is called *Phaisan Normande!*' Andy proceeds to tell me how the pheasant is marinated in cider then cooked with apples.

Hell, I decide, let's try it. So, after returning from the grocers with the apples and cider, Andy sets about creating the family dish while I make the starter, a favourite dish from my own repertoire – *Oeufs Mollet*. This delicious concoction is comprised of soft-boiled eggs with their shells removed, wrapped in smoked salmon, drizzled in mayonnaise and sprinkled with chives. Highly recommended. Trust me.

And since I learnt six years ago how to do a brilliant pastry, I create a delicious, if I do say so myself, strawberry tart. *Voilà!*

This is going to be some meal. And I am with the man of my dreams. Oh boy, am I happy or what?

Later that night, Andy, six guests and I play 'drinking forfeit' with Claret, Beaumes de Venise and Calvados to an adaptation of a well-known culinary tongue-twisting verse:

> I am not the Royal pheasant plucker
> I am the Royal pheasant plucker's son
> I am only plucking Royal pheasants
> Till the Royal pheasant plucker comes.

That is enough Royals. Goodnight.

March 1989

In addition to the privilege of access to Royal Estate game, I one day learn of another perk of working here at the Palace – the Royal Film Club, which is not just ludicrously cheap but you are also allowed to take a guest. Tonight, I am taking a friend I'll call 'Mindy', who works as an estate agent in Pimlico.

What I hadn't realised was the palaver it entails to get clearance for a guest. Mindy, I was told, had to be vetted for security reasons. Who knows, Mindy, a girl from a landed family in the shires, might just fit the profile of the modern terrorist! As I set about filling out a special form two weeks beforehand, I could not help myself wondering how the application was processed and who handles it.

Does a courier whisk it to MI5? Presumably, some secret databank is then accessed. Someone then makes discreet enquiries where she works? They tap her telephone? I can understand the effort for a job application, but for a cinema ticket costing only £1? Anyway, Mindy clearly has no shady past and her pass is ready.

Today holds yet another delight: I am taking advantage of the affections of an admirer, one Dr David Owen, over lunch. No, not the smooth and sexy dark-haired politician who appears on our television screens so many nights, but an ornithologist. David, whom I met in Oxford while I was at secretarial college, is a leading expert on a bird called a chough, pronounced 'chuff', which he has told me about at length and which comes from Wales, just like David.

I know all about the chough, thanks to David. Let's see: it is black, has long legs, a curved red bill and, if I remember rightly, the chough likes to stand in shallow water. It does seem rather extraordinary to dedicate your life to studying such a creature, but I suppose each and every species needs an expert 'authority' and for the chough it is David, who is due to arrive any moment.

I go to the bathroom and check my hair and make-up. I do hope, however, that this time the chough is, conversationally speaking, off the menu. I think David and I have done choughs. Yes, there is definitely no more meat on that bone. I start to giggle at my little joke.

I come out and Victoria tells me that a 'gentleman' is awaiting me downstairs. So down the stairs I go to greet my dashing ornithologist in the Chinese Room.

My goodness, David, I think, you look magnificent. Wild, dark curly hair and penetrating eyes. And such a dandy, too, sporting today a brocade waistcoat with what looks like a Hermes tie. Wow, you are every bit as handsome as your political namesake. However, David, I remain spoken for. Andy is my man. But a girl likes to have admirers who take her out for lunch. And you don't get a more dashing lunch companion than you.

Proudly, I take his arm and off we walk down the Mall to the Oxford and Cambridge Club. Obviously, you can only join this club if you are actually a graduate of either of these universities – which everyone knows are for the brainiest in Britain.

David takes me through this egghead emporium to the Ladies Room, which sounds like the bathroom but obviously isn't. We both order gin and tonics from the *maître d'* and David starts filling out a chit for lunch. The club is one of those wonderfully old-fashioned places, rather like the Palace, I suppose.

Being so highly educated, David knows everything about wine and is soon telling me about the Sancerre and the Burgundy that he says will accompany our dishes.

'So what are we having to eat?'

'It's a surprise. You will like it, I promise.'

The *maître d'* returns in ten minutes to tell us the first course is served. We enter a huge dining room and sit down to smoked salmon. David is a marvellously kind lunch companion, but sometimes I wish he wouldn't be quite so clever, because I can't understand half of what he is saying. So I just smile, nod and stare into his lovely eyes.

Next course arrives. What is it? Pheasant! How hilarious. Brilliant. Now I have something to tell David and off I launch into the story of my near disaster with my two Royal Windsor pheasants. Towards the end of the *histoire*, I suddenly detect David is becoming a little withdrawn.

What on earth have I said? The bulb lights up! Oh, Sarah, you idiot! You mentioned all that stuff about Andy. How could you be so insensitive? Think hard now: what are you going to do to save the day? My mind remains a blank. Oh, Sarah, how could you have fouled this up? I am inspired. Foul. Fowl.

I reach out my hand and touch his, then, my eyelashes fluttering, look at him demurely.

'Now, David, you haven't told me yet. I want to know. I am fascinated. What are the latest developments on your research on choughs?'

David's eyes light up. I bet he hasn't had a date who has ever said that to him before.

The lunch continues happily again and I learn yet more about choughs. Poor David, I am really not worthy of you. You deserve another egghead, I think. Yes, she will be really chuffed. Sarah, stop this!

After this fabulously delicious lunch, lovely David walks me back and we agree to stay in contact. I give him a tender kiss on both cheeks. Phew!

Later that evening, I meet up with Mindy and proudly lead her into Buckingham Palace. She is as agog as I was on first entering the inner portals.

'You are right, Sarah. It really is like a village.'

We go to the bar, order ourselves a wine and soda each and sit on the purple banquette.

'This is such a treat,' she says. 'Hey, have I some gossip for you!'

She leans forward and whispers into my ear.

'Did you know that your employer's wife is getting riding lessons from an Officer in the Life Guards?'

'So?'

'It is not just riding lessons with horses she is getting!'

'That is outrageous! It can't be true.'

'They can hardly keep their hands off each other.'

'No!'

'Oh yes. Quite a goer is our Diana. Seemingly it's been going on for some time.'

So my frivolous speculation was spot on. It's no wonder that Diana's Protection Officer, dear Ken Wharfe, comes and sees us so often in the office. He can hardly hang around outside Diana's bedroom while she's at it, can he?

'What's he called?'

'James Hewitt. Rather dishy.'

'Is this James Hewitt her first lover, do you think?'

'No. Now, let me see. Two years ago at Bunty Worcester's wedding she was brazenly snogging this chap called Phillip Dunne on the dance floor. She was quite public about it.'

'That doesn't mean she was doing anything else, though.'

'Then there was Major David Waterhouse, but he was supposedly just a companion.'

'No!'

'And about two years before that, she had a fling with Juan

Carlos, the King of Spain!'

My eyeballs are about to pop out of their sockets. 'The King of Spain!'

'Yes, the King of Spain.'

'And two years before that she apparently had something going with her Protection Officer.'

'Not Ken Wharfe?'

'No, not him. Somebody called Barry Mannakee.'

There is a moment's silence as I absorb Mindy's outrageous revelations.

'His Royal Highness wasn't best pleased about that affair. Virtually walked in on them. He thought Diana was exercising really bad judgement.'

'Bad judgement! Wasn't he furious?'

'Yes, of course he was, but the marriage had started to hit the rocks by then. I am told that was the blow that, for him, finally broke it.'

'What? Over bad judgement?'

'No, it killed the feelings he still had for her. And yes, the bad judgement issue is serious, too. Look, Sarah, the future Queen of England cannot go round bonking the staff. The Princess should stick to her own class. It is not a snob thing. It's practicality.'

'You come from a humble background and then by outrageous chance you have a fling with the Royal Princess who is destined to be our Queen. Suddenly, you are sitting on a fortune. A story like that is worth hundreds of thousands – possibly even a million. For people with little money, it is irresistible. Look what happened with Princess Anne.'

'Don't tell me she had a thing with her Protection Officer?'

'Yes. Well, apparently she had an affair with her Personal

Protection Officer, Peter Cross. The story was printed in *The Sun.*'

'Did he sell the story?'

'Maybe, maybe not – but the story got out.' Mindy takes another sip of her wine and soda.

This is all a bit much to take in. First, I have just learned that the Princess of Wales, the nation's iconic heroine, has been having affairs, and now I am debating the advantages and drawbacks of having it off with a bodyguard – all in the space of a few minutes. I suppose this is the definition of being 'sophisticated'. I try and imagine myself as a rich and pretty estranged wife. On hand is your bodyguard. Hmm.

'I suppose that having a hunky and fit police officer at your permanent beck and call *is* a bit tempting!'

Mindy now points out the drawbacks. 'Yes, but Princess Anne having an affair doesn't imperil the monarchy. It can be brushed off as a foolish indiscretion. Princess Diana, our future Queen, having a dalliance with a Protection Officer is another matter.'

'So this Barry Mannakee business could blow up any moment?'

'It's fine now. Threat over. All brushed under the carpet.'

'How?'

'He's dead. Killed on a motorbike. Two years ago.'

I put my hand over my mouth.

'You don't think . . .'

'Diana apparently does, but it couldn't have been arranged. The circumstances were too extraordinary. It was just a horrible accident. One of those things.'

'But the timing?'

'Yes, the timing was strange. The hand of providence,

perhaps?'

She cocks an eyebrow. Mindy takes another sip of her wine and soda. I feel my jaw still bouncing on the floor. Mindy continues. 'The greatest story on Royals and rough, though, is Margaret and the gangster.'

'Gangster?'

'That's right. Tough cockney boy. Once killed someone. Margaret met him on holiday in Mustique, where she was a guest of Colin Tennant. He used to entertain everyone by pulling out his thingy. Apparently, it is famously huge. He does this party trick, balancing three pint glasses along its length. What's his name? John Bindon, that's right. But, funnily enough, he has not admitted it yet to the press.'

'What, the balancing act with the three pint glasses?'

'No, Sarah, you fool. His fling with Princess Margaret.'

'So then, if he has not admitted it, how do we know it's true?'

'Because she has told friends!'

What? This is too much. Mindy is kidding me. Surely?

'Mindy, how do you know all of this?'

'From Susie.'

'Susie? How does Susie know?'

'From her mother, of course.'

'Her mother! How does she know?'

'Her sister's a Lady-in-Waiting.'

'So?'

Mindy rolls her eyeballs as if I am an idiot, which I probably am. 'Sarah, don't be silly. She is at the centre of Court gossip. There are few secrets here at the Palace.'

My head is spinning. Presumably, then, Mindy knows more.

'So how is my Boss taking this thing with Diana and this Captain Hewitt?'

'He's delighted. Means her attention is devoted elsewhere and she is not screaming and shouting at him any more. Poor fellow, when she screams and shouts, his nerves can't take it.'

'I think he knew the marriage was impossible the night she picked up a huge, heavy Bible and slammed it over his head.'

I think for a bit.

'But people in relationships often do crazy things. All right, they were having a row. So she hits him with the first thing that comes to hand.'

'He was kneeling in prayer when the attack happened,' says Mindy.

'He was kneeling in prayer?' I repeat, aghast.

'That's right. He is very religious, you know.'

'And she attacked him when he was praying?'

'Yes, it shocked him even more than when she went for him earlier with a knife!'

'You're joking?'

'Yes, and she then deliberately cut herself!'

'Come off it!'

'Yes!'

'So when did this all happen?'

'The early days of their marriage.'

'How early?'

Mindy looks up at me over her wineglass. 'Their honeymoon.'

Wow. This is a bit much to take in.

'So is their marriage dead then, do you think?'

Mindy shrugs. 'Never say die!'

There is a pause as Mindy fixes me with a look. Die!

Princess Di! Never say Di! I nearly collapse in giggles.

'Anyway, I wouldn't worry about your Boss. He is occupied elsewhere.'

'With who?'

'Camilla Parker-Bowles.'

'Yes, I have heard about her. Isn't she married?'

'Yes, but they are all very close. Her husband Andrew once had a fling with Princess Anne before either of them were married. In fact, they are all so close that they live opposite each other in a mews, Clareville Grove, next to the Palestinian Liberation Organisation Headquarters.'

'Sorry, Mindy, you have lost me. Who lives opposite who?'

'James Hewitt lives opposite Andrew and Camilla Parker-Bowles. And after their respective assignations, they drive back to Clareville Grove, occasionally arriving at the same time. They always greet each other with a "Good morning" or "Good night", depending on the time.'

'So the respective lovers of His Royal Highness and Her Royal Highness are friends as well as neighbours?'

'Not close friends, but of course they know each other.'

'Because of the fact they are each having it off with one half of the Royal couple?'

'No,' says Mindy. 'Not for that reason.'

'What reason, then?'

'Camilla's husband Andrew is James Hewitt's Commanding Officer. They see each other in the course of their military duties. So of course they are friendly.'

Mindy titters. 'One of my friends, who knows James Hewitt well, told me something really funny.'

This gossip is quite amazing. I am agog. 'What?'

'The other morning, our young Captain Hewitt opened his

bedroom curtains after a late session. He gazed across the mews and saw a naked woman doing some light housework in the house opposite!'

I put my hand to my mouth.

'Don't tell me. It was . . . Camilla!'

'Yes. Apparently, she was completely oblivious to everything around her.'

I take another sip of wine to take this all in.

'So the Prince of Wales knows his wife, the Princess, is having it off with this Captain Hewitt. And the Princess knows that her husband is having it off with the woman opposite Hewitt, the wife of his Commanding Officer, whose husband is the former lover of her sister-in-law, Princess Anne. So then, all parties are happy, I take it.'

'Er, not quite. Diana doesn't like the fact Charles is so fond of Camilla. In fact, it infuriates her.'

'Even though, from what you are saying, she started having affairs first and she is fully occupied with Hewitt?'

'That's right.'

My goodness, how extraordinary. How fortunate then there are no other Royal scandals! Mindy appears to read my mind.

'Oh, and there's all kinds of other stuff with other Royals, too,' she adds.

'What! Tell me.'

Mindy leans forward and whispers in my ear for five astounding minutes.

Goodness gracious me! Even rabbits might sit up astonished at what the Royals get up to! But this is surely just scurrilous tittle-tattle.

Then, what if it's not? My mind goes back to a favourite nursery song. 'They are changing the Guards at Buckingham

Palace.'It should be 'They are changing their partners' and the first syllable of Buckingham should rhyme with something rude beginning with 'F'.

I walk up the stairs to the Royal Film Club in a state of shock, my innocent impression of my employers'fairy-tale marriage and those of the other members of the Royal Family shattered into a thousand pieces.

Thank goodness we are going to a movie for light relief – some comedy with Dudley Moore and Goldie Hawn. Mindy and I enter a large, beautiful room with cabinets of porcelain. At the back is a projector. There are two armchairs in the front and behind are three of four rows of canvas chairs.

I look around to see if there is anyone I recognise. No, only officials from Buckingham Palace. And no Royals. But that hardly surprises me. They are probably all too busy having sex.

We sit down and I find myself whispering to Mindy about how I so nearly fouled up the lunch with David. She can barely stifle her giggles at my further education on choughs. Then she starts laughing some more. I know the story is funny, but surely it is not *that* funny?

'What?' I ask.

'Just look at the film credits,' she says, her hands covering her mouth.

I look at her but still don't understand.

'The movie we are about to watch is called *Foul Play.'*

I laugh in appreciation at the joke she clearly sees and sit back. I still don't know what Mindy finds so funny.

May 1989

Today is a strange day. Very strange. Not five minutes ago, I saw an extraordinary sight. It would be extraordinary anywhere, but in a palace it is really weird. A middle-aged man with a shock of white hair, dressed in a white boiler suit and covered in gold jewellery, has entered one of the offices. Have they put something strange in my tea, I wonder? Am I hallucinating?

My goodness, I see him again. He is being presented to the Lady Clerks next door. He has in his hand a large cigar, which is strange because no one here is allowed to smoke. Who is he? What is he doing here? Why is he wearing that peculiar costume?

Oh my goodness, he is coming into my office now. My colleagues and I look up aghast at this strange apparition. He fixes us with a smile then wiggles his unlit cigar next to his face and emits a curious warbling noise from the back of his throat, like Red Indians do in cowboy movies.

Is he ill? Is he disturbed? Has security made a terrible mistake and allowed a loony to wander in our midst? They can't have. Who is it, then? Is it some form of practical joke? That must be it. Of course. I remember Mindy telling me that HRH just loves practical jokes. So he has sent this prankster into the office and he is probably watching our reactions right now through some spy hole, laughing his Royal boxer shorts off. Yes, Your Royal Highness. Very funny.

The prankster introduces himself to a stupefied Victoria. He lifts up her hand as though to kiss it, and then he does the most extraordinary thing. He starts to run his tongue across her fingers; he is licking her hand. I can see Victoria freezing. Poor girl, she looks horrified. Rather her than me!

Oh my God! He is coming over to my desk. He takes my hand and does the same thing. His tongue flicks backwards and forwards across my knuckles and fingers. Yuck! This is disgusting. He is looking up at me and grinning in a lascivious way.

'Oh, oooh, oooh! Whoarr! Lovely girl.'

Go away, you horrible man, I inwardly scream. If this is a joke, Your Royal Highness, it is a joke too far. This man is revolting. Somebody get rid of him!

As cool as a chilled cucumber, Geraldine is beside him. She looks completely unruffled by the antics of this boiler-suited weirdo with his flashy jewellery.

'You probably recognise Mr Savile from television, Sarah.'

Oh my God! It's *him*. He is the presenter Jimmy Savile of *Jim'll Fix It*! But what's he doing here? Some sort of television show perhaps? 'Be a Lady Clerk at the Palace for a day'? I give him a warm grin and think to myself, please never do that to me again, Mr Savile. I don't like it. In fact, I hate it.

Mr Savile then bestows his weird attentions on Esther. Flick, flick goes the tongue. From the look on her face, Esther has clearly never experienced anything like it. None of us have. It is all too much. Quietly, I get up and go to the bathroom, where I vigourously wash my hands with soap.

Later, I speak to Geraldine in the kitchen about the appearance of the famous television star.

'Why did he come into the office?' I ask.

'As far as I know, he is working with the Princess on a project for Stoke Mandeville Hospital. Maybe he dropped by to collect some of the unsolicited gifts left here for the children.'

'Do you think he will be a frequent visitor?' I enquire nervously, thinking I could not bear another incident of him flicking his tongue up and down my hand again.

'I expect so,' she says. 'He is quite an important person here at the Palace.'

'Important! Why?'

'Well, besides him working with the Princess, he is here in another capacity altogether. Very hush-hush. Don't repeat a word.'

'And what's that?'

'It's not common knowledge, but he did try last year to help the Boss and the Bossette to work out their marriage problems. He arranged for them to meet in Dyfed in Wales so they could comfort flood victims together in public. Their Royal Highnesses weren't speaking at the time, so to bring them together was quite a feat.'

My jaw hits the floor.

'I don't believe it!'

'Yes,' says Geraldine. 'He's been their marriage guidance counsellor.'

Then she winks at me.

'Jim'll fix it.'

I stand there stunned, trying hard to absorb this piece of extraordinary information. It is incredible. Jimmy Savile, the television personality who utters curious warbling noises, dresses in weird clothing and slobbers over hands, is the advisor to Their Royal Highnesses, the Prince and Princess of Wales, on their relationship issues!

This cannot be true. Of all the people in the United Kingdom they could go to for advice, they go to *him*? Jimmy Savile may do great work for charity and children and stuff, but he hardly seems the best qualified or most appropriate marriage counsellor. Now I have heard everything. I shake my head. What possible chance do Their Royal Highnesses have, I think despairingly, as my right hand, with an uncontrollable impulse, delves into the biscuit tin for comfort.

June 1989

I am sitting with Victoria and our respective mothers at the Close Hotel in Tetbury having coffee. We are all in a state of great excitement because in ten minutes we are going to Highgrove, HRH's beautiful Georgian house in Gloucestershire, which he bought in 1980 from Maurice Macmillan, the son of the former Prime Minister, Harold Macmillan. We have both been invited by the Boss and Bossette for a barbecue. And as we can bring one guest each, Victoria and I have chosen our mums.

Before the journey, Victoria and I were both a tiny bit nervous about our mothers meeting. Would they get on? Do they have anything in common besides their daughters being the fan-mail correspondents for the Prince and Princess? Well, they are chatting away famously. Big relief.

My other big concern is whether HRH will recognise me. My inner nanny tells me not to be so stupid. How could he remember you? Who do you think you are? You are just a foot soldier in his huge army of staff and attendants. You are at the bottom of the pile. You are nothing. Prepare to be disappointed, because disappointed is what you will be.

But he repeated my name. Come on, he likes me. He even expressed a concern that my work was 'tedious'. How sensitive is that? Obviously, I have touched him.

Stop being a fool, you silly girl!

My inner voices continue to battle it out while we climb into Mummy's Polo and off we go. Ten minutes later, we arrive at the car park. As we get out of the car, we all catch a glimpse of the young princes, William and Harry, who are running about the garden. The scene seems so natural yet so surreal.

We are directed to a large field, where the barbecue is situated. There are plastic tables with chairs for us all, but most of us are standing up right now, mingling. There must be about two hundred people here. Then, from out of nowhere, our little group suddenly encounters His Royal Highness.

Gasp! Control yourself, Sarah. My heart palpitates. My goodness, doesn't he look so handsome in his beige linen suit and blue shirt? He opens his mouth. He is going to speak to us. All of a sudden, I feel giddy.

Whatever you do, Sarah, says a familiar voice, don't faint! He looks at us all. Why doesn't he look directly at me? Stop being an idiot, Sarah, says my inner nanny.

'Hello. Welcome. The food is over there. Oh, and drink as much as you like,' he says, gesturing with his arm to the bar.

Darling HRH, who could ever fault your generosity? His Gorgeousness then catches Mummy's eye and proceeds to engage her in conversation. I stand by demurely and listen. They talk about the weather (excellent) and her drive from Shropshire (tolerable). Does he ask her how she came to be here? No. Does Mummy mention me as one of his Lady Clerks? No. Presumably he knows. The conversation runs its course. HRH smiles, then gives me a nod and leaves to speak to the myriad other guests. Wonderful, he actually nodded at me!

My inner voices then restart their neurotic debate. OK, he may have nodded at you but did he recognise you? I am not sure but, be fair to HRH, he was very busy. He has other guests to see as well. But the Prince and future King did not engage you in conversation, did he? Perhaps it was all that 'very, very, very, very' stuff from the Christmas lunch that put him off? Maybe, then again, maybe not.

I am going in circles now. I then look at Mummy, who is now radiant, and I smile. HRH has worked his magic. She is on Cloud Nine. Long may she remain there. And, with that, I forcibly consign my insecurities, if only for now, to mental Pluto.

We join a queue for hamburgers, chicken and sausages. As we sit down with our food and Pimms, we notice from afar the Princess in a powder-blue summer dress. My goodness, she does look glamourous and so pretty. Stunning looks, two handsome boys, an intelligent and sensitive husband, staff to attend to her every need, no money worries, and houses and palaces galore! What's more, she is a princess and the future Queen! She has everything. Where is the problem, girl?

At the other end of the field now is HRH. Who knows? Perhaps I am underestimating Jimmy Savile? The Royal couple are at least here together, if physically apart. And at least she is not shouting at him.

I tilt my head back and savour the scene. Oh, to be in lovely Gloucestershire on a beautiful English summer's day as guests of Their Royal Highnesses, the Prince and Princess of Wales. A jazz band has struck up some Dixieland melody. I am holding a Pimms and building a tan. Utter bliss. Moreover, I have an entire weekend of leisure at home with Mummy and Daddy to look forward to. What more could a girl ask for?

Two hours later, with the summer sun having warmed and (hopefully) bronzed my face, we gather the Mendhams to take them back to their car in Tetbury. They have a drive to Essex ahead of them and we have our journey to Shropshire. I glance around at this magical Royal vista. The band is playing. The guests continue to knock back the Pimms. HRH is still circulating, doing his glad-handing as the perfect host that he is. The young princes are larking in the garden. I capture it one last time as a picture in my mind's eye.

I look around for the Bossette. How interesting. She has remained at the far end of the field the whole time, not circulating at all. It is like she is in self-imposed exile, very much sticking with her own crowd of friends and favourite courtiers, making a very public point of her distance from HRH. Oh dear, I think, as we head for the car, Jim has his work cut out.

September 1989

Do I have the most fantastic boyfriend or what? Right now, I am up on the Scottish island of Skye in the Hebrides. I am staying in a beautiful white-painted cottage with a blue door two miles out of Portree in the shadow of the Cuillin Mountains with my jolly friend Caroline and her mother and father. Ten minutes ago, the most enormous bouquet of flowers arrived for me with a note from the utterly adorable Andy. The bouquet is bigger than me! Caroline and I are now busy cutting the flowers and arranging them in vases. The cottage is hardly big enough to contain them all.

'Aye,' says the florist from town, the *only* one here in Skye. 'The order is so big that we will have to return tomorrow with the rest when extra supplies are brought in from the mainland. The order has cleaned out the shop. It is completely empty now.'

Darling Andy, you certainly know how to make a girl

swoon!

'You should have told me it's your birthday,' says Caroline. 'We would have done something.'

'That's really sweet of you,' I reply. 'But having me up to stay is quite enough.'

And I really mean that. Yesterday, I attended the famous Skye Ball, all thanks to Caroline and her parents. The Skye Ball takes place over two nights. It is held in the village hall in Portree and only the cream of Scottish society is supposed to get tickets. On the first night, the girls wear a white dress with a tartan sash. Mine, last night, was Johnston, as I discovered recently that I am descended from them. I also discovered, yet more recently, that I am really related only to the Irish Johnstons. However, in the absence of any other Scottish relatives, I have embraced the Scottish Johnstons as family.

The men wear white tie or kilts. Men always look marvellous in kilts, to my mind. And I bet there's not a girl who has never wondered at least once about the size of the tackle underneath the bouncing sporran of her dancing partner. White tie is so rare these days but visually it is such a treat. It is so elegantly Edwardian, a good counterpoint to the kilt. Even the village hall is dressed up. Inside, it is festooned in purple heather and strips of tartan. And it is all lit up with the buttery illumination of candles.

Trestle tables are placed on the dance floor at the beginning of the evening and parties take it in turn to sit down and be served. The menu is simple – lobster or grouse. Pudding is *crème brûlée*. After the food is finished, the trestle tables are swept away and the dance begins in earnest. All of us have filled in our dance cards.

The band breaks into the Eightsome Reel and soon I am swirling round the floor with four oh-so-handsome men. So what's under *your* kilt, dear dancing partner? The crown jewels? Probably, for some lucky girl!

Next dance is the Foursome Reel. There is something about the names of Scottish dances that is redolent of group sex, don't you think? Grab your partner for a foursome! So suggestive it makes a girl feel giddy. After that, it is the Duke of Perth. No, not my dancing companion but the dance named after him.

We dance and dance until seven in the morning. Totally exhausted, those of us still standing have a delicious breakfast of kippers and porridge on the reassembled trestle tables before we wend our respective ways to our homes and bed.

The next evening, we return for another marathon session of reeling. What fun. Dawn has broken. We return to our respective homes and bedrooms. I look in the mirror, wrecked again after dancing and drinking with all those lovely handsome men. You are twenty-six now, Sarah. You are so *old*! Never mind, you will cope somehow. Count your blessings.

I look at the huge vase of beautiful flowers by my bedside, then I lay my head down on the soft goosedown pillow and proceed to dream of adorable Andy, my number one blessing. Darling Andy, I love you.

Goodnight.

Early December 1989

Her Royal Highness, the Bossette, has come up with a new idea. The Christmas season should start, she has decided, with a Royal Staff breakfast party at a pub near St James's Palace in Victoria called The Albert. We are all summoned to be there at a ridiculously early time: eight in the morning. This means getting up extra early, which is a total pain for those of us who treasure our sleep.

Also, we are all being charged for the breakfast! A memo came round inviting us to participate. Naturally, we are all fascinated. Yes, we want to come. A given. But then it said those accepting the invitation would have £5 deducted from our wage packets. That's a bit mean, don't you think? Surely the Royal Household could stump up for breakfast?

Now it is seven in the morning and I am struggling to find something to wear. I am feeling like poo and I am having an anxiety attack. Honestly, what can a girl wear when she is having breakfast in thirty minutes with the World's Number One Fashion Icon? I am referring, of course, to our hostess, the Bossette. Eventually, I manage to struggle into something that I hope won't embarrass me in front of our, no doubt, radiant Princess. Off I set to The Albert.

I arrive there to see all kinds of familiar faces and I sit down with chums from the office. The Princess of Wales, looking predictably gorgeous, this time wearing yellow, is at another table and HRH is sadly absent. The food is standard egg, bacon, toast and stuff. Frankly, it could be a greasy spoon meal anywhere. But at least we are drinking champagne and the staff are really, really sweet and make a huge effort.

Forty minutes later, the radiant Princess bids us goodbye. Slowly, the others peel away until there are only eight of us left and seven bottles of champagne. That's right: seven. We all raise a glass to the now absent Princess. Good on you, Your Royal Highness. Excellent initiative! We look at the remaining seven bottles. Shame to waste them, especially since we are paying for them! So we, the tough diehards, hating to see any waste, proceed to make many more Royal toasts.

Christmas is upon us. Festive greetings, one and all!

Mid-December 1989

Such excitement! Tonight, I am taking adorable Andy to the Royal Staff Dance. I don't know why, but everybody in the office pronounces staff on this occasion not like 'starff ' but 'naff ', and we also say dance not like 'prance' but 'ants', i.e. in a Northern accent. 'Cooming to the Staff Dance, then?' we say. And inexplicably we all fall about laughing.

You have to have been employed at the Palace for over a year before you are entitled to go to a Royal Staff Dance, which is obviously why I didn't go last year. Each year it alternates between Windsor Castle and Buckingham Palace. This year it is at the Palace.

It was only four days ago we had the annual Christmas lunch for all of HRH's staff. This year it was at the Hyatt Carlton. Talk about no expense spared. The decorations were amazing! It was like a Santa's Grotto for adults. This time the Boss did not sit next to me. Sigh. But he made the same lovely speech as last year and we all applauded wildly.

Afterwards, as we were leaving, someone had the bright idea of taking home some of the Christmas decorations, as the room was decorated solely for our lunch party, or so we were told. So imagine, I found myself walking out with a Christmas tree! And very nice it looks too, here in the drawing room of 30 Buer Road amidst all the flowers that Andy keeps giving me, bless him. Oh yes, we also all received a present from HRH: a tray with one of his lovely watercolours printed on it. It is a memento to treasure. Thank you, darling HRH.

Andy is at the door now and he comes in looking so smart in his dinner jacket. He hands me yet more flowers and extravagantly compliments me on my evening dress.

'I am feeling a bit nervous,' he confesses. 'you know how dreadful I am at dancing. I have two left feet.'

It is true that Andy is not brilliant at dancing, which is why he wouldn't come to the Skye Ball with me, but I have insisted he partner me at this event. After all, this is not Scottish dancing, which can be complicated if you don't know the steps. Tonight, it will be your basic side-to-side shuffle. What can go wrong?

'You will be wonderful,' I assure him, while smoothing his hair and adjusting his bow tie. Then off we go.

Thirty minutes later, we are inside the Palace, and there have to be about three hundred people present. First, we are all offered some red or white wine. I take one sip of the red, then I try a sip of the white. Now, I am no wine snob, but, frankly, this has to be absolute plonk. You are served better stuff in art galleries or pubs, I think. And I know; I have been to a few.

Surely Her Majesty could spoil her underpaid staff with something a little better? The event comes but once a year. I bet she wouldn't dare serve such plonk at state banquets. The country would become diplomatically isolated.

But I mustn't be churlish. I am here to enjoy myself. I am so proud of Andy – all six foot three of him – and I show him off to all my friends from the office. Geraldine is particularly impressed.

There is a slight hush and in walks Her Majesty, Queen Elizabeth, followed by the Duke of Edinburgh, Prince Philip.

Behind them steps Prince Andrew, his bride, the Duchess of York, then Prince Edward. Pecking orders at the Palace, I am learning, are totally rigid. As they pass through, we all bob or bow.

No sign of His Loveliness, HRH, unfortunately, or of his glamourous wife Diana. They are presumably at Kensington Palace throwing things at each other, being counselled by Jimmy Savile, or off with their respective 'confidantes', which I now understand is the smart word round here at the Palace for lovers.

Two things I notice. The first is that the Queen looks so tiny in person. The second is that someone should tell the Duchess of York, who looks lovely otherwise, not to walk around with her mouth open. Really, she looks as if she is trying to catch flies. You need some poise, girl. Remember who you are. You are a Royal princess not a slack-jawed serving wench!

We all sit down at tables and have chicken fricassee, which is all right but smacks slightly of a standard school dinner and is not up to the standard of hospitality offered by the Prince of Wales.

I must stop this flow of negative thoughts. Grab some more wine, Sarah. Yes, it may be distinctly inferior, but it will loosen you up. The band strikes up with a Glenn Miller melody. Big band stuff. Very danceable. Great! I take my reluctant Andy, my confidante, don't you know, onto the floor. Poor chap, he looks terrified.

Now, Andy, I will teach you to dance, whether you like it or not. Yes, Andy, that's better. Swing your hips. That is marvellous. You have the hang of it, my boy. Another song and then another and then the classic, without which no dance in this era would be complete: 'Tie a yellow ribbon round the old oak tree'. What the lyrics mean is beyond me but the tune is catchy, and now we are really going for it. Well done, Andy! I will make a John Travolta out of you yet. Oh yes! *Saturday Night Fever* at the Palace. Yeah!

We have one more dance then I reward him with a break. We sit down at a table and pour more of Her Majesty's Royal vinegar down our throats. Perhaps the Queen bought it from Homebase, getting her wine supplies confused with paint stripper? Château B&Q, perhaps? Still, not even disgusting plonk can stop Andy and me having fun.

We hit the dance floor again and I decide to be adventurous. Oh yes! I am going to teach Andy the basic manoeuvres of rock'n'roll. Taking his hands, I show him the steps. See, Andy, it is really quite easy. That's right! It is just a matter of confidence and practice. Bravo! Soon we are swirling around the floor. Move over, Fred Astaire and Ginger Rogers, is what I say!

Suddenly disaster looms! Oh dear, this cannot be happening! Oh dear, it is. Andy has lost his balance and appears to be falling. Oh no! He is tumbling right on top of me. I can't hold him. He is too big. Aaargh! I feel my head slide down someone else's body, as Andy's weight drives me down. We land. Cripes, Andy is heavy.

The couple dancing next to us, whom I presume are the ones I nearly brought down, have stopped. What a spectacle we must present as we unsteadily disentangle ourselves and get up. Oh no, I can't believe it! This is too much! The couple in question is Prince Andrew and his lovely flame-haired wife, the Duchess of York. They are both gawping at us. Andy and I manage at last to resume a perpendicular bearing. We give them a sheepish grin. The Yorks continue to gawp. Will someone please tell the Royal couple that it is rude to stare, and tell the Duchess just for once to close her mouth?

Salvaging our wounded dignity, we repair to our table and help ourselves to more of the Royal paint stripper. The last song strikes up. It is *'New York, New York'*, a favorite of mine. We decide to go for it. Who cares if we fall over again?

We don't, and somehow we manage to get home safely.

Happy Christmas.

4

The Naughty Nineties

January 1990

Wake up with a distinct hangover. Make mental note: Don't mix wine with spirits ever again. You should have learnt by now. You pay for it the following morning with a throbbing headache. Silly girl. Still, I have other things to compensate. I am at home in glorious Shropshire and I have had the most wonderful Christmas and New Year.

Goodness, I seem to be popular these days. I am invited everywhere! Some of the people back home seem to have the idea that, because I work for the Royal Household, I am a bit Royal myself. These days, people listen to me in respectful silence: they are frightfully deferential and if I say something only mildly funny they roar with laughter. I cannot remember it being like that before.

'And how *is* His Royal Highness?' they ask me, as if I am his wife or something. 'Tell me, what does he have for breakfast? Where does he buy his shirts? Turnbull & Asser still? Does he buy his shoes from Lobb's? How are the young princes these days? The Princess is looking so glamourous. Who does her hair?'

As if I would know. In truth, the only things I really know

about either the Boss or Bossette are what I read in the newspapers. Oh yes, there are Mindy's stories of course, but I can hardly repeat any of those, can I? So I answer that Palace protocol forbids me to say anything, which seems to get them even more interested. Still, I can hardly deny that I don't enjoy my new-found popularity. Long may it last!

Downstairs, I go to breakfast. Daddy has returned from the shops with the newspapers and I pick up one and start to casually scan the news. Oh my God, my nemesis is staring out of the front page at me. *That* man! I cannot believe it. He has been given a knighthood! Sir Jimmy Savile OBE, the shell-suited finger-licking TV personality has become a Grand Man of the Establishment. What on earth is the world coming to?

Now, Sarah, you're not being a snob, are you? It says here he came from a humble background, that he worked down the mines, was a wrestler, presented *Top of the Pops*, is the voice of British Rail, still presents a hit television show and that he has raised tens of millions of pounds for charity, in particular Stoke Mandeville Hospital, where he also does volunteer work as a porter. That is a fantastic achievement. Moreover, if he is still charged with that hush-hush duty (shoosh, the walls have ears!), he might even succeed in saving the marriage of the Boss and the Bossette. He deserves his knighthood. Don't be so mean-spirited, I tell myself. What is your gripe?

My gripe, I argue, is that I hate it when he licks my hand! Can't he read body signals? Does he think his television success makes him so attractive that he can do things that others would never dream of?

Only a couple of weeks ago he came into the office again. Was there the same fanfar and flamboyance? Yet again he cornered me, this time wearing an absurd Union Jack shirt while emitting curious Red Indian warbling noises and wiggling his cigar.

'Hello, my lovely. Oooh, oooh, oooh! Whoarr!'

I was like a rabbit petrified in the headlights of a car. There was nowhere for me to run. I was trapped. Again, he grabbed my hand and proceeded with his disgusting ritual of licking it. I wanted to slap him. Really, I did.

Lick, lick, lick. I grinned, but inside I was wincing. And to think he imagines I am being charmed. Bear up, Sarah, I told myself. You can get through this. Thank God the ordeal was soon over as he advanced on his next victim.

But it got me thinking . . . surely there was some way to avoid this. My brain started to whirr. Then a bulb illuminated. That's it! I would simply have a pressing need to visit the lavatory each time he came to the office. That way I could avoid being upset. It seemed the only thing for it. Don't mention the idea to your Lady Clerk colleagues, though, I told myself, otherwise there'll be a stampede every time we hear him coming.

But back to the papers. I scan the headlines further. The Royal Family is up at Sandringham. The Boss and the Bossette are there, too. That's nice. I hope there has been no unpleasantness or rows. Put on a front of Happy Families, please, Your Royal Highnesses, if only for the sake of the children and us, your loyal and devoted subjects.

I gaze at the front page of a glossy supplement. Alongside a saucy picture, it reports that we are entering the 'Naughty Nineties'. Are we just? Well, if even half of what I hear from Mindy is true, then we are just continuing a tradition that has been going on for decades – from the 'Sexy Sixties' to the 'Sensual Seventies' through to the 'Amorous Eighties'. And the inhabitants of the Royal palaces have been the leaders. Critics say the Royal Family is behind the times –not in that respect, they're not. Oh yes, they could certainly teach the rest of us a thing or two about being naughty . . .

The telephone rings and Mummy summons me. Goodness, I have yet another invitation! I hardly know these people, but isn't it wonderful to be so liked?

March 1990

Back in London, I have recently moved out of Buer Road as my flatmate, the divine Kate, also my landlady, is selling up. Lucky girl, she has found love and is now engaged. *Bonne chance*, Katy. Bye, bye, lovely flat. Bye, bye, handsome young Viscount and pretty girlfriend from across the road, neither of whom I have met but who I have all too often thought of. Bye, bye. I shall treasure the memories.

Hello, 50 Averill Street and a new and jolly landlord, Charles Dring, gentleman Chartered Surveyor.

It is time for another change as well. Slowly, I am realising that I am no longer in love with Andy. The other day he came round and, yes, he was marvellously sweet as ever and, *naturellement*, we ended up making love. It was quite a session, I can tell you. In the morning, though, I found that our frenzied love-making had broken the bed! No wonder I had such a disturbed night's sleep. Well, no one can sleep properly at an angle of 20 degrees, can they? Oh dear. That took some explaining to Charles! My bed is now propped up with my collection of slimming magazines.

Later, Andy invited me to Paris and it suddenly dawned on me how serious things are. Big question: Would I be prepared to commit for ever to Andy, lovely as he is? Sadly the answer has to be no.

This may surprise you, indeed it surprises me but I am fast developing a crush on someone else.

So who is this new man who has so entranced me recently? He is, of course, exceptionally handsome. He has salt-and-pepper hair and reminds me hugely of that sexy heart-throb Richard Gere from that naughty movie *American Gigolo*. He works in the City in something like insurance. He is half Swedish and his name is George Wintour, first cousin, if you can believe it, of the ultra-famous and oh-so-cool Anna Wintour, the Editor of *Vogue* in America.

We kissed at a Wedding Reception where we met last week. I confess I got a little tiddly. (Well, it's not my fault that the waiter kept re-filling my glass!) I guess there's just something about the combination of Weddings and champagne that makes us girls feel amorous, or at least it does me.

Oh, George, that kiss still lingers. I do hope that you still have my number. Just in case I have been sending him telepathic messages reminding him of it.

My thoughts of Gorgeous George distract me from the builders' dust and pots of paint that I am now living with while Charles finishes renovating the house.

Tonight, we are having a small supper party and I am meeting lots of new people. How wonderful. Suddenly, the telephone rings. Could it be George? I feel a surge of excitement rush over me. Don't be silly, Sarah, it is bound to be a friend of Charles's. Or if not, it will be Mummy. Charles picks up the phone.

'Sarah, it's for you. Some chap called George.'

Aaahh! I don't believe it! OK, Sarah, be cool. Remember:

chaps don't like women who sound over-eager. It is probably best that you turn him down for the date – that is, if he is even offering one! Yes, it is probably best to say that you are busy for the next three weeks: other boyfriend commitments, engagements at the Palace, and so forth. Yes, that way he will be much more eager. I pick up the telephone and do my cool drawl.

'Hello,' I say in a sexy siren voice.

'Is that you, Sarah?'

'Yes,' I reply. Of course, he knows it is me. What game is he playing at?

'Sorry, I thought I must have called the wrong Sarah. It isn't how I remembered your voice at all!'

Oh, Sarah, you silly girl. You will have to drop trying to be a vamp; it is clearly never going to work.

'Well, it is me.'

'Well, that's great. I would really like to see you again.'

'Really?' I sigh.

Hold your nerve, girl. Remember, you are ultra-busy for the next three weeks. Turn him down and he will be oh so impressed.

'Listen, I was wondering what you are doing tomorrow. I rather fancy the idea of taking you out to a favourite restaurant of mine called The Nick round the corner from where I live in Balham. Are you free by any chance?'

This is outrageous. George is expecting to take me out at absurdly short notice to some place that sounds like a prison! Does he imagine that I have no serious social life? Does he think that I will accept just like *that*? Does he think I am desperate?

'Yes,' I find myself saying breathlessly.

'Good, I'll give you the address then.'

I find myself shaking with excitement as I put down the telephone. Only one thing disturbs my ecstasy. What did he mean by the 'wrong' Sarah? How many other Sarahs does he possibly know? Hmmm.

June 1990

Huge excitement. I am back at the Boss and Bossette's summer barbecue at Highgrove. It is a glorious day, just like last year. The band has just struck up. The hamburgers are sizzling. I am wearing my ultra-cool Ray-Ban sunglasses and a carefully selected dress that won't embarrass me (I hope) if and when I encounter the World's Number One Fashion Icon.

This year my guest is Daddy. How proud I am to have him on my arm as we walk round and I introduce him to my Lady Clerk colleagues. Suddenly, from out of nowhere, appears His Gorgeousness himself. As ever, I feel my heart fluttering.

'Hello, everyone! I do hope you are enjoying yourselves. Would any of you, by any chance, care to come with me on a tour of the garden?'

A tour of the garden? I can hardly believe our luck! Gardens only happen to be Daddy's greatest passion. In the summer months, he practically lives outside. Daddy is as much an authority on gardens as Percy Thrower. What he doesn't know about seeding, planting and cultivation is frankly not worth knowing. Oh, kind and wonderful HRH, you could not have offered a more appropriate invitation to my darling daddy!

'Well, let's be off then!'

So our small group of six sets off, following a respectful four paces behind His Royal Highness.

In horticultural circles, the Highgrove garden has become famous, yet few have had the privilege of actually seeing it. When HRH bought Highgrove in 1980, it was all grass with a few yew hedges, some statues and an overgrown walled garden. Now, under the guiding hands of Rosemary Verey, Lady Salisbury and Dame Miriam Rothschild, *the* acknowledged experts, the garden has been transformed.

How exciting! Daddy and I feel like two explorers suddenly entering Shangri-La. *And* we are getting a personal tour from HRH himself. It could hardly be better.

We cross through the rose garden to the side of the house, then onto the terrace at the back. We carefully pick our way around a circular bubbling pool. HRH then takes us along the Thyme Walk. It really is wonderful. It is a lovely path that stretches off into the distance with thyme creeping along its edges. By now, we have been joined by the two young princes, Harry and William, who fondly call their father 'Papa'. How endearing.

We arrive at the swimming pool on the other side of the house. Daddy, forgetting respectful protocol, is by this time nearly alongside His Gorgeousness. Suddenly, HRH swings round and nearly knocks into Daddy, whom he doesn't realise is so close.

'Look closely into the swimming pool,' he commands us.

We do so.

'See that bronze plaque there. It was given to us as a wedding present. I didn't know what to do with it, so I stuck it at the bottom of the pool.'

I can see Daddy is impressed by this ingenuity. Clever HRH, how inspired you are. On we move with His Royal Highness, the Pied Piper.

We are now in the shady part of the garden. Suddenly, I see Daddy looking rather concerned. He swings round to address the startled Prince of Wales, who is again amazed that Daddy is at his side. Pointing to a plant with flowers like cow parsley, he remarks, 'Gosh, you have rather a lot of *alchemilla mollis, Sir.*'

HRH appears taken aback by his strange guest coming out with such an intimidating display of horticultural erudition. How is HRH going to take this? Does he realise this man is my father? Could it jeopardise my position? Hardly likely, I think. He probably doesn't even know who I am.

HRH looks hard at my father. 'Oh, do you think so?' he asks.

'Well, yes, Sir. I do,' continues Daddy in a concerned way, as if this plant about which he is talking could choke all of Highgrove. 'It seeds very freely.'

The Prince looks at my father, absorbs his advice and, appearing somewhat mystified, continues the tour. Poor HRH, he probably doesn't know which plant Daddy is talking about. Daddy could at least have given it its English name, Lady's Mantle.

Our group then passes through an area planted with rare trees between which have been placed lovely statues. I nearly jump out of my skin with surprise when suddenly we are under ambush! The two young princes, who had quietly peeled off earlier, are now shooting at us with plastic sub-machine guns from a treehouse high above. Rat a tat tat! Rat a tat tat!

We take our lead from their father and pretend not to notice the continuing assault from the camouflaged Royal aggressors. Promising commando material there, I think to myself.

We then come to the walled garden. Oh, how wonderful! We can see it has been completely restored to its medieval scale – little box hedges with vegetables growing in between, curving arches of roses in the middle, paths edged with apple trees growing sideways on. Right in the centre is a semicircular painted wooden seat. Ah, I imagine this must be where HRH contemplates his princely existence. After that, the heir to the throne leads us out and back up to the house, passing some wild grasses and flowers. He loves the natural state of things, I note.

'Sir...' Suddenly, my father is making another remark. 'I think there is slightly too much ivy up some of these trees. It's not good for them, you know.'

HRH clearly doesn't feel up to arguing the toss on such matters with a subject of his realm who not only knows obscure plants but can also name them in Latin.

'Oh, but I like the ivy because the insects like it.'

My father appears lost for a retort. That has stumped you, Daddy; you hadn't reckoned with that as a response, had you?

How sweet of HRH, I reflect. I repeat his reply in my mind. This shows such a sensitive streak, caring for the creatures of the insect kingdom. It is very Buddhist, really, the kind of concern you might expect from the Dalai Lama. How surprising to hear it from a Royal Prince. You have risen even higher in my affections now, darling HRH. I would not have thought that possible before.

August 1990

It is ten o'clock in the morning and I am bowling down the motorway to Gloucestershire in one of the Royal fleet cars.

And just to think, I thought I would not see Highgrove before next summer's barbecue: now, I practically live in the place!

The whole thing has come about because of an event that occurred in June. Imagine, there we were in the office when we saw a worried Equerry whispering to Dreamy Dave Wright. We all sensed something was up, but as it is terribly uncool to ask anything here we continued with our duties. Then the next morning, we read all about it in the newspapers.

Dearest HRH, the nation learnt, had broken his arm being heroically bold at Cirencester polo club. Just for once, the Boss rather than the Bossette commanded the front page. I then read a comment from some stupid man criticising darling HRH for being reckless. I threw down the paper in disgust. How dare that horrid journalist! How dare the equally horrid Editor who let him say such things! And how dare the publisher employ such people, I thought to myself!

Two months down the line, I am on a rota of Lady Clerks who drive down to Highgrove to attend to secretarial duties while HRH recuperates. Sometimes, if we have to work late, we stay overnight in a nearby farmhouse along with various other Highgrove minions, policemen and flunkies. Staying over can be tedious and the best way to get through the evening, by consensus, is by drinking. Oh dear, many a hangover I have suffered as a result of a Highgrove stay-over, I can tell you.

I park the car, then walk over to a glorified Wendy house attached to the side of Highgrove. In truth, there is really not much to do. HRH has taught himself to write with his left hand, though there is not much for him to write in his state. But I am so impressed that he has taken the trouble to learn. There is no end to the man's talents. And imagine: his heart even embraces insects. Canonise him, that's what I say!

I enter the Wendy house. Then suddenly I trip, nearly falling over completely. Cripes, I stumble over him again! Will I ever learn? Tigger, HRH's Jack Russell, has decided that the Wendy house is the place he likes to relax these days. I suppose a Royal Jack Russell should have a kennel the size of a palace, but I wish he wouldn't adopt this recently assembled Lady Clerks' office as his preferred abode. The problem is that he blends in rather well with the seagrass matting, so, in spite of Tigger being rather porky, I never see him.

The other day I witnessed a remarkable and rather touching scene. It really is worth relating. Bernie, one of the butlers, visited me in the Wendy house. He was looking for Tigger.

'Oh, there you are,' says Bernie.

'I suppose you have been instructed to take him for a walk,' I say.

'No,' he says. 'I am taking him to meet His Royal Highness.'

That is strange, I think. Has Tigger perhaps not formally been introduced to HRH as yet? Has Tigger all this time been on probation to see whether he would be suitable as a Royal pet? Perhaps there is a strict protocol about Royals meeting animals just as there is for them meeting non-Royal humans?

Bernie looks at his watch. 'I better take him right now. His Royal Highness will be arriving here any moment. Tigger should be on hand to greet him.'

I nearly jump out of my seat.

'His Royal Highness is coming here? To the office?'

'No, here to the house. His Royal Highness had to go away for twenty-four hours. When he is away from Highgrove, he misses Tigger.'

Just then, we hear an extraordinary noise overhead. It is deafening. It feels apocalyptic. What on earth is it? Are we being invaded?

'Better go now,' says Bernie, looking up. 'He is arriving.'

I can't help myself. I follow Bernie out of the Wendy house. Above us is a large, red helicopter. It is hovering over the front lawn. Slowly, it descends, blasting the air around us with the strength of a force-nine gale. Bernie is standing not forty feet away in his smart blazer, calmly holding Tigger, the hair on both flying about. Now landed, the helicopter blades slow down.

I then watch Bernie release Tigger onto the ground. He waddles enthusiastically towards the helicopter. Just then, the helicopter door opens and out steps HRH, one arm in a sling. From the drawn look on his face, I can see he is in a lot of pain after the accident on the polo field, but when he sees Tigger at his feet his face lights up. Tigger then rolls over onto his back for what I can see is the customary Royal tummy tickle. All smiles, HRH bends down and rubs Tigger's pot belly with the hand of his functioning arm. It really is so touching. It is the first time I have seen HRH look truly happy, instead of the forced smile he wears at those functions he goes to. I then swing back to my office. Another sight to remember and treasure.

How wonderful, I think, would it be if the same scene could be re-enacted, this time with the Bossette greeting the Boss as he drops in from the sky? It is strange that I haven't seen her at all. You would have thought, as his wife, the Princess could visit him at least once while he is injured.

The best way to get through a slack day – and today looks

like a day of particular indolence – is to look busy. My fan-mail duties have had to be taken over by Victoria, who, poor thing, has to work extra hard at St James's Palace while I am here at Highgrove doing nothing. Still, I must *appear* industrious, so I make a few personal calls (to George), and shuffle and reshuffle the papers.

Shortly afterwards, I am given something to do. One of the butlers appears, a dapper chap called Paul Burrell, who is pleasant enough though slightly insipid. He appears with some jottings from HRH, places them on the desk and leaves. My job is now to decipher them. Goodness, if I don't interpret his writing accurately, I think, I could cause some frightful stink.

I remember once typing too fast and instead of writing HRH has no problem, I wrote HRH has 'bo' problem. For St James's Palace to state that the Prince of Wales emits a displeasing body odour would have caused uproar! Thank goodness, I caught that before it was dispatched. But there was another one I didn't spot in time. I spelt Sydney as Sidney. Goodness, HRH was cross. A big red pen had gone over it. Whoops! I won't forget that in a hurry. Please remember, HRH, I thought to myself, I am only human. But I have learnt my lesson. Never again. I shall be meticulous always.

I scrutinise the handwriting and I must say I am again impressed by HRH. I could never be so legible with my left hand. I briskly make my way through the correspondence.

At 12.30, I head off to the kitchen. Chris, the chef, has prepared a fabulous pasta dish with a wonderful salad – grown at Highgrove – followed by a fruit salad. As usual, I am eating on my own, so I watch daytime television, which is always, always on. How relaxing it is to watch the dramas of Australian folk in *Neighbours*, I think, and how very unlike are the characters' lives to the life of my own dear master, His Royal Highness.

At 3.45, I prepare myself to leave. Oh to be back at the Palace again to resume my duties as a fan-mail correspondent. Stop complaining, Sarah, this is a fabulous job and tonight you have a drinks party and gorgeous George to look forward to. Yippee!

As I head towards the car, I suddenly realise my bladder is full. Too many cups of tea. Oh what a bore! That means I have got to go back into the house and use the lavatory. What if Paul Burrell or Michael Fawcett see me and I get drawn into conversation, or, worse, they suddenly produce a letter from HRH for me to type? I really, really don't want to be late for the party, and motorway traffic at this time of year is so unpredictable. Perhaps I should turn off at a motorway petrol station and use their conveniences? Then I remember the disgusting state of the last lavatory I used in a petrol station. Yuck!

I have a brainwave. There are not two alternatives. There are three. Before me is a huge garden. I gaze around. It appears deserted. It is a warm afternoon. I shall follow the course of our ancestors – discreetly, of course. I stroll over to the wooded part. I look around. No sign of human life still. Excellent, now where do I pee?

Frankly, I am tempted to lift my skirt and drop my panties right here, but it is close to a path and there is, of course, a possibility that a gardener might come strolling by. That wouldn't look good, would it? How do you do? You must be Mr Mellors. Me? Can't you see by my attire that I am Lady

Chatterley, and, as you can see, stripped and ready for action?

I see some yellow shrubbery nearby. That should provide me with camouflage from any Highgrove wanderers. I lift my aquamarine cotton skirt and pull down my skimpy white panties. I leave them resting at my ankles as I squat. I start to pee. Ah, the relief!

Suddenly, I hear footsteps. Oh no! I imagine the worst. They have seen I have left the office, but they have also noticed my car is still here and sent out a search party. Oh my God, this is a disaster! Reason in the form of my inner nanny steps in. Don't be so dramatic. It is probably just someone having a walk.

I stop panicking. The steps are now getting closer. I start panicking again. I clench my inner muscles and stop peeing, which is damned difficult. I shut my eyes and pray hard that the shrubbery is all the cover I need. Thank goodness it is summer and everything is in full bloom! But what if there is a detectable trickle of pee, or, worse, what if it is a staff member walking a dog?

My God, what if it is Tigger? He will come straight over immediately. He virtually lives with me during the day. What will I do if he comes snuffling up to me with my knickers round my ankles?

Half of me says stand up quickly, simultaneously pulling up your knickers. Yes, it would be embarrassing and it would definitely require an explanation. What that explanation would be, I don't know, but I am sure I could gabble out something. The other half of me says stay put. Freeze into immobility.

I take the paralysis option. So, here I am, crouched down with my panties round my ankles and my naked bottom just four inches from HRH's precious *alchemilla mollis*, peering through the protective shrubbery. Who could it be? A Protection Officer? A gardener? Michael Fawcett or Paul Burrell? Get on with it, please. Come on, whoever you are!

Suddenly, a figure comes into view. It can't be. I don't believe it! This cannot be happening! What are you doing here? Shouldn't you be inside the house convalescing? What are you doing strolling in the garden? Oh please, please don't look in this direction. Please, great and wonderful Boss, don't come over here. Stick to the path. God, I feel sick! I am so damned nervous, it is all I can do not to start peeing again.

HRH passes by slowly. He is wearing beige cords and an expensive blue shirt. I look at his furrowed brow. He appears deep in contemplation. Perhaps it is the pain from his polo accident that is troubling him? Or is it possibly the burdens of his princely office? Who can tell? Oh, darling HRH, if only you realised that you have a loyal and faithful but terrified Lady Clerk just feet away from you with her panties round her ankles!

I then notice he is clutching a bucket. Oh my God, he hasn't brought that out for me, has he? Perhaps the sensitive Prince spied me from one of the Georgian windows, divined my intentions and has, in kindly and sweet consideration, brought me this portable privy? Don't be ridiculous, says my inner nanny.

He continues up the path. But what is it with the bucket? I then see him take a turning towards the chicken coop. Of course. How wonderful! He has feed in the bucket. What is more, he has come to feed the chickens personally. Just to think, he could have dispatched a minion. But oh no, the great Prince feeds the Royal Highgrove fowl himself. I then watch him clamber into the coop. What dedication.

At last! I relax and the *alchemilla mollis* below me gets it hard. A right tropical rainstorm bursts upon it. I remember now my father telling His Gorgeousness earlier this year that lady's mantle seeds too freely. Well, this batch here won't. Not any more, I can tell you.

Phew! That is better. I slowly get up, pull up my panties and gaze around this heavenly Cotswold garden with its ripe foliage warmed by the afternoon summer sun. I take a step and then I hear something. I stop. The voice is unmistakeable, its tone quite distinct. My goodness, it is HRH. Who is he talking to?

I freeze. My eyes have not left the chicken coop all this time and, as far as I know, unless he is Houdini, the Boss is still in there. I listen carefully. It then dawns on me. I feel a sense of wonder at this moment of historic realisation. I am the sole witness to something quite magnificent. I, Sarah Goodall, am hearing the Prince of Wales having a conversation with his Royal Highgrove chickens.

I pick up a word here and there and detect from his timbre that he is offloading a lot of his angst, which has been exacerbated no doubt by the pain of his polo injury. Well, what is he talking about, you ask? It is obvious, isn't it? His marriage.

Here we have a thoughtful and sensitive Prince married to the World's Number One Fashion Icon. From all reports, she neither really loves nor appreciates him, which is so sad. More than that, she hates him. So, in moments of anguish, what is the poor chap to do? In such moments of distress, he has to confide, but to whom? Who can he trust? It could be me, but I am beneath the lofty Royal radar screen. Sir Jimmy

Savile is not on hand. Is there a close member of staff to whom he can unburden himself? Probably not, it would be too compromising. What if word ever got out? Perhaps these compliant egg-laying Gloucestershire fowl, so feathered, plump and vulnerable, are, at this moment, the best ears for his Royal woes? Perhaps these sedentary, friendly clucking creatures and the Boss commune on a level unknown to the rest of us?

It would, I think, take someone of deep spiritual insight to comprehend the therapeutic benefits of such a communion. After all, no one thinks it's odd to gabble intimately to fur-covered creatures. Who of us does not talk emotively at some point to dogs and cats? What about HRH's formidable and magnificent sister Princess Anne, who communes so brilliantly with horses? Why not equally converse with creatures festooned in feathers?

As I stand here in the Boss and Bossette's garden, I feel a strange moment of oneness with the universe. How fortunate and privileged I feel that I am witness to my future King bearing his soul to his chickens. During the conversation he had with my father last summer, I learned that HRH cares for insects. We have all read of the news that he talks to plants. He loves dogs passionately and I know full well how much he is concerned for the troubles of people everywhere. But few realise that HRH's heart is truly universal, embracing even the world's culinary mainstay, the chicken.

I slowly walk back down the path, clamber into the car and head off for London, leaving behind my darling Prince in therapeutic feathered dialogue.

September 1990

How thrilling! All the office staff have been invited this evening to a go-carting competition in Clapham, south London. This apparently is the brainchild of Ken Wharfe, the singing policeman and Princess Diana's trusted and devoted Personal Protection Officer. It is a competition not to be missed, in spite of the fact that at dawn tomorrow George and I are catching the ferry from Dover for a holiday in a *gîte* in northern France.

So it is that all of us – or at least those who want to – are coming to the race, which is to be held in a converted bus garage. What fun!

But this event provokes another wardrobe crisis! What to wear when appearing next to World's Number One Fashion Icon in grimy motor contest? After preening in front of the mirror with various combinations, I plump for one of my favourite patterned sweatshirts and jeans.

I arrive at 7.30, feeling really nervous. Should I have worn the other patterned sweatshirt of which I am usually so fond? But then I am presented with a red jumpsuit. So all this neurotic anxiety about what to wear was for nothing! Aha, I am now competing with the fashion goddess on equal sartorial terms.

I have been seeing the Bossette rather a lot recently. Last week, Victoria and I were asked to help Harold Brown, the butler, hand out canapés at an event at Kensington Palace. Though this cut into my personal 'quality' time, I didn't mind at all, as I had never been to Kensington Palace before. Their Royal Highnesses often have drinks parties for people from the various societies or organisations of which they are patron or president. It is a way of saying thank you. That night, it was the Abbeyfield Society's turn (Hurrah!).

Unlike St James's Palace, which is medieval and where the rooms are cramped, the proportions in Kensington Palace are classical and generous. In the drawing room, there were flowers everywhere and an abundance of framed family pictures (the Bossette's evident influence). There is a grand piano, and the plush carpet is light beige and patterned. The furnishings are very luxurious. I thought of the modest lodgings with which I had made do, so far, in my adult life. Oh, to be a Prince or, indeed, a Princess! I went into the kitchens to receive my orders and found that all that was required of me was to take round the nibbles – canapés neatly prepared by Mervyn Wycherley, the Kensington Palace chef.

Mervyn is a legend. Ken Wharfe tells a story that once Tigger was annoying Mervyn so much in the kitchen at Highgrove that he popped him into an oven that was still warm. He was about to let him out when suddenly HRH entered the kitchen enquiring as to Tigger's whereabouts. Everyone shrugged while Tigger quietly baked. Only after HRH left did Mervyn dare open the oven door. Fortunately Tigger was fine. But a minute more and Hot Dog would have been on the menu that night. Naughty Mervyn!

The canapés looked delicious. The assembled throng thought so too and dived into them. Victoria and I were soon back in the kitchen for further supplies. I was inwardly pining that they didn't eat them all. Please, please, let there be leftovers, I repeated to myself like a mantra.

Harold took care of the wine. Paul Burrell, his under butler, I learned, was based more and more at Highgrove because he preferred it there. HRH circulated, being dutiful and charming and talking to everyone, but where was the Bossette, I wondered?

I soon found out. Returning to the kitchen for more canapés, I bumped into her.

'Hello,' she said, flashing me a warm smile.

Immediately, I curtseyed.

Next thing I know she was pulling out a bowl of jelly and custard from the fridge. She picked up a spoon and proceeded to dig into it. How extraordinary!

'Oh!' she suddenly exclaimed. 'I must go and get the fake tan on!'

Why, I wondered? Had she another engagement? Or had Sir Jimmy Savile worked his magic, so she's dolling herself up for HRH? Wouldn't that be marvellous! I returned to the drawing room with more canapés.

I came back minutes later, and guess what? Her Royal Highness was eating from *another* bowl. Amazing! How can she eat so much yet stay so thin? The Princess should give her secret to *Slimming* magazine.

'Does anyone know what's happened in *EastEnders*? I've videoed it but have simply got to catch up,' asked the Bossette.

None of us could help her.

I continued my chores as a waitress. By the time I next looked at my watch it was 8.30 p.m. and I had sacrificed my evening for the Prince and Princess. But I loved it. I felt indispensable and wanted. As I left, Harold beckoned me over and presented me with a lovely reward – a bottle of Châteauneuf du Pape. Scrumptious! That nicely supplemented the pasta dish I ate with George the following night. Oh dear, I thought at the time, why have I let Andy go? His recipes are so much more imaginative.

Anyway, here at Clapham, I get into my go-cart. We are all being timed. Off I go. Now, I am confident behind the wheel of my Metro. I can go quite fast – really, I can – but the go-cart is another kind of vehicle altogether. Perhaps it is something about being so close to the ground and having no shell to protect you. The straights are fine. It is the corners that terrify me. I feel the torque is about to tip me over. I am pathetic. I overtake no one. Really, Sarah, sometimes you are such a dweeb. The contestant who is most impressive is, unequivocally, the Bossette. My God, she almost has a maniacal glint in her eyes as she roars past me. She overtakes everyone!

I am eliminated early on and soon battle commences between the finalists. The Bossette is just about to hit the finishing line when all of a sudden Sergeant Nigel Owen, a Welsh orderly who fetches and carries at the Palace, bumps the Princess's go-cart. She loses the lead and Sergeant Owen wins!

Nigel Owen is teased pitilessly afterwards by the Bossette. How we all laugh. He is presented with the Cup and we all cheer heartily. Well done, Ken Wharfe! Well done, Your Royal Highness! Congratulations, Sergeant Owen!

We then have a group picture taken – and, oh my goodness, I am kneeling right next to her. That is right, here I am bang next to Her Absolute Gorgeousness. She really does have a magical vibrancy about her. No wonder men swoon. There is Victoria in the picture, Dickie Arbiter, the Buckingham Palace Press Officer, and all my mates.

This picture is a part of our personal history. I am so glad that we have a momento of the occasion. All of us chasing the Princess of Wales around a track and she so nearly wins! But for just a little bump she would have been the champion. Who would have thought it?

I escape quickly. George is waiting for me in Balham and our ferry to France leaves early in the morning.

Bonnes vacances!

December 1990

We are all assembled at the Hyatt Carlton. This year, we have gone traditional, as HRH is not up to a themed event. His Royal Highness, I have to report, has been suffering a lot of pain recently and last month had to have yet another operation for his broken arm. This was performed at the Queen's Medical Centre in Nottingham. HRH was very tough about the whole thing but, goodness, he is looking down these days. I do worry for him. No wonder he is taking four months off his official duties.

Mindy, my secret source close to the ladies-in-waiting, tells me that HRH is also very depressed about his marriage. But I can't help wondering why: maybe I am naive, but the Boss and Bossette both have their confidantes, so why can't they find a working accommodation, a modus vivendi? Other couples do.

And, after all, they are not living in an average house. In fact, they don't live in houses at all. They live in palaces. Surely they can just avoid each other if they can't bear to be with one another.

But the marriage problems of the Boss and Bossette appear beyond a civilised arrangement. The counseling of Sir Jimmy Savile OBE has come to nought, I fear. Jim cannot fix this one.

Sir Jimmy has indeed been coming to the offices of late,

still exhibiting his boundless desire to slurp over our hands. I wonder if it is a foreign custom he picked up when he was presenting *Savile's Travels*? Someone should tell him, really they should.

Anyway, his clarion call of 'Now then, now then!' always gives me sufficient time to propel myself from my desk to the safety of the bathroom. After twenty minutes, it is normally safe to return.

I was out of the Palace a lot last month as I was one of the Lady Clerks sent up to Nottingham for secretarial duties while HRH was hospitalised. I was billeted at the home of Lord King, the famous chief executive of British Airways. It was almost as grand as staying in a palace. Talk about tight security! There are more police at his gates than there usually are at Highgrove.

After three days, brave HRH, his arm in a sling, appeared in a lovely check dressing gown and slippers decorated with the Prince of Wales feathers and made a speech to thank the doctors, the nurses and us, his Palace staff. The Bossette was nowhere to be seen. I felt so protective of him that I wanted to go up and hug him. That's what you need, HRH, a good hug.

Oh, he's standing up again! And now he is making the same Christmas lunch speech, thanking us all. He finishes with the same joke and, as ever, we all laugh wildly and applaud.

It's the way he tells them.

5

Storm Clouds

May 1991

I enter the kitchen at the office in St James's Palace to make myself a cup of coffee. Things have been so quiet these last five months. Earlier in the year, HRH went to stay with Baroness Louise de Waldner in the south of France to convalesce and paint. May the brush be with you, Your Royal Highness! Meanwhile, the Bossette took the young princes on a family skiing holiday to Klosters. HRH was supposed to join her and the princes but at the last moment he changed his mind. Don't tell me – more rows. Where are you, Sir Jimmy, when your country needs you?

But it is not all bad news with the Boss and Bossette. They recently returned from Brazil, where they were attending a conference on the environment. Not too many rows on that trip, I hope.

I return from coffee and am sifting through some post when suddenly, to my surprise – and by the look of it everyone else's – we are summoned into the office of the Private Secretary, Major General Sir Christopher Airy. Sir Christopher is our number one chief here at St James's Palace. This has to be seriously important. What on earth has happened?

Sir Christopher, let me tell you, is a wonderful old-fashioned courtier. Because he can be a stickler for formality some of us are a bit scared of him, but he is always beautifully mannered and we love him for that. His undoubted strength is organising occasions where there is pomp and ceremony. No one does it better or with more enthusiasm. He loves his work and it shows.

We all crowd into his office. We are agog with anticipation. Sir Christopher then stands up. He is extremely tall. We take one look at him and prepare ourselves for the worst. His whole frame is shaking with emotion. There are tears brimming in his eyes. My goodness, what has happened? Has someone in the Royal Family suddenly died? Has there been an assassination? What?

'I have called you here to tell you that, as of now, my services here are no longer required and, as such, I have tendered my resignation. I have only been in this post a year, but I want to tell you how much I have enjoyed working with you all . . . very much!'

And with that, he sits down. We are stunned. There is silence. There has been an assassination after all. A Palace assassination.

We quietly file out of the office and return to our desks. We are too shocked to say anything. A minute later, Sir Christopher comes out of the office. He then proceeds to stop by each of our desks. He formally bends down and shakes our hands and repeats his farewell, tears still in his eyes.

Even those of us who recently joined or did not greatly warm to him cannot but feel a huge rush of sympathy for this bewildered, proud old man. When he comes to me, he repeats again how much he has enjoyed working with me. How kind. How warm. He then completes his tour.

I find I am crying, so I totter to the bathroom to compose myself. There are four other Lady Clerks in there all doing the same. We are overcome with emotion.

Was he bad at his job? No. So what happened? Does anyone know? One of my colleagues turns round and in a whispers a name: 'Richard Aylard.'

We look at her perplexed.

'The Boss wants him in charge now.'

'Why?'

'Because the General irritated HRH by trying to organise things in what he thought was a proper manner.'

'Really,' interjects another Lady Clerk. 'I had heard that the opposite was true and that it was the Bossette who was behind it!'

So, two contradictory rumours. Clearly the collapsing marriage of HRH and the Princess has now created opposing camps - one blaming the Boss and the other blaming the Bossette for this horrid episode. Where does the truth lie? Who knows? And does it really matter now, except to poor Sir Christopher?

Slowly, we all leave the bathroom, the tissues depleted. Sir Christopher is packing his belongings. Still no one is saying anything. The mood is as sombre as if we had just heard of the death of a much-loved family member. Some of the Lady Clerks are still sniffing, myself included.

There has been intrigue at the Palace throughout history but to see such a decent, faithful and trusting stick like Sir Christopher falling victim, through no direct fault of his conduct, is a terrible thing to behold. I can only consider myself fortunate that nothing like this could ever happen in my pool of lowly Lady Clerks.

We watch Sir Christopher leave. Goodbye, General. You may be wounded but you have served your country and your Prince with honour and distinction. Keep your well-trained military bearing and your head held high. We, the Lady Clerks, salute you.

Other news now, on a much lighter note: Victoria has started to look so svelte and I am deeply envious. We both read the same slimming magazines and the same case studies. Before, we were equal in size. Now, she is an 8 and I am a 12. And on a bad day, I am a 14. Eeek!

Why has Victoria got more willpower than me? Why can I not resist Graham's offerings of calorie-rich dishes in the Royal Officials' canteen at Buckingham Palace? Could it also be something to do with the fact that George and I ingest indecent amounts of pasta in the evening? Maybe.

Nature designed me for comfort rather than speed, I ponder. Look at yourself, girl, you have the bosom of a barmaid. Let's face it, Sarah, you were never going to be a model or fashion icon like the Bossette.

Ah, the Bossette. She looks more and more beautiful. These days, I cannot get away from her. Not that I see her in person. She just stares out at me from every magazine cover in the world. Well, there is one leaf I can take from Her Royal Highness's book: I am going to become blonde, just like her. Well, not precisely like her because she is a natural blonde, I think. Isn't she? Anyway, my brunette locks have to go. Goodbye, Sophia Loren! Hello, Kim Basinger! All right, I am kidding no one, but it is nice to dream.

Make mental note: stay away from Royal Officials' canteen and book appointment with hairdresser.

July 1991

I shouldn't report every rumour I overhear, but the other day Geraldine told me that, in an effort to mend fences, the Princess visited HRH at Highgrove and he turned her away. But why, I asked?

Geraldine told me it was because HRH was so upset about her turning *him* away when he tried to stay with Prince William in hospital the evening after he had been injured by a friend swinging a golf club into his head last month. To make matters worse, Diana then apparently secretly briefed the press that HRH had left Prince William's bedside because he simply didn't care. This was, of course, a complete lie, but HRH wasn't warned and the next thing he knew about it was the appalling headlines in the papers. And there was inevitable widespread tabloid comment about how heartless he was. What really destroyed HRH, though, was that it sent out a terrible and misleading signal to his injured son. Seemingly, he still cannot forgive her for that.

I tossed and turned, thinking about it all night. Frankly, if I was HRH, I would have turned her away too. None of us like to take sides in marital difficulties, but I am beginning to think the nation's Icon can occasionally be a witch.

Other news: late last year I was moved from fan-mail duties to something far grander. Oh yes, it appears I am climbing the Palace ladder!

I am now the secretary, would you believe it, for the Architecture and Planning Group, which we abbreviate here to APG. The role of the APG is to advise HRH on which projects he should get involved in. Architecture is one of his greatest passions and he has gone to war with trendy architects. He maintains they design buildings with no thought or care for the people who live in them. We are with you there, HRH!

Referring to the German Air Force who bombed Britain during the Second World War, the Boss once said in a speech: 'You have to give this much to the Luftwaffe: when it knocked down our buildings, it didn't replace them with anything more offensive than rubble. *We* did that.'

When he looked at the plans for an extension of the National Gallery, he condemned it as 'a vast municipal fire station . . . like a monstrous carbuncle on the face of a much-loved and elegant friend'. That plan got promptly dumped and the architects responsible went out of business.

He doesn't hold back, does he? You will not be altogether surprised that HRH has made quite a few enemies with this controversial stance. He is not liked at all by these architects and their friends in the press, like Stephen Bayley. Oh no. HRH gets as much flak as the Luftwaffe did.

Nonetheless, the Boss's crusade strikes a chord with many members of the public who see the Prince as their champion. Bravo, Your Royal Highness!

The APG, then, is a collection of his friends who know all about buildings and planning, and they advise HRH when and where he should raise his princely cudgel. They volunteer their services for free and meet here at St James's Palace. My role is to organise the monthly meetings, along with the general duties of a PA.

In the early days, our chairman, Dr Brian Hanson, thought the least we could do was lay on tea and cakes for our gathering of architectural luminaries. So, before every meeting, I would nip up to Fortnum & Mason and buy a selection of fondant fancies. Dr Hanson is particularly partial to these cakes – so much so that behind his back we naughty Lady Clerks call him 'Fondant Fancy'. A decision was recently taken to upgrade from cakes and tea. And my task now is to lay on a case of wine with some crisps and peanuts. As you can imagine, the meetings here become quite noisy by the end!

So who are these knights of the Prince's architectural round table? Apart from the chairman, Fondant Fancy, there are Professor Jules Lubbock, who worked with HRH on the redesign of Paternoster Square; Professor Keith Critchlow, who specialises in Islamic architecture; Christopher Martin, who can be a bit grumpy but certainly seems to know his onions; Christopher Gibbs, a famous Bond Street art dealer; Colin Amery, who is brilliant on monuments and who holidays in Corsica with the Rothschilds, don't you know; and writer Candida Lycett-Green, daughter of distinguished poet Sir John Betjeman.

One of the distinguishing features of the group is that they all look, nearly without exception, a touch eccentric, in the mad professor way. Well, I suppose two *are* professors. Even the lovely Candida Lycett-Green looks a little detached at times, favouring, as she does, the Bohemian look.

The appearance and demeanour of the members of the APG has not gone unnoticed elsewhere in the Palace. While I am returning with a carrier bag full of crisps and peanuts for today's meeting, the Sergeant of the Vestry, a Palace veteran in his 60s, raises a weary eyebrow as he sees me pass by.

'Got the loonies coming in again, then?'

Really, some people show no respect.

Slowly, the luminaries gather – gosh, nearly wrote 'loonies' myself! Fondant Fancy starts the meeting and we quickly go through the agenda that I have prepared. While they are always given a sympathetic hearing, most members of the public who write in asking for support with some complaint or given project are politely booted into touch, and I am instructed to write a letter accordingly. If only they knew what I know. They should write in about churches. The APG is mad for churches.

Today, as no one has written in about a church of some distinction, the conversation inevitably turns to two of the group's favourite topics: the forthcoming launch of the Institute of Architecture and the plans for Poundbury, HRH's visionary plan for a large new village near Dorchester. The idea for Poundbury came from Professor Leon Krier, another of HRH's architectural supporters.

By this time, we are halfway into the case of wine and the conversation as usual is becoming quite passionate. Though I am now finding it difficult to follow, I continue to take notes. Like all professions, architects have their own 'in' words, some of which I don't know the meaning of, let alone how to spell them. But no doubt, I think, I will be able to piece it all together in the morning.

The debate gets noisier. There is a lot of laughter, scornful denunciations and vigourous consensual nodding. They are all saying such clever things, I am sure; I just wish I could understand them.

More wine gets poured. We are on to the tenth bottle and everyone is now a bit blotto. What I don't appreciate is that I am getting a bit blotto myself.

The meeting finishes with the end of the case. What a curious coincidence. Greatly refreshed with the lubrication so generously donated by HRH, we launch ourselves into the warm evening air.

The next day, with an uncustomary hangover (for a workday) I sit down and read my notes with the intention of providing HRH's architectural round table with a summation of their sagacious musings. The early part of the meeting is fine. My handwriting is legible and coherent. But as the wine flowed, my shorthand started flowing too, becoming demonstrably larger and more flowery. By the last twenty minutes, when we were down to the remaining bottles, it is completely indecipherable. Oh dear.

Am I to be deterred? Certainly not. I take a bit of what I can remember and what I liked hearing, attribute these strands of thought to whoever takes my fancy, then distribute the minutes of the meeting to the attendees. Frankly, few of them will bother to read the minutes and those who do were too tipsy to have any clearer recollection than I do about who said what about what and to whom. At least, I hope that is the case. Well, no one so far has challenged my minutes.

At last, I am learning to get on in the world.

September 1991

I have discovered yet another perk of working at the Palace. When the Royal Family is not using it, we have free access to the Royal Box at the Albert Hall! That's not something you can pass up lightly, is it? Tonight, I am attending the Last Night of the Proms with George and some colleagues from the office. We enter the box and help ourselves to the drinks. To think that all the monarchs since Queen Victoria and her

Consort Prince Albert have sat right here, and now it is our turn!

The conductor waves his baton and the orchestra strikes up. Soon we are lost in a reverie of the great annual musical pageant. There are pieces by Beethoven, by Mozart and by Handel. The concert concludes, as ever, with Elgar's great anthem 'Land of Hope and Glory'. It is so patriotic. Shivers run down my spine. Below me people are waving their flags wildly in time to the music. It is wonderful to view the sea of jubilant faces below full of emotion and love of their country.

Those of us in the box jointly decide it is indecorous to wave the Union flag in quite the same free-spirited way, so I keep my elbows to the side and wave my flag with what I hope is ladylike restraint, as a Royal would do. It makes me feel a bit of a dweeb, but I am at the front of the Royal Box and can hardly let the Royal side down, can I?

The concert is drawing to an end. There is rapturous applause. Suddenly, someone screams out. Then people turn round, point, stare and wave towards us excitedly. What is the commotion? What is happening? Then someone bellows, 'Princess Diana!'

I hear a cheer! Gosh, I can't believe it. I start blushing. Just think, I am being mistaken for the World's Number One Fashion Icon! This is amazing, utterly amazing. I think I am going to faint. It must be the new blonde hair! Treasure this moment, Sarah!

Another voice calls out. 'Get yourself some glasses, mate! That's not Princess Diana. Look at her. Far too fat!'

The crowd turns away.

I retreat into the box, red-faced. I am going to forget that this happened. No, I won't mention this to a soul. I don't know why I am even recording this. In any case, I am sure they must have been talking about someone else. Surely they could not have been referring to me? Surely not. Start that diet *tomorrow*!

March 1992

Victoria and I have found another way to lose weight. Have a sandwich, then shop! As our lunch hour is precisely one hour and twenty minutes, what we do is speed over to BP (seven minutes), create sandwich from roll, salad and cold meat, wrap it in napkin (three minutes), and set off again. In and out in twelve minutes!

Today, we are joined by Poppy, another Palace shopaholic. As we make our way briskly through Green Park, I am personally relieved we are also avoiding one particular Lady Clerk colleague who is always trying to get me to sign up to the Cats Protection League. I am fond of cats, but their protection is not something that ranks in my priorities. In fact, the notion is absurd. Cats can survive perfectly well without mollycoddling from humans. Aren't nine lives enough?

The trouble is that she is senior to me and I never have the guts to tell her I am simply not interested. Instead, I pathetically nod my head in agreement when she regales me yet again with more cat protection propaganda. There are obsessives everywhere – even in palaces.

Four minutes later, I arrive at my Mecca – Bond Street. We have precisely fifty minutes to indulge our retail fantasies. What do I buy? Very little, of course. The Palace wages are linked to inflation, so there is no proper pay rise as you might get in other jobs. Every year, we get a letter from Richard Aylard to inform us of 'the increment' to our wage packet. My take home wage is now £205 a week. Wow! Bond Street, watch out!

But, my goodness, we enjoy entering the portals of high fashion: Asprey, Garrard, Hermes, Gucci. We gaze at their offerings and salivate. Occasionally, we succumb. Right now, we all have an obsession with gilt animals on our shoes and belts. The bank manager and Daddy simply have to understand that this year gilt animals are essential!

Sometimes, I must confess, I am a bit naughty. I pretend that I have mislaid my checkbook and my credit card. I then present the shop assistant with my work card. Invariably, the assistants confer with the manager. Next thing I know is that my 'acquisition' is wrapped up while the manager informs me that he will drop the small matter of the bill directly to me at the Palace.

It arrives. Oh dear. How unfortunate that it falls into the wastepaper basket. The bill then gets chased up six weeks later. The irritated accountant eventually docks the sum from my wages. Well, I reason, at least it has helped me on cash flow.

On other occasions, I have to present the bills to Daddy. Usually, when I next visit Shropshire, he makes me sit down at his study desk and draw up a financial plan. Poor Daddy, he must get so exasperated.

But, truth to tell, we impoverished Lady Clerks have other ways of surviving and keeping our end up with our Royal masters. The Princess, bless her, is our kind and sweet benefactor. As the World's Number One Fashion Icon, she is, of course, the target of every manufacturer of every beauty product ever made. Who in high fashion marketing would not want to claim that the Princess favours their product?

Consequently, every week the Bossette receives loads of sample perfumes and new face cream products from the top beauty houses. Of course, the Princess already has all the beauty products she could possibly want. So what does she do with them? Why, she passes them to Victoria, her devoted Lady Clerk, to do with as she pleases!

It does me no harm, of course, that I am one of Victoria's best friends. This week, I am so lucky. Victoria is giving me some wonderful perfume – *Knowing* by Estée Lauder – and matching body lotion.

Then, of course, there are the amazing discounts that Royal staff are entitled to. The best has to be Bronnley soap. The discount is 90 per cent. Can you believe it? All the Lady Clerks have cottoned on to this perk and at Christmas time St James's Palace resembles a dedicated Bronnley soap department store, with boxes and boxes of the stuff arriving continuously.

Other discounts include Royal Brierley glass, Royal Doulton china and Barbour jackets – all at 40 per cent off. Also, with Barbour, you can send them back later for re-waxing. Simpsons department store on Piccadilly gives us 30 per cent discount. I am not mad about Pringle jerseys or golfing socks, but I am tempted by their Leonidas Belgian chocolates, which so far I have successfully resisted. But, hooray, they have recently opened up their Red Door Salon. Getting 30 per cent off my hairdressing bill is a bargain I cannot afford to pass up.

Finally, there is the flower van that comes from Windsor Castle every week, bringing bulbs and poinsettias in the winter and bedding plants in the spring. I occasionally buy some for friends. You pay just 30 per cent of what you would have to spend in a flower shop. It is always tempting to go out into the courtyard when the van arrives, just to see what is on offer and also for the fun of saying 'Hi' to everyone. The flower van then goes to Buckingham and Kensington palaces before returning to the Royal Gardens at Windsor.

May 1992

This is so exciting, I can hardly believe it! I am driving, or should I say I am being driven, down the motorway in a cavalcade. I am sitting with the swanky Foreign Office smoothie Peter Westmacott. He is a Deputy Private Secretary and for some reason we Lady Clerks have nicknamed him Peter 'Wally-ma-cott'. Why? I don't know. It just sounded funny and so it has stuck. Also with me is Anne Beckwith-Smith, the Bossette's lovely Lady-in-Waiting.

The road has been cleared, so we whizz through traffic lights. How strange this feels. We are heading down to the M4 to board the *Queen's Flight* at Heathrow. It is all so presidential. I cannot believe it is happening. Talk about feeling grand and important!

Police motorcyclists ride in front, behind and alongside. The two limousines ahead of us are Rolls-Royces carrying the Royal couple. I should imagine Their Royal Highnesses are in separate cars, such is the state of enmity between them. Their marriage looks as if it is seriously collapsing. The press coverage of their recent tour of India was dreadful, with photographs of the Bossette looking theatrically disconsolate outside the Taj Mahal while the Boss attended an official prearranged lunch.

It wasn't his fault that he couldn't be with the Bossette. The lunch was part of his schedule. Why should he disappoint all the Indian businessmen who were waiting to meet him? But the newspapers gave it the slant that he didn't want to be there with her. Presumably, the Bossette briefed them.

A new book by Lady Colin Campbell, *Diana in Private* has appeared. It has whipped up a storm, not only here but all over the world. She says that there are real problems in the relationship; that both Charles and Diana have lovers and that the marriage has been over in all but name for years which, of course, all of us at the Palace know to be the truth. We have all surrepticiously bought copies. The word around the Palace is that Diana initially co-operated in the book but pulled out when she realised that Lady Colin wasn't going to do a hatchet job on my lovely HRH, but rather would present a more balanced view of their troubles. After all, neither of them are saints. Oh dear, where is this all going to end? It is unthinkable that they divorce.

I knew things were getting really bad last December when the Bossette refused to turn up to a party at Kensington Palace for suppliers in protest, apparently, at the Boss inviting Mrs Camilla Parker-Bowles to represent her at a funeral. Oh dear, I did think that was a bit provocative of you, HRH. You must have known she would go ballistic: inviting your confidante to be her representative. How would you appreciate it if she asked Captain Hewitt to be yours? Lapse of judgement there, I think.

So will the Boss and Bossette use this trip as an opportunity to patch things up? Or will it be more of the same? Something tells me not to hold my breath.

We are off to Seville in Spain, where we will be attending something called Expo '92. Naturally, I am absolutely thrilled, but I am, all the same, slightly nervous. Why?

Because I have never done a Royal tour before and normally two Lady Clerks travel out but this time it is just me. What if I make a mistake? What if I do something wrong? I don't even speak Spanish.

Inner nanny cuts in. Don't be silly, Sarah, remember you are a Virgo. You are, by astrological design, very organised. Everything will be fine.

I run through the tasks I have to perform. Yes, everyone has their passport. They also have their full tour booklet, which comes in two different sizes with information on Seville, time differences, weather forecasts, contact numbers, times and dates. I had to work weekends to put the booklet together. But I didn't mind because I got to choose the colour of the cover. I settled on royal blue, which I thought was appropriate given the circumstances. The girl in me wanted pink. I know that the Princess would have been amused, but I think HRH would have got cross. So royal blue it is.

A part of me remains fretful. Now, Sarah, have you forgotten anything? Think! No? All right, then. All you have to do is ensure the temporary office on location runs smoothly and type a few letters. What can possibly go wrong? Relax.

My goodness, we are at Heathrow already. We are whisked into the VIP lounge, as we have no luggage to check in. Our suitcases have been taken ahead for us. This has been arranged by the Travelling Yeoman, Sergeant 'Sarge' Ron Lewis. This is the way to travel!

Now we board the *Queen's Flight*, a small jet for the exclusive use of the Royal Family. We, the officials, step on first. Is this amazing or what? I buckle myself in. The last to board are the Royal couple, who are seated in a separate cabin. The plane takes off and we are in the air.

This whole experience reminds me of something. What is it? Yes, I remember. A scene out of *Goldfinger,* the early James Bond movie. Here I am, flying high above the skies with the World's Number One Fashion Icon, her lovely Lady-in-Waiting, the gorgeous heir to the throne and a suave Foreign Office gentleman. Then there is little me. What am I doing here? How did I get here?

Don't ask such silly questions, I tell myself. Just relax and enjoy yourself. Then I have an anxiety attack. What if, just like in *Goldfinger*, some dastardly rogue tries to hijack the plane? After all, two of the passengers are about the most high-profile people on the planet. What if one of the cabin staff or the pilot himself is a villainous Blofeld? Don't be stupid, Sarah. You are being melodramatic.

But what if something went wrong? Like what? Like the pilot and the co-pilot both have heart attacks! Now you are being really stupid, Sarah.

Of course I know perfectly well that, besides being an expert on architecture, the inspiration and leader of a great and effective charity, a champion of all faiths, lover of all creatures (including insects), HRH is also a man of action. Oh yes, he has commanded naval battleships and is a qualified fixed-wing *and* helicopter pilot. Why, he could step into James Bond's loafers any day! He would calmly take over the controls and land this jet on a small coral atoll if he needed to. And he would dispatch a mythical Blofeld with one sweep of his princely arm. Moreover, James Bond exists only in fiction, while His Royal Highness exists in fact!

Reassured, I shut my eyes and try to sleep, which is ridiculous because I am far too excited.

After landing and disembarking from the plane, we are

now speeding along the road into town in another cavalcade. I gaze out of the window. My goodness, Seville is stunning. We sweep up to the Hotel Alfonso XIII, which is big, beautiful and oh so expensive. And, fantastic, I am not paying!

I am shown to my bedroom. It is amazing. It is more like a suite. Apart from my double bed there is a spare single bed, a huge television and a long table on and below which are metal boxes containing office supplies, computers, a printer and so forth. Well done, Travelling Yeoman. My bedroom is to be Their Royal Highnesses' office. Come in day or night, Boss and Bossette, your Miss Moneypenny awaits you!

You know your duties, girl, so set about them. As I start to unpack the boxes, in comes the Travelling Yeoman himself.

'Mind if I watch television?' he asks. Doesn't he have one in his room, I wonder? He is possibly a little lonely and wants company.

'Go ahead,' I say.

Sarge then makes himself comfortable on the single bed, while I continue my task of setting up the office.

Voilà! Everything is organised. Now all I have to do is switch on the computers and the office is ready for action. Their Royal Highnesses can depend upon me, Oh yes! I press the requisite buttons and . . . er, nothing. I press them again. Still nothing.

I emit some Anglo-Saxon utterance for which you get sharply rebuked as a child. Sarge looks up at me from the bed. 'Oh don't worry, dear.'

That is all very well for him to say. I have an office to run! I fiddle around with a few wires and double-check everything is in place, then press buttons again. *Still* nothing! Repetition of Anglo-Saxon utterance.

'Oh don't worry, dear,' repeats Sarge.

Sarge, I think, you are getting on my nerves. I frantically go and check the connections again and finally the plugs. Aha! one of them is a bit loose. I press requisite buttons again. Lights flash, the computer whirrs.

At last! Everything is fine. I can relax. Then, all of a sudden, there is a loud popping noise and all the computers go off, the bathroom light goes off and so does the television. Oh my God! At least three more repetitions of Anglo-Saxon utterance.

This is my first and probably my last ever Royal tour. I can't even set up a simple office. I have failed everyone: the Palace, my colleagues, the Boss and Bossette, and myself. I am an utter, miserable disappointment and am about to burst into tears.

'Don't worry, dear,' says Sarge. 'It can all be fixed later. I think what you need right now is a nice lunch.'

And with that, avuncular Sarge steers fretful me out of the room, which is now devoid of any electricity.

I am greeted at the pool by the rest of the team, who are so sweet to me and ply me with champagne. Soon, I am taking in the midday sun of Seville and thinking what a lucky girl I am to have such an amazing job. Yes, the electricity failure is a small matter and can wait. After all, Their Royal Highnesses will not be returning until much later. I was being silly, overreacting like that. Sarge and the team are right. When I think about it, my sense of panic is a bit embarrassing. You need to mature a bit, girl. Chill.

Feeling a little light-headed after the sun and champagne, I meander back to my room. Phew, it is hot in here. What's happened to the air conditioning? Sarah, you dolt, there is no electricity, remember? Oh well, that will soon be fixed. Nothing to worry about. Remember, chill.

Suddenly, I remember something else. Oh my God! This is too dreadful. I cannot believe it. There certainly *is* something to worry about. I had completely forgotten. In three of the unopened metal cases there is everybody's emergency supply of blood. They are clearly marked with our different blood groups. In the event of an accident or a terrorist outrage, these cases can make the critical difference between life and death. It says clearly on the boxes: VITAL: KEEP AT ROOM TEMPERATURE.

Is this room temperature right now? Hardly. The room is like an oven! Aaargh! How long have I been away lounging by the pool? Two hours at least! Two hours in which you have jeopardised the lives of your wonderful colleagues and the world's most glamorous couple. The life of everyone on this Royal tour is at risk because of you, Sarah! Forget about your own life, girl. It is hardly worth living now.

With tears welling up in my eyes, I look despairingly at the three metal suitcases. Our blood supplies are probably by now some sticky congealed confection of black pudding. Don't stand there and gawp. Do something!

I pick up the telephone and jabber a command to the receptionist.

'Please speak slowly,' she replies. 'I cannot understand.'

Speak slowly? Can't she speak English? Calm down, dear, says my inner Sarge. English is probably her fourth language. Remember, we are in Spain.

I take a deep breath. '*Por favor*, I need a handyman right now!'

'Please tell me. What is handy man?'

This is ridiculous. I take another deep breath.

'I am with the Prince and Princess of Wales, *comprende*? As of now, we have an emergency because there is no electricity. And this could, for reasons too complicated to explain right now, endanger people's lives.'

'So you need an electrician?'

Phew! We are getting there.

'Yes. And, *por favor*, this is an emergency!'

I congratulate myself for not shrieking out the last word like some dysfunctional hysteric, which, at the moment, is what I am. Please, God, don't let there be some Basque terrorist outrage or a traffic accident right now. Please.

Five minutes later, there is a knock on the door and in walks Señor Hotel Maintenance Man. He looks at me, blinking. I quickly realise he can't speak even a word of English. This is a disaster. I am Sybil in *Fawlty Towers* and before me is uncomprehending Manuel. Inside me is demented Basil, flailing his arms around and losing it.

Be calm, Sarah, my inner Sarge tells me. Take control. The poor man can see anxiety etched across you. He looks agitated. Smile at him, then speak slowly and use sign language. I proceed to point and give encouraging signs. He looks bemused at first but then, by jingo, he is on the job. My goodness, this curious Esperanto has worked!

A minute later, the lights blink on, the television comes alive, the computers fire up and the air conditioning starts blasting. Well done, Manuel! You have saved my life, not to mention possibly the lives of the future King and Queen of Great Britain. The United Kingdom will not forget you. I feel like giving you a kiss, I am so happy! Yes, I am giving you a kiss right now. With that I place my lips on his left cheek and then on his right. God bless you, Manuel. *Muchas gracias* from Great Britain.

Oh dear, Manuel looks nervous, as if I am attacking him or something. Gathering his tool kit, he starts to make a hasty exit. I am only being warm and appreciative, Manuel. I don't mean to scare you, my eyes plead. Being Latin, I thought you would be familiar with a demonstrative expression of emotion. Oh dear.

'*Adiós, señorita*!'

This is cultural miscommunication for you. Manuel probably thinks I am some lonely randy foreigner who has invited him up for some fuse-fitting as a pretext for something different altogether. Yes, I know, Manuel, you are a maintenance man, not a gigolo. I only wanted to say thank you.

I take a deep breath. Look on the bright side, I tell myself. Crisis has been averted. The blood supplies won't boil over, and the computer and printer are ready for action. You are Miss Moneypenny and you are back in control.

My workload over the next forty-eight hours is light: typing the odd letter, normally late at night, presented to me by Peter or Anne. During the day, I am free to lie by the pool and work on my tan. In the evening, I watched television with Sarge.

Then it is over. We fly back landing, this time, at RAF Northolt. No customs or anything. Amazing. Limousines from the palace are at hand to whisk us away. I gaze out of the window of the car as we sweep into London.

While it has been an amazing Royal Tour for me, it has not, I fear, been a good one my Masters, the Royal Couple, of whom I caught only a few glimpses. But I can report their body language says it all. No need for any evidence of rows or anything. They clearly can't stand each other right now.

Well, it can't get much worse, can it?

November 1992

How exciting! I am being driven up to Norfolk now with Sarah Ward, another Lady Clerk. Sarah is also HRH's goddaughter. She is getting married and I am being 'shown the ropes', as they say, of working for HRH at Sandringham, the Royal Family's house and estate near King's Lynn.

I don't dare ask, because it is personal, but I wonder whether it is Sarah's great-grandmother who was the cruelly discarded lover of HRH's great-uncle Edward VIII when he became smitten with Wallis Simpson.

Geraldine tells me that I should see this tour of duty at Sandringham as a form of promotion. Apparently, HRH has decreed that I am a 'good egg' as a result of my work on the Royal tour in Spain in May. This is flattering, but HRH barely caught even a glimpse of me. Indeed, the last time we talked was when I first met him, nearly four years ago. But who am I to fathom the workings of the great Royal mind? Luckily, neither HRH nor anyone else ever found out about the Royal blood supplies nearly boiling over into black pudding.

Will the Bossette be in attendance, I wonder? I doubt it. Not after all the mud that has been flung and reported so gleefully in the media. I remember it starting. Who cannot?

In June, another book comes out about the Bossette, this time by Andrew Morton and it is serialised in a Sunday newspaper. In short, the book portrays Her Royal Highness as a put-upon victim trapped in a loveless marriage and betrayed by her adulterous husband who doesn't love her and never did. The nation was shocked. There are even rumours at the Palace that Diana herself cooperated in the book and that this is the hatchet job on Charles that Diana had been plotting. She had, of course, hoped Lady Colin Campbell would carry it out. But that lady was sufficiently strong-minded to refuse the Princess her wish. Morton's book commands all the attention now but, having read both accounts of the rocky Royal marriage, my vote goes to Lady Colin. As she presents the evidence, there is fault on both sides. As Morton presents it, the fault lies solely with HRH.

Why is this? Consider the backgrounds of the two authors. At the time of writing his book, Morton was a reporter on the *Daily Star*, a red-top tabloid for blue-collar workers. He was spoon-fed propaganda solely from Diana's friends. On the other hand, Lady Colin is an aristocrat with easy access to many royal sources. Verdict: you get closer to the truth with Lady Colin.

Then in August there is the newspaper publication of transcripts of the notorious 'Squidgy' tapes. This is a recording of the Princess talking on the telephone with a man who refers to her as 'Squidgy' recorded up at Sandringham at New Year in 1990.

The nub of it is the Bossette says being with HRH is torture. It transpires the man's voice belongs to an old boyfriend of hers, a rather dashing chap called James Gilbey, whom the Princess met and was seeing as a lover long before HRH. So much for the virgin bride myth!

So here we are now with the world condemning the Boss as a cold-hearted adulterer and the Bossette as a hot-blooded tart. And they don't even know about the Bossette's other lovers yet! How did it come to this?

I gaze out of the window. We have been driving for nearly three hours. Goodness, the scenery round these parts is drab. It is all flat and featureless. Who wants to live round here? Pheasants and partridges, I suppose. Apparently, it is rather depopulated in north Norfolk. I am hardly surprised. You wouldn't get me voting to live here. Oh no.

Eventually, we arrive at some gates. After being checked in by security, we go down a long drive and are at last about to arrive. I trust Sandringham is beautiful. Of course, it will be. This is, after all, Her Majesty's residence in East Anglia. I have already pictured it in my mind. It is palatial and romantic with turrets, rounded towers, a drawbridge and moat, a country palace fit for a queen.

Oh dear. Instead, looming in front of us is a large, nondescript red-brick Victorian edifice with nothing endearing about it at all. In fact, it puts me in mind of one of the grim boarding schools that I so unhappily attended as a child.

How unlike Highgrove. That is beauty and style for you. The Georgians were so much better at country houses than the Victorians, which I can say with some authority as the secretary on HRH's Architecture Committee. Still, it has to be jolly nice inside, I muse.

We enter the inner portals. I am briefly introduced to some other members of staff and then I am taken upstairs. We climb two flights of stairs right to the top. I am then shown my room. It is built into the eaves. Oh my God, it is so small! It really is just like boarding school. There is an old-fashioned enamel sink and an ugly metal bed.

Have I done something wrong? Am I being punished for

something? To think I have to spend ten days here and not have Gorgeous George around to console me. How utterly depressing. What I am told next astounds me further. The corridor I am in, Sarah says, is the woman's quarters. Another corridor on the other side of the staircase is the men's. I was right. This *is* boarding school.

Sarah then shows me the office. There is a huge amount of work on at the moment because Windsor Castle just nearly burnt down and HRH is sending out a whopping three-page letter to nearly every firefighter who came to the rescue and saved the great castle from being reduced to an incinerated ruin.

It appears fire brigades came from all over the country, so there are a lot of people to contact. I set to my task. I must say, it really is considerate of HRH to thank all these people with such a long, considered letter. How many other people would even bother to send so much as a postcard?

As I bash out the correspondence, I idly wonder whether I will see HRH. Probably not. After all, who am I in the great Royal scheme of things? I am nobody, just a humble Lady Clerk.

In the evening, I am re-introduced to Bernie the butler, who is one of HRH's staff, not her Majesty's. Bernie presents us all with a huge stiff gin and tonic, by which I mean it is a large tumbler of gin and ice with the merest hint of tonic.

That hits the spot. I then sit down to some spaghetti bolognese. There is nothing good on television so I try to break into conversation with some of the local staff, but they appear rather reticent. I don't know where Sarah is. I presume she is dining with her godfather, the Boss. Ho hum, I might as well go back to thanking firefighters.

The Princess of Wales kneeling for a group photograph during
the staff day out go-cart racing in Clapham. That's me next to
her in my earlier days as a brunette.

St James's Palace,
my place of work.
(Associated Newspapers)

Major James Hewitt, former Life Guard and lover of Diana, Princess of Wales, walking his dog. (Associated Newspapers)

Princess Diana with her Personal Protection Officer, Ken Wharfe. (Associated Newspapers)

Mervyn Wycherley, Diana's ex-chef, in the gardens outside Kensington Palace, home to Princess Diana. (Associated Newspapers)

Jimmy Savile with Princess Diana after he persuades her to do a walkabout in Clifford, North Yorkshire, in September 1988.

HRH's Architecture and Planning Group taken during the day out in Strawberry Hill. Left to right: Brian Hanson ('Fondant Fancy'), Christopher Martin, Candida Lycett-Green, Prof. Keith Critcklow, HRH, a local councillor, Colin Amery, Prof. Jules Lubboch, Christopher Gibbs, Mary-Anne Malleret, me.

Sandringham: my office was above and behind the courtyard on the right.
(Associated Newspapers)

My colleague and friend Victoria Mendham with Princess Diana.
(Brendan Beirne)

Balmoral Castle. (Press Association)

Michael Fawcett, the indispensable former
valet to the Prince of Wales.
(Associated Newspapers)

Flowers outside St James's Palace the day
after the funeral of Diana, Princess of Wales.
(Associated Newspapers)

Candida Lycett-Green, a star of the
Architecture and Planning Group.
(Associated Newspapers)

Me with a South African Airways steward
during the Royal tour in 1997.

Above – Royal tour group photo taken in the garden of the British High Commissioner's Residence. Left to right: (front row) Royal surgeon, Nick Archer (Assistant Private Secretary), HRH, Sandy Henney (Royal Press Secretary), John Lavery (Equerry), Peter Clarke (high-ranking Metropolitan Police officer); (back row) Iain MacRae (HRH's Personal Protection Officer – a Mel Gibson lookalike, Iain is now Prince William's Motorbike Protection Officer), Carolyn Robb (HRH's chef), Clive Allen (HRH's valet), Amanda Neville (press), Superindendant Colin Trimming (HRH's Protection Officer), me, Lee Dobson (HRH's valet), Juliet Franks (Lady Clerk), Ron Lewis (Travelling Yeoman).

Right – Tiggy Legge-Bourke, 'Royal gopher'. (Associated Newspapers)

A typical tour of the Highgrove garden. In the forefront is a pond designed by Willy Bertram, edged by Lady's mantle, the pervasive *Alchemilla mollis*. (Associated Newspapers)

Left – Karen Humphries and me at the Cavalry and Guards Club just after I was decorated with my MVO.

Above – HRH with his friend, the Duke of Westminster, Mr Sexy Woodentop. (Jim Bennett)

Camilla, Duchess of Cornwall, and her daughter, Laura, watch the first race of the Cheltenham Festival in 2006 with Prince Charles. (Associated Newspapers)

Me, reflective, in 2005. (Les Wilson)

In the morning, Commander Aylard comes to see me. This is a welcome surprise. I have been invited to help out at a shooting lunch where HRH and his pals will be gathered after their exertions blasting pheasants and partridges. I wonder if Royal Sandringham pheasants will be on the menu some time during my stay up here. I hope so. Yes, Your Royal Highness, I am more than happy to serve you as a waitress as well as a secretary.

Sarah drives me to what appears to be a village hall. I have butterflies in my stomach again. I enter the room all ready to perform my catering tasks and find that the shooting party is already here. A round table with stools for seats has already been laid out. Presumably, I will be having a sandwich next door with Bernie.

Bernie is handing out the drinks. I find myself brushing shoulders with His Magnificence. Eek! How exciting is that? Swoon, he looks so handsome in his shooting togs! I glide up to Bernie and whisper in his ear.

'What do you want me to do?'

Bernie looks at me, bemused. He is serving right now and cannot say anything. Please will someone tell me what I am supposed to do! I look to Sarah Ward, but she is busy talking with one of the guests. That is all very well for her. After all, Sarah is practically family. But I am not. I am a nobody who doesn't know anybody. I am overwhelmed with panic and feel like crying.

The Commander comes up to me and smiles. 'Just help yourself,' he says, pointing to a drinks tray.

Nervously, I pour myself some red wine. Should I be doing this, I wonder? I start gulping down my drink. My God, I have finished the entire glass in hardly a minute. This is dreadful.

The Royal shooting party will think they have a dipsomaniac in their midst. Too late now. I look around. Everyone seems engaged in shooting banter. I pour myself another. I take another gulp and then another. Yes, I am feeling much better now, thank you, and, imagine, this second glass needs a refill. I go over and pour another. This is better, much better. Yes, the panic has dissolved.

Oh dear, HRH is looking straight at me! This is too much. I am about to be fired. I know it. I am to be dismissed for getting drunk. What a disgrace! I will never live this down. Please God, command an earthquake and let the Norfolk earth swallow me up. My miserable and pathetic existence should be extinguished. Oh Sarah, how could you?

He opens his mouth. I steel myself for the inevitable.

'Sarah,' he says.

I look at him transfixed. Oh dear. He even knows my name. His god-daughter must have told him who the alcoholic is in his midst. I hold his stare. I am numb and petrified. I cannot speak. He looks at me closely.

'It is Sarah, isn't it?'

I nod. Prepare yourself, girl. Your humiliating moment is about to happen.

'Would you care to sit down?' He points to a stool.

Oh no. He is going to denounce me. Please, HRH, I am so sorry. I know I have to leave your employment now. I didn't mean to do it. Really, I didn't. But I know my fate. I don't expect any notice. I will go quietly and slink off to somewhere far away. But please get it over and done with. I can't bear it any longer. I think I am going to cry! My inner nanny steps in.

Don't be stupid, girl! He is just inviting you to sit down for lunch. See, look around. Everyone is sitting down and you are included. I am? Yes, you silly girl, you are. And stop gawping at him like that. You are a Lady Clerk, not a fish.

I sit down and then this huge man sits next to me. He is massive. His bottom spreads over the stool, which seems to almost disappear. Poor chap, he must be so uncomfortable. And who is sitting next to me on my right? I turn round.

Oh my God! It's him! His Magnificence himself. And because the table is so small and the man on my left is so big, my body is practically pressed against his athletic Royal frame. I have heard of shoulder-to-shoulder but this is ridiculous!

HRH is turning round. He is looking at me and now he is opening his mouth. Please, Sarah, whatever you do, don't clam up, not like last time. You are an intelligent (sometimes, at least), well-educated (sort of) young woman. You know how to form a sentence and hold a conversation. I do? Yes. Now get to it!

'Hello, Sarah. Are they treating you all right?'

Who are 'they'? He must mean the staff? How considerate. How sweet. Here is my future King bothering to ask if I am being looked after. I can hardly complain about the room and ask to be upgraded to a suite, can I?

'Oh yes, Your Royal Highness, they are treating me quite splendidly.'

'Good, I am glad,' he says.

We all then adjust ourselves to tackle the baked potatoes, quiche and salad being served by Bernie. Should I get up and help, I wonder? I should, I think. But I can hardly do so when I am being addressed at this personally historic moment by my future King.

'I say,' he says with a twinkle. 'A bit squashed here!'

I gaze into those gorgeous blue eyes, give him a wan smile and nod.

'I don't mind at all, Your Royal Highness!'

The inner alarms go off. How *could* you, Sarah? You sound like some tarty vamp. You are a lowly Lady Clerk, not Mae West. What is he going to think of you, giving him a saucy comeback like that?

'So, Sarah, I imagine you have a boyfriend, don't you?'

I am about to pass out. Quick, get some smelling salts someone! A huge river has just been crossed. It is a river that I thought would always, always stand between me and my Royal and exalted master. Not only does HRH honour me by sitting next to me and even bothering to address me, he has the kindness and the warmth to move from the safe and general (shooting and the weather) to the personal (the boyfriend).

'Yes, Your Royal Highness, I do have a boyfriend. His name is George.'

HRH contemplates the name with a furrowed brow, no doubt ruminating on the many Georges in the illustrious Royal Family.

'Now, tell me about George.'

So I tell him, briefly of course. After all, the last thing I want to do is bore the Boss.

'To be truthful, Your Royal Highness, I am not sure what George does. He does something in the City, I think.'

HRH looks at me and nods. God, what else do I say?

'But, Your Royal Highness, the thing for me is that he is lovely and he looks like Richard Gere.'

Oh dear. HRH is furrowing his eyebrows. He doesn't have

a clue who I am talking about.

'Sarah, I hope you don't mind if I say something.'

I feebly shake my head. I feel the rest of myself shake too. My bosom is wobbling all but two inches from his chest. Has he smelt the wine on my breath? Do I absolutely reek of claret? Oh God, what is he going to say?

'Please don't get me wrong, and I *really* hope you don't mind me for saying it.'

He pauses. I am about to faint. I have BO. I stink of alcohol. He is trying to be kind. I can see he wants to tell me I smell like a lush. He is trying to find the diplomatic words to inform me. Don't bother, Your Royal Highness, I know what I am. I am a disgrace.

He continues. 'After you have called me "Your Royal Highness" once, it is sufficient for the day. Afterwards, you just address me as "Sir".'

I gulp. 'Yes, Sir.'

'Good. Are you in love with George?'

Wow, we are moving from the personal to the intimate!

'Well, Your Royal Highness – sorry, Sir – it is difficult to say. I certainly have strong feelings for him!'

'Good. Do you think you will marry him?'

No one has put this to me before!

'Sir, I really don't know. It is as much up to George as it is up to me.'

HRH ponders.

'Yes, it is a tricky thing, marriage.'

Suddenly, he looks so sad. I feel overwhelmed by emotion. You can see the pain surging through his face. He is so obviously such a decent man. The Bossette is just not the woman for him. But I cross my fingers. Who knows? They could still work it out.

'I take great solace from the Bible, you know.'

He pauses again. I feel like crying. Poor man, he is in such pain. I cannot bear it. I pick up my napkin and dab my eye. HRH looks at me with concern.

'Don't worry, Sir. An eyelash must have strayed into my pupil.'

'Oh I do hope you are all right!'

'I am fine, Sir, really, I am.'

'Oh good.'

And with that, HRH proceeds to sketch out his religious beliefs. I am particularly taken with the notion of death being the next great journey. I don't know whether he is right or not, but I am utterly convinced of his sincerity. And I am so touched he is sharing it with me. Imagine, a one-on-one with the future King!

The man on my left bellows out and soon the table is back to jolly shooting speak about the speed and altitude of the morning's partridge and pheasant.

I look around. I feel so utterly reassured and confident now, with my body wedged between His Splendidness on my right and His Hugeness on my left. Quite often the two banter across me. I don't mind at all. I can sense the tangible warmth and affection between HRH and this enormous chap.

Good, I think, you need solid friends around you, Sir. And who better than this portly fellow the size of a sumo wrestler and with a voice like a foghorn? I wonder what his name is? Do I dare ask? No, definitely not.

Suddenly, His Massiveness turns round, smiles and addresses me.

'Hello. We haven't met. My name is Nicholas, Nicholas

Soames.'

If I wasn't so firmly wedged, I would have fallen off my stool in amazement. This is *the* Nicholas Soames. Wow! Now, I never follow politics because it is boring, as far as I am concerned, but even I know of the great and colourful Nicholas Soames, Conservative Minister for Agriculture and grandson, would you believe, of the greatest Englishman of all time, Sir Winston Churchill.

I have even written the great Minister a few letters, not of course from me but on behalf of His Gorgeousness. What an honour, Sir, to meet you, even if your right buttock has spread itself onto my stool. Let it spread further, if you wish. You can park it on my lap! I don't care. It is a privilege and an honour.

What I want to say to you, Mr Soames, but obviously I can't, is how delighted I am that you are a friend of HRH. With a stout fellow like you at his side, I should imagine that HRH can survive the slings and arrows of the outrageous media and that shameless Mr Morton, who has been portraying the Boss in such a bad light in his one-sided book.

The Glorious Panjandrum that is the marvellous Mr Soames is suddenly addressed by a funny-looking fellow across the table. He turns from me to reply. Whereas Nicholas Soames has a round head, this chap in front has a square one. Indeed, the top of his head appears flat, rather like that of the creation of Doctor Frankenstein. I half expect to see bolts on either side of his skull. But apart from that, he is really rather dishy. At least, I think so. He has dark bushy eyebrows, which meet in the middle, and an abundance of floppy dark hair like the gorgeous actor Hugh Grant.

Who is this sexy woodentop, I wonder? I catch his eye. But he surveys me as if I am some kind of lower life form and looks away to talk to someone else. We are not big on the charm stakes, are we, Mr Woodentop, whoever you are? Perhaps you are just rather shy and I am misjudging you. Suddenly, I overhear somebody address Woodentop as 'Gerald'. Aha, we have a name.

Minutes later, the shooting party gets up and prepares to leave. Wildfowl of Norfolk, your executioners are on their way. Prepare for a glorious death. Royal dinner tables await you!

Sarah and I then help Bernie clear up and we drive back to the house.

'Who is that chap Gerald?' I ask her.

'Oh, that's Gerald Westminster.'

I look out of the window, pretending I am neither interested nor impressed. That would not be cool. Inside, I am screaming. I thought I recognised him. Of course, it is him. Woodentop, the Duke of Westminster. And he is no ordinary duke either, not that there could ever really be such a thing as an ordinary duke. No, this Gerald is the richest duke in the world! By zillions! He is worth something humungous like five thousand million pounds. Yikes. No wonder I find him so attractive, with his handsome looks and effortless superiority born of refined breeding and barrels and barrels of money.

I reflect on the shooting lunch. I feel I have just eaten at Madame Tussauds. Nearly everyone I have been with today is famous. The difference is that I have encountered them in the flesh rather than as wax effigies.

'Nicholas Soames is funny,' I say.

'Yes,' replies Sarah. 'He can be hilarious.'

Back at Sandringham, Sarah picks up her bag then drives off back to London. She has the arms of a future husband to look forward to and I have another nine days in this depressing mausoleum. Still, those firefighters must be thanked.

As I go to sleep that night in my horrid bedroom, I dwell on the sadness that is all too visible in the Boss. How can His Royal Lowness become His Royal Happiness? That is the question. Perhaps Camilla Parker-Bowles is the answer. Like most men, HRH needs unqualified love and support. And, from what I have seen and heard, he certainly has not been getting that from the Bossette. Not for years and years, if ever.

Then what of Camilla's husband, Colonel Parker-Bowles? He needs someone in his life. Maybe he could reignite his flame with Princess Anne? That would be a neat solution, wouldn't it? The Colonel and his wife divorce. Camilla marries HRH and the Colonel marries HRH's sister Princess Anne. They would become brother and sister-in-law! No, that won't work. Princess Anne is already married.

What of the Bossette? She has quite a stable to choose from already. Frankly, with her allure, she can have any man on the planet, lucky woman. In the Morton book, she claims she loves the Boss, or did. Does she love him or does she want to just control him? There is a big difference. If what Mindy says is true, she certainly has never behaved as if she loves him. Could the finger-licking Sir Jimmy yet save the Royal marriage, or is it beyond him? Will it all unwind? Where will it end? The complexities fascinate me.

I turn over in my creaking little bed. Another thought: will I ever meet this now infamous Camilla? Probably not. After the public abuse she has been suffering since the publication of Mr Morton's book, she is doubtless in hiding. I should imagine HRH has Camilla safely squirrelled away somewhere very remote.

I drift off to sleep.

When I wake up, I have breakfast and go back up to my room to smarten up, as Commander Aylard tells me I am welcome to join the Royal party for church. Yes, of course, I want to go. I need to ask God whether I should marry George (if George wants me) and I also want to thank Him for this amazing job. I look at myself in the mirror. Yes, you'll do, Sarah.

I walk down the stairs to join the party. As I come into the hall, I blink and then I blink again. Right now, a Prince of Wales feather could knock me over. Keep your composure, girl. Steady! Remember you are in Royal Wonderland. Nothing, but *nothing*, should surprise you. That is right. Smile, act breezily and talk as if everything is normal, which of course it is. You may be astonished, but you must act as if nothing whatsoever is amiss.

'Good morning, Your Royal Highness.'

'Good morning, Sarah.'

I go over to Commander Richard Aylard. 'Good weather!'

'Yes, it is agreeably clement for November. Seems we are having a bit of an Indian summer.'

HRH asks if we are all gathered and then the Royal party, about eight of us, sets off to Sandringham church in the crisp November air. The sun is shining and there is a slight breeze. Walking calmly in front, not three feet from me, is the woman herself, the one everyone is talking of. Yes, it is she, Camilla Parker-Bowles!

How did she get here? When did she get here? Has she perhaps been with HRH all weekend?

I continue to chirrup away to Commander Aylard about the

vagaries of the weather, pretending everything is quite normal.

What on earth does HRH think he is doing, I inwardly scream? I appreciate he wants to be with his confidante but surely not in public? I want to rush up to him and tell him to turn back. Quickly, before it is too late!

What if there is a reporter, photographer or cameraman at the church gates? Don't he and Camilla appreciate that after all this speculation and unpleasantness in the media there will be an absolute uproar if they are seen together? Just a single picture of the two of them at this moment in time will confirm everyone's worst suspicions.

I steel myself for the pop of a light bulb. But there are no reporters, photographers or cameramen. Phew! And no one else in the church so much as bats an eyelid at the presence of the scandalous Mrs Parker-Bowles. Yes, I suppose, Sandringham is about as remote as you can get. But what a risk they are taking.

After the service, we all walk back and then Camilla and HRH disappear into the cavernous depths of the Royal House, to rooms and corridors where Lady Clerks never go. And for the rest of my visit I don't see either of them again.

December 1992

It is Christmas Day and I am in Shropshire with my family. We are having Christmas lunch. Nothing ever compares to my mother's Christmas lunches. She just does them brilliantly. But a fortnight ago, I must say, HRH surpassed himself in his choice of surprise venue for the staff Christmas do. He chose a recently converted church, now a restaurant called Mossiman's. Mossiman's is in West Halkin Street in

Belgravia. And Belgravia, as everyone knows, is owned by the Duke of Westminster, Mr Sexy Woodentop, himself!

We were all in a slight state of trepidation because the Prime Minister, that nice Mr Major, announced the separation of the Boss and the Bossette just seven days previously. Would the Boss and Bossette both come?

Friends outside the Palace are not altogether surprised by the Royal separation because of the Morton book and the publication of the 'Squidgy' tapes. Some of my friends blame Camilla and others denounce not dashing Mr Gilbey, but Captain James Hewitt, who is having a right rough time of it in the press, I can tell you.

Why do they pick on him? Why do all the other lovers get off? The press is intent on nothing less than the Captain's destruction. Recently, I was even approached at a party by a former Army Officer, now a journalist, who had the gall to ask me if I had any dirt on Captain Hewitt? How should I know anything, apart from what Mindy tells me, of course, and I am not going to reveal that. In any case, I have never even met the man.

It is open season on poor Captain Hewitt, who served, I understand, with distinction and bravery in the recent Gulf War. Perhaps the press don't know that his relationship with the Bossette was actually *welcomed* in Royal circles. Or perhaps they do know but they simply don't care. I should imagine the Captain would prefer to be back in Iraq right now facing enemy gunfire than having to endure the onslaught from the British press. At least in Iraq he could fight back.

Anyway, both the Boss and the Bossette appeared, separately of course. We were up in the Belfry looking down on the restaurant. It really was so lovely.

The theme this year was animals and I was placed on a table called Duck. No HRH to sit next to me, unfortunately. But the food at Mossiman's was superb. Yes, their Christmas lunch matched Mummy's and I can't give higher praise than that. Well done, the Palace!

Over lunch here in Shropshire, we unwrap our presents and, with tingling excitement, I open the gift from Their Royal Highnesses. Yes, this year, at the request of my family, I have waited until Christmas Day to unwrap it so they can share with me the thrill. It is childish, I know, but I think if you don't have a child inside of you on Christmas Day, then there is something wrong with you.

First I open the Christmas card, which is personally signed by HRH. Now it is time for the large red box wrapped up with a green ribbon. I undo the bow. The family peers around me. I delve into the box and pull out two goblets with the Prince of Wales's crest beautifully engraved on the octagonal bevelled glass. There is a gasp of admiration from the family. Oh thank you, Your Royal Highnesses.

Yes, it is the identical Christmas gift as the year before. My collection has now gone from two to four. Fantastic. I intend to hide them away in the bottom of my chest of drawers with the other two glasses. They will be perfect for a display in my future home, I think, possibly when I am married . . . as I hope soon to be to George.

At three o'clock, we switch on the television to watch the Queen's Christmas Message. She tells the world through a language no one has spoken for a thousand years – Latin – that she has had a horrible year. Yes, we all know she has. There was the recent fire that destroyed nearly a quarter of

Windsor Castle; the separation of Prince Andrew and Sarah, the Duchess of York; and then the formal separation of her eldest son and his wife, the Boss and Bossette.

Goodness, how the world sniggered at Fergie's toe-sucking antics with her Texan 'financial adviser' John Bryan on holiday in the South of France. It is bad enough for adultery to be reported but to be photographed is total humiliation. Still, the worst must be over for Her Majesty. Before the dawn comes the darkest hour, as they say.

When Her Majesty famously declared she had had an *'annus horribilis'*, I could see from the horrified looks of my family that they thought she meant something different. I had the impression that, if only for a second, they thought their Queen was admitting to suffering from a disagreeable condition to do with her bottom. 'Annus' and 'anus' are remarkably similar.

How many of her subjects in the United Kingdom and the Commonwealth speak Latin? Less than one in a thousand. While *I* understood Her Majesty (thanks to a patient Classics teacher), most other viewers were, I bet, left bewildered. What a waste.

Hear the words of a humble Lady Clerk, Ma'am. This is my Christmas message to you: tell your loyal and devoted subjects like it is – straight. You have had a *rotten* year (dramatic pause). Yes, it has been horrible.

Uneducated as the Bossette is, with not even an 'O' level to her name, she understands this well enough. Forgive my impertinence, Your Majesty, but take a leaf from the book of your daughter-in-law, Her Royal Highness, the Princess of Wales.

Happy Christmas.

6

Cocktails and Passion

February 1993

How life can suddenly turn. Twelve hours ago, I was still hoping that George would make an honest woman of me. Then, eleven hours ago, I meet this suave monster who takes my breath away. Literally. Goodbye, Richard Gere. Hello, Hugh Grant.

Of course he is not *the* Hugh Grant. But from the explosion of feeling I had last night he might just as well have been the great movie star himself. Now I am lying naked in his arms as the morning light filters into his bedroom, reflecting on what a slut I am and how frankly, my dear, I don't give a damn. What has happened to me? This is extraordinary. I look into his dreamy eyes, ponder his cheesy pick-up lines and tell myself this is one big embarrassing mistake.

It happens to all girls at one stage of their life, having a one-night stand. And, actually, if we are going to be honest, it happens many more times than once, doesn't it? I trace my fingers up and down his slim and gorgeous frame. Who is he, this dreadful Lothario who has lured me back to his flat and seduced me? What did he say he did? Oh yes, he is an entrepreneur. He buys and sells companies.

He said it with such assurance that I believed last night he was some kind of Jimmy Goldsmith or George Soros. Now, looking around his flat, I have deduced he is not quite in their league, otherwise I would surely be waking up in one of the Belgravia apartments leased from Mr Sexy Woodentop, Gerald, the Duke of Westminster, Britain's Ducal Donald Trump. As it is, I am in a strange place; on the other side of the river, if you please. Yes, I think what we have here is a corporate Del Boy, a man on the make, a smooth opportunist with balls.

Talking of balls, what do we have here? Well, since I am now condemned as a slut, I might as well make the most of it!

An hour later, having satisfied my fleshly wants and his, I avail myself of his shower. Then I dress. I look at my watch. Cripes! It is getting on and I am expected at St James's Palace at 10 a.m. for a meeting with Fondant Fancy. I hope he is not going to tackle me on our last meeting's Minutes.

'Where precisely are we?' I ask my unshaven Don Juan.

He hands me a cup of coffee, looks me straight in the eye and replies, 'Docklands.'

Docklands! Oh my God. That's miles and miles from anywhere. What the hell am I doing with a man who lives in Docklands? It is not just geographically far from my home and office, it is culturally the Kalahari Desert. What do we have in common? Nothing. This certainly is one big mistake.

I grab my bag and shoot out of the door. Thank goodness I have plenty of cash in my bag; £40 should cover the taxi fare from where I am in freaking nowhere.

Oh Sarah, how could you? Falling for a spiv who lives here of all places. And how are you going to explain your late arrival to Fondant Fancy? An appointment with a doctor? Oh come on, he is not going to fall for that old chestnut. In any case, you used that excuse the last time! Oh Sarah, your career at the Palace is about to collapse – all for a bout of lust with a smooth-talking chancer.

I frantically hail a taxi and jump in.

'Look, I know it is a long way, but please take me to the other side of London!'

'Yes, madam, where?'

Well, I have prepared him now. 'St James's Palace.'

The taxi driver gives me an odd look and starts driving. Well, he has probably never driven to the other side of the city before, I muse. I check my watch. Oh dear, I am right. It is far too late to go home and change. This will be really embarrassing. What will my colleagues think? What will Fondant Fancy make of me in my tarty evening wear? He probably won't even notice: after all, I am not a building.

Suddenly, I find myself travelling over a bridge. That's odd. I thought the last bridge on the river was Tower Bridge. Shouldn't we be going through the Blackwall Tunnel?

'Excuse me,' I say to the taxi driver. 'I know this sounds a silly question, but where precisely are we?'

'Well, madam, behind us is Battersea and in front of us is Chelsea.'

I sit back in the seat absolutely stunned. Anglo-Saxon utterances explode in my head. Not only does this, this, this utter creep seduce me, he deliberately lies to me about his whereabouts. Battersea is miles from Docklands and only ten minutes from my flat!

'Change of plan, please. Can you take me to 50 Averill Street?'

Four hours later, I am still seething. I have finished my

meeting with Fondant Fancy and I am now furiously bashing out some correspondence on the computer. Wait till I get hold of that creepy Casanova! In fact, I have a good mind to ring him right now and give him a piece of my mind.

Inner nanny cuts in. That will be difficult, Sarah. And why will that be difficult, I reply? Because you don't have his telephone number. That's true enough, but, then, there is always directory enquiries. That is also problematic. Why? Because you don't have his address. True. And then there is another problem. What? You can't remember his name. I find myself blushing. It is true, I can't. Sarah, you are a shameless hussy. You let yourself be picked up by a stranger, you have a night of frolics that would raise the eyebrows of a call girl, and you can't even put a name to him. Yes, this is one of those disgraceful episodes you should quietly put into a folder and then delete. It never happened. Remember, you don't have one-night stands, do you? No. All right, then.

Geraldine comes over to my desk.

'There is a call for you on line four.'

'Who is it?'

'Someone called Eddie. I didn't catch his last name.'

Eddie, I think, Eddie who? Perhaps it is another loopy recruit for HRH's Architectural and Planning Group.

'The Prince and Princess of Wales's office,' I chime. 'It is Sarah Goodall here. Can I help you?'

'I didn't know you worked at the Palace,' says a vaguely familiar voice.

'That's because you never asked me,' I reply crisply. 'If you remember, you only talked about yourself. Anyway, how did you get my number?'

'Since you ask, I got if off my bathroom mirror.'

'Your bathroom mirror?'

'Yes, you wrote this number on it with your lipstick. It was a devil of a job to get it off, I can tell you.'

Good. 'Why did you tell me your flat is in Docklands?'

'Oh that was just a joke.'

'Yes. Very amusing. You had me in a state of panic.'

'Oh, sorry about that. Will you forgive me?'

'Absolutely not.'

'Oh dear. I was actually ringing up to find out what you are up to tonight. Are you free, by any chance?'

'No, I am not free,' I icily reply. 'I am busy.'

'Really, what are you doing?'

'I'll tell you what I am doing, since you ask. I am being picked up at eight o'clock by a man who *could* just be a gentleman, if he made the effort. He is going to arrive with a very large bunch of flowers and then he is going to take me to an expensive restaurant, where he will spoil me rotten with champagne and fine wines to make up for his dastardly behaviour. The address is 50 Averill Street, SW6, and you better not be late. And one more thing . . .'

'Yes?'

'What's your surname?'

I put down the telephone. A surge of desire is rippling through my loins. What a wanton woman I am. Roll on eight o'clock.

April 1993

I am up at Sandringham again, doing a week's secretarial duties for HRH. I haven't seen him as yet and I probably won't. I suspect he is wrapped in the arms of Camilla Parker-Bowles, whom he has hidden in one of the rooms of this huge red-brick monstrosity.

I wouldn't mind being in someone's arms myself right now. Last month, I came clean with George and told him it was over. We have now parted for good. He is a decent and lovely man, but the fizz had evaporated. If only he had asked me to marry him last February, I would have accepted like a shot. When it comes to matters of the heart, a girl can't wait. Goodbye and good luck, George. You will make another woman so happy. If you want me as a reference, call any time.

As for Eddie, he does love to play his games. He calls me, if I am lucky, just twice a week. He doubtless has a string of girlfriends. I am sure I am just one of the fillies in his stable. And since I have been up here, he has not once returned my calls. Bastard. Why do I fancy him so much? I hate to admit it, but I think I have been dumped.

So here I am in the early evening having a stiff gin and tonic in the absolutely huge kitchen. HRH's Valet Michael Fawcett is regaling us with some hilarious stories. Mervyn is whipping up a dinner for HRH, and 'Bob', his replacement chef for tomorrow, is sitting down with me enjoying Michael holding court. Bob has teamed up with Susannah and me a few times for the occasional game of tennis at Buckingham Palace, so I have come to know him quite well.

We then go through to the staff dining room. The local Sandringham staff all sit together at one table and outsiders like us at another. Supper here is ridiculously early. Six o'clock to seven. It is just not civilised, is it? I imagine it is this way so that the kitchen is free for the Royal dinners. What, I wonder, are Royal dinners like? There is no chance that I will ever be invited to one of *those*. Helping out at the odd shooting lunch is one thing, being invited for dinner with the Prince is another. You would have to be HRH's god-daughter as well as resident Lady Clerk for that. I know my place in the Royal scheme of things and it is somewhere very low.

But I am not complaining. I wouldn't trade my job for anything in the world . . . although that's not entirely true. I wouldn't mind trading places with Michael Fawcett and have the chance to actually dress His Magnificence. I would be good at that. I wouldn't mind at all if he got cross and impatient, which I understand he sometimes does. I can handle a temper – even a Royal one.

Dinner finishes and I go up to my horrid room. Yes, I am in that one again. I try to read my book, *A Handful of Dust* by Evelyn Waugh. But it is no good. I just cannot get into it. So I go downstairs to see how things are going in the kitchens.

Mervyn hands me another gin and tonic with ice and a slice. Bless you, Mervyn. Wow, I think you have forgotten the tonic! Bob and I continue to natter about this and that. I really like Bob and, unlike a lot of other men who work for the Palace, he is not gay, so even though we are just friends there is still that little frisson.

Goodness, this drink is making me feel woozy. Bob is now helping out Mervyn, so, having pestered them with my presence for long enough, I decide it is about time that I retire.

'Don't go to bed just yet,' says Bob. 'I tell you what, why don't we continue our chat upstairs somewhere between our landings? I'll knock on the door when I am finished here.'

That's sweet of him to keep me company. So I go upstairs, bouff up my hair and try to read the book again. This time Evelyn Waugh ignites me. I am on chapter six when suddenly there is a knock on the door. I have been so engrossed in the story that I had clean forgotten about Bob.

Poor fellow, he looks exhausted. My goodness, he is clutching a bottle of vodka and two large bottles of tonic. We are in for one big session, are we? What fun.

'Find any rooms between our landings?' I ask.

'Can't say I did,' he replies.

'Never mind. We'll drink here.'

I empty the glass of water that a maid has thoughtfully provided, then wash out the tooth mug. Bob does the honours with the vodka and tonic and soon we are merrily chatting on the bed about this and that and goodness knows what. It is amazing how vodka just sinks inside, isn't it? Another funny thing that I have noticed all of a sudden, which strangely I have never taken on board before, is that Bob is really very attractive. In fact, his attraction increases with each sip.

He is smiling at me now. That's nice. He is stroking my hair. That's even nicer. He is leaning over me now. Gosh, what a sexy mouth he has. His hands are running up my body. Oh no, Sarah, you must stop this. His lips come down on mine. It is no good, he is just too goddamn sexy. Our tongues now meet. This is just heaven. Desire is coursing through me. This is wrong, so wrong. What am I doing?

You know perfectly well what you are doing, inner nanny reminds me. No, I don't. Yes, you do. Look, you are unbuttoning his shirt. I am? Yes, you are. You are now running your fingers down his naked back. I am not, am I? You are now undoing his belt. I can't be! This is outrageous. I must stop this right now! You want to stop? Yes, I definitely want to stop. Well, it might help if you weren't pulling off his pants. I am not doing that, am I? You most certainly are. My goodness, I am naked. How did that come to be? It must be magic. My clothes appear to have dematerialised. No, Sarah, they have not dematerialised. If you weren't swooning and gasping right now and could be bothered to open your eyes, you would see them scattered on the floor. When did this happen? What happen? Losing my clothes. That happened about fifteen minutes ago. I am not going to be able to stop this, am I? I very much doubt it. Oh, he's so good at this. I must try and make him stop *now*. Well, it might help if you closed your legs. But it is so difficult. He is stroking me so nicely. I must stop this before it is too late. Go on, Sarah, make an effort. He is a friend, for goodness sake. You work with him. This is not right and you know it. All right, but he can continue for another five seconds, *then* we will stop. Whoops, too late now.

Oh my God. This is just incredible. You certainly know what you are doing, don't you, Bob? Yes, I am in the hands of a master chef, all right. Oh Bob, I can be your meal any day. Wow.

The morning light splashes through the curtained window. Did I dream that or did it happen? It must have been a naughty dream. Of course it was. I wouldn't do anything like that, would I? Absolutely not. So it was a naughty dream.

Goodness, I feel rough. I sit up on the bed. The room is spinning. I look down on the floor. Oh dear. There are my clothes scattered around the floor like wind-blown confetti. It wasn't a dream at all, was it? No, Sarah.

Oh dear. How am I going to live this down? I really don't feel well. No, I don't feel well at all. In fact . . .

I launch myself across the room to the sink and am violently ill. Bye bye, vodka and tonic and last night's meal. Thank goodness for old-fashioned large sinks, is all I can say.

I am a little shaky as I head downstairs, but I feel so much better. I quietly have my breakfast and go to the office for another day of secretarial chores. At eleven o'clock, I find I cannot help myself. I sneak past the kitchen door and catch a glimpse of Bob's sexy *derrière* enveloped in wonderful black-and-white chef's trousers. Bob is chopping vegetables at breakneck speed and his bottom wiggles involuntarily in unison as he does so. It is all I can do not to rush in and yank his trousers down right now.

Restrain yourself, girl, says inner nanny. You are a refined Lady Clerk, not a rampant nymphomaniac. Well, perhaps things have changed. But remember, men don't go for over-keen women. But I had sex with him not twelve hours ago and it was amazing. That was then, this is now. And you know perfectly well that back in London he has a girlfriend. It is a one-night stand and he is your friend. Can't I just go over and give his butt a squeeze? No. But I want him so much. I am sure you do, but the feeling will fade and you have work to do. Sigh. You are such a spoilsport sometimes. I know.

At midday, Bernie the butler enters. He looks at me with a smile. Oh my God, he knows. Bob has told him all about our session last night, hasn't he? Of course he has. He could hardly resist, could he? I bet word is spreading round the staff quarters like wildfire. This is too awful. I'll be known as the Sandringham Slapper. They'll be forming queues outside my bedroom door. I will never live this down. I will have to resign.

'Good morning, madam.'

'Good morning, Bernie. So do you have anything from His Royal Highness?'

'Indeed I do, madam.'

Come on, man, spit it out. Yes, I know that you know I am an utter slut. Have your giggle and let's get on with the business of the day.

'His Royal Highness presents his compliments and invites you to join him for dinner this evening.'

I blink in disbelief. Surely HRH is confused. He must be. I know. That's it. He has the wrong Sarah, of course. That's right, he is thinking of his god-daughter, my Lady Clerk colleague, Sarah Ward. I smile at Bernie sweetly.

'I think His Royal Highness has me confused with another Sarah, Bernie.'

'Who would that be, madam?'

'Sarah Ward, his god-daughter.'

'I assure you, madam, that it is you whom he is inviting.'

'Me? Sarah Goodall?'

'Yes, madam.'

Suddenly, a wave of paranoia hits me. I know what it is: they are having a joke at my expense. That's what it is. Bastards. I better check first before I throw this vase at him.

'Is this a joke, Bernie?'

I can see he is looking confused.

'No, madam, I assure you it's not.'

I can tell by his expression this is for real.

'Wow!'

'And what would you like me to say to His Royal Highness?'

'Sorry?'

'Are you accepting his invitation?'

I can hardly refuse, can I? The Prince of Wales does not invite. He commands.

'Please tell His Royal Highness that I thank him for his

kind invitation and that I am absolutely delighted to accept.'

'Splendid, madam. Dinner is served at 8.30. His Royal Highness will be receiving you and the other guests at 8.00 in the drawing room.'

'Bernie, one last thing . . .'

'Yes, madam?'

'You couldn't be really kind and show me where the drawing room is when the time comes, could you? I only know my way around the staff quarters.'

'It will be a pleasure, madam.'

Bernie bows out. I sit at my desk stupefied. This is amazing. I am shagged by a Royal chef one night and I dine with a Royal Prince, the future King of England, the next. Who would believe it?

I remain in a daze for the rest of the day. I even manage to forget about Bob's bottom, which is extraordinary because before Bernie came in I could think of little else.

At six o'clock, I go into the kitchen and help myself to one of Mervyn's stiff gin and tonics. Bob gives me a sideways look and a half-smile. Yes, I know, Bob. It is just a one-night stand. Don't worry. I won't molest your gorgeous taut buttocks. I do hope you haven't told anyone but frankly, if you have, I don't care. Not any more I don't, because tonight I am dining with His Royal Highness. I wouldn't give a hoot if my night of passion was broadcast on national television.

I go upstairs to my room to change. But change into what? I flick through the choices on my wardrobe rail. After thirty minutes, I have tried every combination and am now down to a choice of two. Hmm, I definitely like the vampy number with the slit on the side. That would go very well with my high heels, my tart's trotters, as the Princess of Wales calls them. How do I look? Sensational. I carefully apply my make-up. I adjust a few strands of hair and take one last look in the mirror.

I am about to walk out of the door when my inner nanny cuts in. Sarah, you cannot wear that outfit! Why ever not? Because it is inappropriate. You are not going out on a hot date. You are joining the Prince as his guest for dinner, probably only to make up numbers. You are supposed to be a demure Lady Clerk, not a geisha girl. In any case, the post of Royal mistress is already filled.

Reluctantly, I change into something modest then go downstairs. Bernie takes me into the Royal quarters. Am I nervous or what? I enter the drawing room. Wow! It is hung with beautiful tapestries. At one end is a minstrels' gallery. Will minstrels suddenly appear and serenade us, I wonder? Almost anything is possible in Royal Wonderland.

'Good evening, Sarah,' says HRH.

My goodness, I have been so entranced by the tapestries and gallery I have failed to see him. He is wearing a blue damask Nehru suit, very fetching indeed. I have a moment of anxiety. Is this a fancy dress party? I quickly scan the other dinner guests. Phew.

I then do my Regency curtsey, which I have been practising for years now.

'Your Royal Highness is most gracious to invite me to dinner.'

Steady, Sarah. That was a bit over the top.

'Not at all,' he says, walking me over to a 1970s hostess trolley. 'What do you want to drink?'

Wow. The Prince of Wales is offering to serve *me*. I cannot believe this.

'A gin and tonic, please, Sir.'

'Good for you!'

And with that, HRH pours me the stiffest gin and tonic I have ever seen.

Cripes, it must be a Royal thing, these stiff drinks.

'Thank you, Sir.'

'Are you all right? Are they treating you well?'

'They are treating me splendidly, Sir.'

'Oh good.'

I think wistfully of Bob's bottom. They could hardly treat me better.

I drink the killer G & T and join in conversation with the other guests, who include Commander Aylard. I quickly realise my role is to be the background girl. Speak when you're spoken to and be quiet otherwise. In terms of pecking order, I am at the bottom of the Royal heap. I am not quite a guest but a bit more, I suppose, than just a member of staff. It is a curious rôle to occupy.

HRH checks his watch and in we go to dinner. The dining room is enormous. On one side of the room are Georgian windows that face the garden. The other side is covered in Sèvres plates. The table is oval, about eighteen feet long and six feet wide, and is festooned with porcelain *objets d'art*. There are eight lit candles on four pretty china double candlesticks. It is all so beautiful.

We sit down to eat. There is soup, followed by lamb cutlets, and then lemon tart. My only criticism would be that we are spaced so far away from each other that it is sometimes difficult for some of the diners to follow the conversation. There is a lot of 'Sorry, can you repeat that?' Well, I suppose the table is designed more for thirty people than six.

I would love to say what the wines are, but I am just not knowledgeable enough. I surmise they are French. Bordeaux or Burgundy? Difficult to tell. However, this much I can accurately report: they aren't the Château B&Q Her Majesty serves up at Royal staff dances. No Royal vinegar on the Prince of Wales's table!

After dinner, we retire to another room and sit around a large roaring fire. We drink coffee and nibble Royal Duchy orange thins.

This is magic. I am in a reverie. HRH suddenly addresses us, asking, 'Would any of you care to join me for a film show?'

Well, I am hardly going to pass up this opportunity, am I? Richard Aylard and another guest plead tiredness and go to bed. HRH then leads the remaining three of us back to the drawing room.

A screen has been erected during dinner. I see one of the Sandringham staff with a projector in the gallery. Goodness, what are we going to see? How exciting!

HRH then motions the three of us to sit down. I plonk myself down on a sofa. Goodness, this is relaxing and nice. Hmm. Those drinks have had a wonderful calming effect on me. Whoosh! I feel a sensation in the sofa. What is it? My goodness, HRH, the future King, is sitting next to me. What an honour!

The movie begins. Oh my goodness, I know this movie. It is *Howard's End*, starring Anthony Hopkins. I have seen it before. A good period drama that HRH will love, I am sure of it.

The movie begins and I reflect on Bob's bottom and the Boss's aftershave. It is Trumper's, I bet. Yes, HRH would go for something like Trumper's. Goodness, how smart the Boss looks in his snazzy Nehru suit.

The next thing I know is that the lights are on! My God, what has happened? There is no one here. Where have they all gone? I hear a noise in the minstrels' gallery. I look up. There is the projectionist packing away a reel.

'What happened?' I bleat.

'You fell asleep, madam.'

'In front of His Royal Highness?'

'Well, actually, madam, beside him.'

My God, how did that happen? Why did I fall asleep? My inner nanny answers. You fell asleep through a combination of the following: HRH's ultra-stiff G & T, the wines at dinner, the fact that you have seen the movie before and, finally, the tiredness stemming from your insatiable demands last night on Bob.

My head hung in shame, I slink out of the room and go upstairs to bed. Well, that's blown it, hasn't it? No more invitations to Royal dinners. How could I insult His Royal Highness by slumbering in his presence? Did I snore as well, I wonder? I bet I did! What am I to do? Let's face it, I am finished now. Tears are rolling down my cheeks.

But that stern voice interrupts my thoughts. Come on, girl. It's not so bad. You have done five years in Royal service. That's quite an achievement. I know, I weep. But I love this job and I adore him. You do? Not in that way, of course. But whenever I see him, I feel that deep down he is in so much pain. Yes, and? I just want to go and . . . Yes? Hug him. Well, that's all right. And now I have to resign. That's a bit melodramatic, don't you think? No, it's not. I showed disrespect. Can you imagine anything more insulting than falling asleep next to the future King? I can imagine plenty more insulting things. Now go to sleep. It is nothing in the scheme of things. And one more thing. What? Even if you do have to resign, you will have one big boast that you can take with you to your grave. What's that? How many women are there in the world who can honestly say they slept with the Prince of Wales? Yes, now there is a point.

Clinging to it, I drift into sleep.

The following morning I wake up, have breakfast, stride to the office and prepare my resignation letter. I try various combinations. They range from the mawkish (sentimental and pathetic) to the steely (cold and formal). Oh dear, none can capture the compound of dignity and emotion that I wish to convey.

Bernie the butler enters the office. What has he got for me, I wonder? A letter of reprimand? The letter of disengagement? My P45? Oh well, I might as well get it over and done with. Come on, Sarah, steel yourself.

'Yes, Bernie. Do you have something for me?'

'Yes, madam.'

I grip the side of the chair. My stomach is a hollow pit.

'What is it?'

'His Royal Highness wishes to thank you for your attendance at dinner at such short notice yesterday and wishes to extend the invitation again this evening.'

I am knocked back into my seat. So HRH is not angry with me at all! Not just that, he wants me at dinner again! I don't know what it is like to be told that you have just won the Lottery but I can imagine it now. It is as if my fairy godmother has waved a magic wand. All my anxieties have been dispelled in a puff of heaven's dust. Oh, did a butler ever bring such good news as this?

'Please tell His Royal Highness I am delighted to accept.'

'I will, madam.'

'One more thing, Bernie. We have known each other for, what, two years? When did you start to call me madam?'

'Yesterday.'

'Precisely. Beforehand you have always called me Sarah. Then, when I am suddenly elevated to dining as a guest of His Royal Highness, you call me madam. Please, Bernie, I know the lines of demarcation are difficult, but I am one of the staff like you, so if that's all right, please keep calling me Sarah.'

'I know, Sarah. But when a Lady Clerk becomes a guest of Their Royal Highnesses, everything changes. Most of the staff here choose to be safe and make an immediate adjustment in their dealings with her, given a shift in her position. It is difficult, I am sure you will appreciate, for all of us. But thank you for telling me to continue calling you Sarah. I will inform the others. Sarah you are and Sarah you will remain.'

With that, the great unsung Jeeves of the Royal Household leaves. I feel I am crossing not just bridges but mountains. Later that evening, I meet again with HRH and his guests in the drawing room. I curtsey.

'Your Royal Highness, good evening!'

'Good evening, Sarah.'

'I simply must apologise, Sir, for my deplorable manners. I am so sorry for falling asleep during last night's film.'

'Oh please, Sarah, think nothing of it. Can I get you something to drink?'

'That is so kind of you, but if you don't mind I will pour it myself!'

'Oh. As you please.'

I pour in plenty of tonic and a drop of gin, not the other way round, as seems the normal practice here. At last, I am in control. My future King stands before me and, just this once, I am neither drunk nor neurotic. There we go, girl.

'Yes,' continues HRH. 'We tried to shake you awake last night at the end of the film but nothing seemed to rouse you.' He looks at me with a twinkle. 'Yes, er, I thought you were *dead*!'

My heart melts once more. Darling HRH, I simply cannot help myself. I love you. He continues.

'And the funny thing is that, before you went to sleep, you took off your earrings and placed them on the table by the sofa. I am glad you feel so at home here.'

Thank goodness, I was wondering where they were. I was frantically looking for them all day. HRH points to the table in question. 'I would take them now in case you forget them.'

Not just that – people might reach some scandalous conclusions as to how they were left here and under what circumstances. It is bad enough developing a loose reputation on my side of the green baise door, I can't afford to let one develop in the Royal state rooms as well, now can I?

I scoop them up.

December 1993

Hurrah, today is one of my favourite days of the year, the office Christmas lunch! Yes, we are off to Simpson's-in-the-Strand! What will it be like?

Clambering out of our coaches, we enter this incredibly grand dining room with heavy wooden panels. The waiters give us a choice of amazing pre-lunch cocktails. One has a stick of cinnamon, another has dark berries and there is a pure white one, which the waiter informs me is a Snowball. I suspect this Snowball should be done under the Trade Descriptions Act. When snow melts, it is pure water; this, however, will turn to pure alcohol, I bet.

Which do I choose? No, this time I am going to stick to champagne. Predictable, but at least I know what I am drinking and can pace myself. I still feel extremely embarrassed about my moment of shame at Sandringham. I personally blame the stiff cocktails. Do the Royals have their alcoholic beverages anything but stiff, I wonder? I am not going to take the risk. Laurent-Perrier, please. Yes, that will do nicely!

Their Royal Highnesses enter the restaurant and we all bob and bow. She is looking stunning, as ever. And dear HRH looks so handsome. Will they ever get back together as husband and wife, I muse? Who knows? The omens don't look good.

Rumours persist of the Bossette's flings. And then, of course, there is the now infamous tape recording of an intimate telephone conversation between the Boss and Camilla Parker-Bowles, which got published earlier in the year. The press had a lot of fun with that one, didn't they? How they lampooned poor HRH just because he expressed a desire to be in the womb of his lover. What is wrong with that? I think it is imaginative and honest and sweet. It reveals a man who is truly in love. Yes, I concede that he phrased it in an unfortunate way, saying he wanted to be her tampon. But can't people be allowed to exchange mushy intimacies without fear of them being broadcast around the world? Is nothing sacred?

How did the press get hold of the recording in the first place? And who recorded it? And how was it picked up? I sometimes wonder if there aren't some sinister people in high places plotting and planning the Royal Family's downfall.

I look around the room. I see so many people I know here. There's my lovely friend Victoria Mendham. She has now moved over to Kensington Palace to work exclusively for the Bossette. She tells me the Bossette is rather demanding – sometimes she cannot leave until nine in the evening. I personally think that is a bit hard on Victoria, as she gets no extra pay. And not just that, she then has to take the train back to Essex.

To the Bossette's credit, she does at least acknowledge Victoria's hard work and calls her 'my rock'. Mind you, she calls quite a few of her staff 'my rock': Mervyn Wycherley, her chef; her recently departed Protection Officer, the operatic Ken Wharfe; and her butler, Paul Burrell. That is a lot of rocks.

Victoria tells me the Princess also teases her, calling her 'Ralph' because these days she rarely wears anything but outfits from Ralph Lauren. Well, Victoria certainly has the figure for designer clothes. In *Slimming* magazine parlance, Victoria is now the giraffe. I remain the hippopotamus.

I have learned from Victoria that it is her parents who pay for these outfits from Ralph Lauren. This is sweet and lovely, but I sometimes wonder how they can afford it. It is one thing to keep up with the Joneses; it is quite another to keep up with the World's Number One Fashion Icon.

Anyway, some of us here at the Palace think Victoria is now looking as pretty and stylish as the Bossette. I am glad Her Royal Highness is not the jealous type!

So, who else is here? Ah, there is funny Michael Fawcett. Then I see all the butlers – Bernie, Harold Brown and Paul Burrell. I see Mervyn Wycherley, and over there is Bob! I look quickly in the other direction, blushing.

Over on another table is Tony Burrows, the Royal accountant. He organises the money side of things at the Palace. One of his best friends is one of my favourite characters – yes, Sergeant Ron Lewis. Tony once told me that Ron and HRH adore each other, as Ron has been with the Boss since he was nineteen. Ron was with the Prince on the beach in Australia where a girl rushed up and snogged him. Hmm, I bet they had difficulties prising her off! Someone took a picture of it, which was printed in all the newspapers. Ron once proudly showed me a copy that he has up on the wall in his small bedroom upstairs in St James's Palace.

Geraldine and Esther have left, which is sad. They have 'moved on', as they say. Well, I am certainly not moving on. I am going to be 'staying on'. The only way they are going to get me out of here is in a wooden box! Oh yes. I *love* this job.

Everyone is knocking back the cocktails, which are being speedily replenished by the attentive waiters. Twenty minutes later, we all sit down to enjoy the lovely roast turkey – Simpson's is world famous for its roasts. The vegetarians have a different meal. They don't know what they are missing.

I notice that people seem more tipsy this year than on previous occasions. Some of them look, dare I say it, a bit drunk. I knew it! Those cocktails *are* lethal. Lucky me, steering away from them. Had I been knocking them back, I would probably be planting myself on Bob's lap right now!

I glance over to Sarge, the Travelling Yeoman. At this

moment, he looks more like the Teetering Yeoman.

There is a hush in the room as His Gorgeousness stands up and makes his speech. He concludes it with the usual 'Oh! How many are you? You just seem to grow and grow! Happy Christmas!'

We all clap wildly and HRH sits down. I just love that speech.

Suddenly, a familiar Welsh voice rings out. Oh my goodness, it is Ron! He is attempting to stand up. The room freezes. Ron is swaying from side to side in his alcoholic stupor. Please, Ron, don't do it! Sit down before it is too late!

'Hello, ladeeesh and gentulmen! I jusht wish to make a toasht! The toasht is Hish Royal Highnesh and my good friend Tony Burroashe!'

He flings his arm out to HRH and then to Tony. There is a moment's stunned silence. Then we lift our glasses and repeat Ron's toast. Ron slides back happily into his chair. Well, I suppose there are no two more important people to us than our employer and the man who pays our wages.

To everyone's relief, His Royal Highness appears to find Ron's surprise toast highly amusing. That is wonderful. Can you imagine other members of his family reacting in such a relaxed way?

No, neither can I.

7

Changing the Guard

July 1994

There has been a frightful stink here both at Buckingham Palace and St James's Palace, in fact at *every* palace and Royal home. It concerns a recent televised documentary to promote the publication of Jonathan Dimbleby's authorised biography of the Boss. The Boss has not only gone on record complaining about the lack of warmth he had from his parents as a child, he has also admitted to his relationship with Camilla Parker-Bowles!

This has caused havoc. Camilla and her husband Andrew Parker-Bowles are now getting divorced. The Queen and Prince Philip are upset and furious. According to Mindy (still my source in the inner Palace circle), they are particularly hurt by HRH's public complaint about them. Moreover, Prince Philip says that Charles's confession of his adultery is 'puerile', which I had to look up in the dictionary (it means childish). Prince Philip's argument goes that he would never admit to having any confidantes, so why should his son? He has a point.

Why, dear HRH, why?

Mindy says that Jonathan Dimbleby is one of those

persuasive journalists who gets his interviewees to say things they often later regret. It is bad enough when people admit to things that muck up their own lives, but when it messes up other people's and threatens the future of the monarchy, that is really serious. Oh dear, the cat's out of the bag now, isn't it?

So who is to blame? Mindy says the old Guard at Buckingham Palace who advise the Queen and Prince Philip are pointing the accusing finger at HRH's Private Secretary, darling Commander Richard Aylard, who, as we all know, is devoted to the Prince. The charge is that he failed to stop the Boss from cooperating with the smooth Mr Dimbleby.

Richard's defense to others high up at the Palace is that the truth was bound to emerge sooner or later. He thought it was better to deal with it now, irrespective of the consequent furore, rather than have the Palace suffer the more damaging 'death by a thousand cuts' of innuendo and revelation in the media. His argument is a fair one but, all the same, look at the casualties.

Personally, I have been a bit in the dumps because Mummy has been diagnosed with cancer. She says it is not serious. Why then is she having chemotherapy? I cross my fingers and pray she is right.

I have been cheered by the fun I am having at work. I have been up to Balmoral, the Royal Scottish Estate, twice so far this year. And I still make regular trips to Highgrove and Sandringham. And I have been promoted again!

Besides being the secretary to the Head of the Architectural Group, I have also been made Second Secretary to Deputy Private Secretary Stephen Lamport. Because of the increasing number of staff, I have been sent down to a newly created office in the basement, which I share with Ceri (pronounced

'Kerry'). Ceri Jones, a wonderful Welsh civil servant seconded from the government departments, has taken over from Fondant Fancy and is now my architectural boss.

Everyone was most sympathetic on hearing I was being moved out of the State Rooms. They said how unpleasant it must be for me now to be working in the windowless gloom of the basement, separated from everything going on upstairs. How wrong they are! The atmosphere upstairs has changed for the worse, with clock-watching new appointees monitoring the times we all get in and come back from lunch. Ceri doesn't give a damn about timekeeping, which is a huge relief. As far as she is concerned, I can get back from lunch when I want. And, even better, I can come in when I want, so long, that is, as the work gets done!

It also helps that we are drinking mates now and she takes an avid interest in my romantic activities, which these days are mostly centred on Eddie. But since I still only see him occasionally and I know that he has other female interests, I have other interests too! Oh yes, what is sauce on the side for the gander is now sauce on the side for the goose.

To make life really civilised here in the office, Ceri and I have started a tradition of closing shop early on a Friday. We crack open a bottle of chilled champagne at four o'clock and friends in the Palace drop by for discussions about their love lives while sitting on the yellow silk *chaise longue* that has been thoughtfully provided for us. What we don't get to hear about who is doing what and with whom is hardly worth knowing, I can tell you.

The highlight of the year so far was the launch of the new architectural magazine, *Perspectives on Architecture*, which is to be the mouthpiece of HRH's crusade to give 'new buildings a more human dimension', or so I wrote in the dictated press release.

The editor is the dynamic Giles Worsley, who used to work at *Country Life*. And he has all kinds of smart people writing for him, like the lovely Candida Lycett-Green and the brainy, stubble-headed Australian Clive James. All the loonies of the APG came to help launch it and I can report it was quite a party we had here in the State Rooms. Modern British buildings will be beautiful once more. Well done, HRH!

October 1994

How lovely to be up at Balmoral again. Yes, this is the third time this year. Let me tell you the set-up. Balmoral is the large Royal Estate near Aberdeen in the eastern Highlands of Scotland. There is the castle where Her Majesty and Prince Philip live and where the rest of the Royal Family congregates. Then there is Birkhall. This is the Queen Mother's residence and where HRH comes to stay. I would usually also be staying there, but Birkhall is full at the moment, so I have been put up in a remote three-bedroom cottage on the estate three miles from Birkhall and near Loch Muich. It is called called Tom-na-Gaidh.

Tonight, I am staying here all alone, which is a bit scary, particularly as I have been told there is a ghost. Apparently, a woodcutter once went mad and did something indescribably horrid in the woods just beside this cottage. Now, his ghost is said to roam around. I know it is silly, and of course ghosts don't exist, but all the same I am sleeping with the lights on tonight.

Whereas Sandringham is, frankly, rather bleak, Balmoral is heavenly. It is surrounded by beautiful hills and heather. My office is in the dining room, and when there is no work I sit and gaze happily out of the window at the splendid view.

I have had so many wonderful times this year, but the best so far has to be this morning. Instead of catching a British Airways flight to Aberdeen, I was told I could hitch a lift with HRH on the *Queen's Flight*. I was in a frightful panic because I woke up late with that fearfully sexy beast, Eddie, and nearly missed the plane!

So I arrive at RAF Northolt fifteen minutes before departure and am whisked onto the plane. I buckle myself into my seat and while I gaze out of the window I see a beautiful green Aston Martin glide towards us and pull up on the edge of the runway. Out steps a purposeful, fit, slim man. Is it James Bond?

Nearly. It is the heir to the throne of England, Scotland, Wales and Northern Ireland. Yes, it is His Gorgeousness. Tigger, his Jack Russell, precedes him up the steps and waddles into the cabin. He then decides to curl up at my feet for some reason. I thought Tigger's attentions were solely devoted to HRH. Moreover, in the past he has growled menacingly at me. What has brought about this change of Tigger's heart? I feel really flattered.

The plane revs up and minutes later the *Queen's Flight* takes wing. Bye bye, the cramped streets of London. Hello, the beautiful vistas of the Scottish Highlands. What a life.

Tigger has decided that he is going to stay here by my ankles. Should I carry him back through to his master, I wonder? No, I think that would be breaking protocol. I better wait for his master to come through to me. Fifteen minutes later, HRH enters our cabin.

He looks down at his pooch. 'Oh there you are,' he says,

addressing Tigger. 'I am glad you have found somewhere comfortable.'

I have a moment of panic. Should I unbuckle myself from the seat, stand up and curtsey? I realise that could be a bit awkward given the constraints of the cabin but, even so, Royal protocol should always be respected. It is too late now. I do hope HRH won't be cross.

'Good morning, Your Royal Highness!'

'Oh good morning, Sarah.'

HRH then does the most extraordinary thing. He peers closely at my left hand. My God, is there something wrong with it? Is there dirt on it? Did I not wash my hands properly this morning? Is one of my nails cracked? Does he disapprove of the colour of my varnish? What is it?

'Oh, so you are not married yet?'

'No, Sir, I am not married.'

My heart is palpitating. Why is he asking me such a thing? Is he thinking I might possibly be suitable as a wife, now that Sir Jimmy has all too clearly failed to save his marriage to the Bossette? Is that why he is checking my marital status? This is like all my dreams come true. This is unbelievable.

My inner nanny has had enough. Yes, it is unbelievable. Stop deluding yourself.

HRH speaks again. 'Sarah, since Tigger is so comfortable with you, could you be so good as to look after him a bit this week?'

I find myself blinking. This surely is a step forward in our relationship. HRH is entrusting me, of all people, with Tigger, the dog to whom he is devoted.

'Oh Sir, that would be an honour. I would be more than happy to look after Tigger. He is such a wonderful dog.'

'Good.'

And with that, HRH walks through the door to the cockpit. So here I am, entrusted with the Royal pet. Wow! I wonder whether that is an official designated title, Keeper of the Royal Pet? Now, whether snuffling, growling or biting, Tigger will be for ever embraced to my bosom!

For fifteen minutes, I am in a state of bliss, until suddenly I have a moment of creeping anxiety. Why has HRH been in the cockpit for such a long time? Has something happened? Has something gone wrong?

I look for his Royal Protection Officer, who seems remarkably calm sitting on the other side of our cabin, and ask him, 'Does His Royal Highness often spend so much time in the cockpit?'

'Oh yes,' he replies. 'His Royal Highness is getting in his air miles.'

I am now completely bewildered. Aren't air miles the points you get awarded if you fly a lot? Why would HRH need air miles? Is this some sort of Palace initiative to cut down costs? I think for a second. Surely that can't be right.

'Excuse me, I don't understand.'

The Protection Officer leans forward.

'His Royal Highness needs to keep up his air miles for his pilot's license.'

I am stunned.

'Are you telling me that, right now, His Royal Highness is actually in control of the plane and flying it?'

The Protection Officer nods.

'Yes, and he will be landing it too!'

I sit back in the seat in amazement. Is there no end to HRH's talents? And to think, I thought his flying days were finished after he overran the runway on the Scottish island of Islay a few months ago. Obviously, that was just a little Royal mishap. Anyway, everyone knows how short the runway is at Islay!

Oh, darling HRH, just to think that you are a Commander of the High Seas, the Prince of Wales, Lord of the Isles and, right now, King of the Skies. The Keeper of the Royal Pet salutes you! Oh to be in such masterful hands!

So here I am, six hours later, at Tom-na-Gaidh. The light is now fading. The ghost of the mad axeman will be wandering around the woods outside soon. But the lights are all working and, in any case, I have Tigger with me for company and protection. Oh yes, Tigger, we will see off the mad axeman, won't we? Tigger growls at me in obvious assent.

I also have a rather naughty book to keep me company, which obviously I daren't let anyone see. It is called *Princess in Love* by Anna Pasternak and it's about the affair between the Princess and Captain Hewitt.

I asked Mindy the other week over the purple banquette at the bar in BP how this book came about. She said the Princess had asked Hewitt to cooperate with Anna Pasternak on an article denying the relationship between her and the Captain. He was reluctant but felt that he could not disobey a Royal order from his former confidante. The story was duly written and printed. But all the other newspapers knew he jolly well *had* had an affair with the Princess and consequently got nasty with him.

In fact, he was so vilified that people shunned him; he couldn't get a job and then his horse riding business in Devon started to lose money. So he faced financial as well as social ruin. Back comes Anna Pasternak, who, incidentally, is the great niece of the man who wrote *Doctor Zhivago* (one of my favourite movies). She said that if he admitted the truth, then the whole matter would be cleared up.

Cleared up? It has just made matters much worse for the Captain. He is now called Britain's Number One Love Rat! Why, he is as unpopular now as Camilla, whom people are calling 'Cow-milla'. What a terrible price these two people are paying for being the confidantes of the Boss and Bossette.

Mindy tells me that *Princess in Love* is a vulgar and disgraceful book and that no one in society should ever be caught or admit to reading it. I agree. I certainly don't intend to be found out!

November 1995

I am sitting down on the sofa with Eddie in the cosy terraced house I now live in at 19 Moylan Road, off the Lillie Road in Fulham. *Panorama*, the BBC's current affairs programme, is screening an interview with the Bossette. Goodness, what is she going to say? Why the big fuss? Will she say that she and the Boss have made it up? Oh that would be such wonderful news.

The programme starts. I suddenly have a very bad feeling. She is wearing heavy black kohl eyeliner and she hangs her head to the side in a pose of misery. I have seen that look before. Yes, that's her 'forlorn' look, pictured three years ago outside the Taj Mahal. Eddie and I sit gripped.

As the interview proceeds, I realise this is a re-run of Andrew Morton's book staged live for television. The Princess talks of her bulimia; HRH's friends, whom she maintains are beastly; and Camilla being her enemy in the Palace. Oh no, she also confesses that she has had an affair with James Hewitt!

'I adored him, but he let me down.'

What next?

'I want to be a queen in people's hearts.'

No! I inwardly scream. Stop it! 'The Queen of Hearts'? If even half of the men you've slept with are ever revealed, you'll be known as the 'Queen of *Tarts*'! Please, Bossette, this is not right. There can't be more, can there?

Oh no. I feel my stomach churning as she tells the world that HRH is not fit to be King.

Not fit to be King? Darling Bossette, I realise you are in a huge amount of pain, but that is the maddest, not to say the cruellest, thing you could have done. What are you trying to do, rob your husband of his future throne? Obviously. What will your children make of what you are doing? I know you are not my employer any more, but I and everyone who has known you have always felt huge affection for you. But how can we do so now? This is not an interview; it is a declaration of war. It is a Pearl Harbor strike on the Royal Family. Do you really believe there will be no repercussions?

The interview finishes. Even Eddie is stunned and at a loss for words.

Next comes *Newsnight*. My goodness, they have invited my Sandringham lunch companion, His Massiveness, the great Minister of State for the Armed Forces, Nicholas Soames, to comment. He is now grilled. Will he pull his punches? I can't imagine so. He is not that kind of man.

He says Diana has endured a period of unhappiness that has led to 'instability and mental illness'. Right, he is saying she is partially mad. My super-sized friend then talks of Diana's theory that her telephones are tapped. His response: she is exhibiting 'the advanced stages of paranoia'. No, he is saying she is *completely* mad.

I collapse back into the seat. What has this gained anyone? I reflect on what I was told recently by Mindy. She claims that Diana is different from her sisters, the other Spencer girls, less centred and with a vengeful streak. Mindy had then proceeded to put forward an absurd notion that this might be because she is not actually the daughter of Earl Spencer. My mind goes back to the conversation. It is easy to recall because it is so hard to forget.

'The rumour is that her mother was having an affair with a powerful, well-known man, a very glamorous one who few women could resist, before Diana was born.'

I know Mindy likes to tantalise.

'Go on, then,' I say. 'Who was it?'

'If I tell you he has been knighted and his first name is Jimmy, can you guess his surname?'

I am knocked back. I can't believe it. So *that's* why the Boss and Bossette chose Sir Jimmy Savile as their marriage guidance counsellor. All along, he is the Bossette's real father! That explains a lot. No wonder he felt he had the right to be so familiar with us Lady Clerks.

'Who would have thought it?' I say. 'Sir Jimmy Savile being Her Royal Highness's real father.'

'What!?' retorts Mindy. 'Not Sir Jimmy Savile! I am talking about Sir Jimmy Goldsmith.'

'What, Sir Jimmy Goldsmith, the humungously rich financier and politician?'

'That's right.'

'You cannot be serious.'

Anyway, Mindy insists that Diana's mother had an affair

with Sir Jimmy and that the dates all fit. She goes on to ask whether I had noticed the striking similarity in looks between Jemima, Sir Jimmy's daughter by Annabel Goldsmith, and the Bossette.

Not only *that*, she says, but isn't it interesting that they are close friends and both have fallen for gentlemen from Pakistan – Imran Khan and Diana's current squeeze, the surgeon Hasnat Khan?

Could Imran and Hasnat be cousins? They have the same last name. Rumour has it that they are and, moreover, that Imran and Jemima, actually introduced the Princess to Hasnat.

I repeated to Mummy what Mindy said and her response is unsurprisingly proper and sensible, dismissing it as no more than 'speculative rumour'. And quite right, I suppose. Until a DNA test is performed, it will be what other people call 'utter nonsense'.

December 1995

Huge excitement, not to speak of a bit of tension, here in the offices as we clamber onto the bus at St James's Palace for the annual Christmas Lunch, which this year is being held at The Lanesborough Hotel overlooking Hyde Park Corner. In a quite unprecedented move, the Bossette has decided to ride with us!

The World's Number One Fashion Icon looks absolutely stunning. She is wearing a lovely pink jacket with brass buttons and a black skirt. Her shoes are by Jimmy Choo. The Bossette only ever wears Jimmy Choos these days. Besides looking radiant, she also has an air of triumph. Is this because of the *Panorama* programme, I wonder, or the prospect of a new life once her divorce is settled?

She places herself firmly at the front of the bus, like a warrior princess leading her troops into battle. I can see people outside in the street staring up at her astonished, not believing what they are seeing. I am not surprised. Would you believe your eyes if you saw Princess Diana on a bus?

We arrive at The Lanesborough to be greeted by a huge throng of reporters and cameramen. All of us are photographed. I feel like a star at a Hollywood premiere. It is amazing! This has never happened before. A friend tells me that the Royal Family is such hot news that photographs are required by the press of everyone who works for them, even Lady Clerks. We enter The Lanesborough and are served champagne. *Mais naturellement!*

As I enter the building, I encounter William and Harry's nanny, Tiggy Legge-Bourke. A few years back, Tiggy replaced Olga Powell, who was sweet, a bit like 'Nursie' in *Blackadder.* But Olga was not up to controlling the two young Royal tearaways. I remember a scene at Highgrove with the panting Olga crying out 'Come back here, you naughty boys!' while trying to catch up with her fleeing charges as they tore upstairs. Tiggy is someone to whom the boys would naturally heed. She has a bit of the old-fashioned Field Marshall about her and talks in a brusque military way.

'How's you?'she greets me heartily, as if I was a fellow Commanding Officer.

'Oh very well, thank you, Tiggy.'

Soon we are engaged in meaningless banter. I know quite a bit about Tiggy because she has been in the newspapers a lot. Mindy has also filled me in on the latest goss about how the Bossette detests her. At first, she took exception to the fact that both her sons liked her. Then she objected to the obvious affection between Tiggy and HRH. This much is common knowledge, as there was even a picture of the flirty Tiggy giving the Boss a peck on his Royal cheek. But the Princess and her allies go further. They say Tiggy and HRH are having an affair. Indeed, the Princess maintains that HRH has dumped Camilla and is keen to *marry* Tiggy. Mindy says Diana is so paranoid that she thinks dear HRH will go so far as to have her killed in a car crash so the wedding can happen! Have you heard anything so ridiculous in your life?

Before I realise what is happening, the Princess herself has joined us. I curtsey, but the Bossette does not have eyes for me, only Tiggy. Her eyes are aflame. Her Royal Highness looks Tiggy up and down with evident disdain and in a loud voice declares, 'I am so sorry to hear about the baby!'

The Bossette sticks her nose into the air and moves forward into the crowd with that expression of vengeful triumph she wore on the bus, indicating to every witness that she is 'Number One'. Oh yes! Tiggy and I are left with our jaws hanging open. Did we really hear what we thought we just heard? I am stunned. The Princess has publicly and directly announced that the nanny of her sons has either had a miscarriage or an abortion – and surely the unambiguous implication was that HRH was the father.

I am still rooted to the spot in a state of scandalised shock when I see Tiggy addressing Princess Diana's new Protection Officer, who is lagging behind her.

'Do you know what she just said to me?' she asks him.

He shrugs and looks embarrassed. Wow! I'm wondering how is this all going to develop, when there is a sudden call for us to sit down. Phew! Saved by the bell.

The Princess's entourage is in one room and the Prince's in another. We are like two rival armies. The whole atmosphere is extraordinary. I wave to Victoria, who is now firmly ensconced in the other camp. Can our friendship survive?

Predictably, there have already been resignations tendered over the *Panorama* fiasco. Princess Diana's Press Secretary, Geoff Crawford, has left and her Private Secretary, Patrick Jephson, is said to be packing his bags.

We all sit down at our designated tables. I see Tiggy not far from me. She looks absolutely furious and I totally sympathise. Whatever the Bossette feels, it is dreadful to go and publicly accuse a member of staff of such a thing, don't you think? If I was Tiggy, I would be beside myself. In fact, I would probably have walked out by now.

During pudding a a magician by the name of Fay Presto entertains us. Well, if ever there was a time for light relief, this is it. Fay Presto is brilliant. She makes bottles disappear and does card acts, and soon all the tension of the incident with Tiggy and the Princess evaporates.

Then suddenly I catch sight of something out of the corner of my eye. This surely cannot be happening! Can I really have just seen a bread roll fly past? My goodness, a bun fight has erupted between five or six tables! It is Tiggy and the young princes hurling bread rolls around the room. What is going on? That naughty Prince Harry is having hysterics. My goodness, what does he have in his hand now? It looks like a can. He is not going to throw that, is he? I know he can be a handful, but if young Prince Harry starts throwing cans, there will be trouble. Forget Protection Officers, the princes will be having Probation Officers. My goodness, Prince William has one too. And Tiggy!

Suddenly, to add to the missiles of food being thrown everywhere, foam starts erupting from the cans. Even the Protection Officers are joining in the mayhem. I look at an uneaten bread roll. Do I follow the example of my Royal masters? I suppose I do. I then chuck the roll into the mêlée. What fun. Someone chucks one back. Then I see Tiggy advancing purposefully over to HRH's table. My goodness, she is now spraying the Boss with foam. Everyone is now laughing.

And then I catch a sight that I will never forget to my dying day: as Tiggy is spraying the Prince, she looks over to the astounded Princess in the other room as if to say, 'Look who has the *special* relationship.'

The Princess is livid! Tiggy holds her stare and smiles mockingly.

The Princess declared war with a shock offensive. Field Marshall Tiggy has gathered herself and is coming back with all guns blazing. If the Bossette gets up and comes over, I swear there will be an all-out catfight. The Protection Officers will really have their work cut out. These two women hate each other.

I see the Princess steeling herself to get up. Then Tiggy swings round and returns to her table. The Bossette is still furious, but the opportunity for combat has now passed, so she slips down into conversational gear and resumes her chat with the man on her left. Phew!

We all collect our Christmas presents – two glass tumblers with the Prince of Wales feathers – and then, as St James's Palace is so close, we walk back to the office. Outside the hotel, the throng of photographers snap away at us. The Boss and the Bossette appear to be the biggest story in the world right now. Yes, this Christmas lunch is not one I will easily forget.

February 1996

I am off up to Balmoral for an entire week. How exciting is that? The only problem is that I have worn my clothes so often now that I need a new wardrobe. All I can afford are charity shop cast-offs. But I can hardly wear a cast-off in a palace, can I? My credit is at its limit and I can't borrow any more money from Daddy, especially as he and I both know I will never pay it back.

Thank goodness for friends, is all I can say. Frankly, if it wasn't for Karen Humphryes, a former debutante and magnificent friend, I would be the Palace bag lady by now. Besides being the prettiest girl I know, she is the kindest. Imagine having a beautiful fairy godsister who gives you carte blanche to take *anything* from her wardrobe! That's Karen. Every girl should have one, certainly if they work at a palace and they have peanuts to live on.

Anyway, I am staying up at Birkhall this time, not in the cottage. I am in the office doing some typing when in walks Bernie the butler to inform me that I am invited to dine tonight with HRH and friends. Yes, yes, yes! What excitement. Bernie leaves the room and, since I am by myself, I stand up and do a pirouette of joy. I am just resettling myself in front of the computer when a voice calls out 'Saaraah!'

Who is that? It sounds like HRH but surely it can't be. After all, the Prince doesn't call out. He quietly summons. It has to be one of the staff.

'Yes?' I drawl back in a slightly silly voice.

'Oh can you come into my office, please?'

Oh my God, it really *is* HRH! I rush into his office just down the corridor. My heart is palpitating. I didn't mean to take the mickey, really I didn't. He seems quite unconcerned, though. Phew. I take down a letter. As I prepare to head back to my office, he speaks again.

'Tell me, Sarah, do you like caviar?'

What an odd question for him to ask. Of course, I have tasted caviar. I serve the lumpfish on smoked salmon canapés. I can be quite sophisticated at times, you know. This is my chance to show His Royal Highness my erudition.

'Yes, Sir, I often eat it.'

HRH raises his eyebrows. 'You do?'

I find myself flustered. 'Yes, sir, at £4 a jar it is not that expensive.'

'Sarah, the caviar that I speak of is the egg of the sturgeon. It comes in a tin and costs not £4 but about £400. I've been given quite a few of these tins recently by the Sultan of Brunei. It is Royal Beluga caviar, the best. We are having it this evening. You are in for a treat. I hope you enjoy it,' he replies with a smile.

As I leave his office I think, I hope I do too. Obviously, it is a different kind of caviar to the one I normally eat. That seems rather a lot to pay for fish eggs. Some people have more money than sense! I wonder how different it tastes to the one I buy at the supermarket. Perhaps if I ever meet this Sultan I will pass on this money-saving tip. Go to the supermarket, Sultan. Save yourself some dinars! A sturgeon's eggs can't be that different to lumpfish roe, surely?

Early that evening, I reflect on HRH's good fortune having such generous friends as the Sultan, even if perhaps he is a bit silly with his money. I suppose then that the Sultan is a house guest, which is why he has given HRH these fish eggs. Goodness, I will doubtless meet this exotic man at dinner. How exciting. What will he wear? A flowing robe? A turban studded with precious jewels? Just who *is* he, I think as I try on the lovely skirts and tops donated by Karen, bless her.

Is the Sultan married or is he single? If he is married, is his wife a Sultana? Does he have lots of Sultanas? Does he want another one, I wonder? Do his Sultanas all stuff themselves with this expensive fish-egg caviar? And where on earth is Brunei, of which he is Sultan? Is it far away? Would I like to live there? Well, I will soon find out.

Nervously, I go into the kitchen, nab one of Mervyn's stiff gin and tonics, and ask him if I look all right. Bernie informs me I look fine. I am still anxious.

'It is not too tarty or over the top, do you think?'

Bernie assures me it is not. I resist asking him whether my bottom looks too big in the outfit because that would be improper but, all the same, the anxiety is there. I take a final swig, then set off to the drawing room.

Here I am on my first evening up at Balmoral and I don't know who HRH's guests are. Still, I am quite prepared. Oh yes, I am ready to prattle with Princes and circulate with Sultans. So who is going to be dining here tonight?

I enter the drawing room and look around. Is Sexy Woodentop, the Duke of Westminster, here? No. Is His Massiveness in attendance, the great Conservative Minister Nicholas Soames? No. What, not even a Sultan or a Sultana? No. Perhaps they have yet to arrive? Minutes later, I am introduced to a Duchess and an Earl. I deduce they are neighboring landowners.

HRH calls me over and asks me what I wish to drink.

No, thank you, Boss, you are slightly too generous with the gin! I will get it myself. Of course, I don't say that. I wouldn't dare! I am just demure little me, who knows my place.

We sit down for dinner and I quickly gather that the other guests are mostly local grandees, all with nearby estates, no doubt as big as Balmoral. There are only nine of us. I sit next to one of the women, whose face seems very familiar. Who is she, I wonder, racking my brain. Then I realise. It is *her*! Yes. It is Camilla Parker-Bowles.

Oh my God. The last time I saw her was at that memorable church service at Sandringham. But of course she has been in the newspapers ever since. Here I am sitting with His Royal Highness opposite and his Royal mistress next to me! Who would have thought it?

Bernie now arrives with the caviar. Thank goodness I am not served first. I am clueless as to what to do. This certainly isn't the way I prepare caviar.

Following the others, who have clearly done this before, I first take some small buckwheat pancakes. Continuing to copy, I then put some soured cream on my plate; next some chopped hard-boiled egg and onion, and finally a dollop of the glutinous, shimmering black Royal Beluga caviar on which I squeeze some lemon. So how is this different, I wonder, from the caviar I buy?

I take a bite.

Do you remember the moment you first fell in love? Do you recollect your first bout of passionate sex? Do you recall your first orgasm? Well, I am never going to forget my first bite of Royal Beluga caviar. It is like paradise crash-landing on my taste buds. At £400 a throw, it is beyond most people's pockets but, dear reader, if you win the Lottery and want to spoil yourself, take a tip from the Sultan. Try a feast of Royal Beluga. Just once. But beware. If you get addicted, it is bye bye to your Lottery millions!

So here I am munching away on this divine theft from heaven's larder when Camilla Parker-Bowles starts addressing me. Who am I? A Lady Clerk. How long have I worked at the Palace? About eight years. Do I ask her any questions, like who are you and how do you know the Prince of Wales? As if. That wouldn't be tactful, would it? And if I didn't know the answer to *that*, then I would have to have been living on another planet these last four years.

Bernie then comes round with more offerings of this sublime Royal Beluga caviar. I tell myself I should exercise some ladylike restraint, like my friend Victoria Mendham, but frankly this is a temptation, like certain men's bottoms, I cannot resist. I scoop a great mound of it onto my plate.

At some stage in the conversation, I let it slip that Mummy is battling with cancer. Suddenly, Camilla, as she has insisted I now call her, is *so* sympathetic. She tells me all about her own mother's death from osteoporosis. Soon we are glued together, chatting away.

Goodness, Camilla is so sweet! I think all the nasty things that have ever been said about her are vile; nothing but bilious poison. Anyone who attacks her now is my enemy. I mean that! What a fortunate man is HRH for having such a wonderful and sympathetic woman as his mistress, his confidante, his lover! No woman can be sweeter, I think, as I bite into yet another helping of the Sultan's kind and delicious present.

Later, I go to bed and reflect on the dinner. It quite simply has to be one of the most wonderful evenings of my life.

Imagine, I have eaten Royal Beluga caviar, mountains of it. Not just that, I have had a one-to-one with Camilla Parker-Bowles, who has to be the sweetest woman imaginable. *And*, would you believe it, she is now my friend! When you think about it, it is incredible. I go to sleep.

Three days later, a set of HRH's friends arrive from England. I have been given the task of helping out at a Royal picnic. How wonderful. We rendezvous at the Swiss Lodge, which is near a small mountain pond in the middle of one of the woods. The Swiss Lodge, I learn, is a genuine Swiss chalet that was given as a present to Her Majesty. Goodness, doesn't the Royal Family have generous friends? Imagine, an entire Swiss chalet as well as all those tins of Royal Beluga!

I have gradually worked out who these new friends are, having been to one more dinner. These are the Boss's arty friends, ideal companions now that the shooting season is over, hence no Mr Sexy Woodentop or His Massiveness.

In order to get to the Swiss Lodge, we have to drive into the Royal Estate and gently climb up bumpy tracks through the pine trees, up and up, as I discover, nearly to the end of the treeline.

We all arrive in our respective Discovery Land Rovers. I am with Bernie the butler. Intentionally, we are first so that we can lay out the picnic. It is the same as usual: jacket potatoes, salad and quiche. Do 'real' Princes eat quiche, I ask myself? Of course they do. In any case, my Prince is not just a real prince but a Renaissance one. I place the potatoes and quiche in the Aga to warm up.

Everyone suddenly arrives. But my new best friend Camilla Parker-Bowles is not amongst them. That's a shame. HRH and his friends all pile into the lodge. The atmosphere is relaxed. Well, *I* am relaxed, having helped myself to the rum-and-orange punch, which is served, would you believe it, in small horn cups. Very warming, thank you. I am just pouring my third when I hear a familiar voice.

'Oh Sarah, do you think you could hand round the soup?'

Saved from incipient dipsomania by the Royal command! For a moment, I indulge my little fantasy that, as I play 'hostess', HRH and I are entertaining our friends. I am, of course, more than happy to dish out the cups of steaming broth. Everyone sits down at the big old pine table. I see a space and sit down too. Next thing I know, HRH is placing himself next to me.

Again, Your Royal Highness? Rumours will start flying. They will be whispering that I have replaced my friend Camilla Parker-Bowles as the Royal Mistress.

Don't be silly, says my inner nanny. You are flattering yourself. I am, am I? Then explain why he ends up sitting next to me so often? Inner nanny fires back, HRH is only sitting next to you because he is holding back until last, as a good host should. As the designated helper, you sit down second last. That is why. Inner nanny is right, damn her. Ho hum. A girl can but dream.

I gaze around, absorbing the scene. The sun is warming us through the big panoramic window that looks out onto the dark-green mountain pond. There is a lovely log burner also very efficiently chucking out heat. The conversation is amusing, informed and, if I am honest, over my head. But arty types have such a sensitive and nice way about them that I feel completely at home. I could happily stay here all day.

At the end of the picnic, it is decided that we should go for a relaxing walk. We leave the chalet and look at the beautiful mountain pond. I learn that this August Tiggy Legge-Bourke was up here with the two young princes. One of them went for a swim – though whether he dived in or was pushed, I don't know!

HRH stands proudly and contentedly surveying the beauty of the forest. Just then, some ramblers walk in front of us and cross the little bridge over the pond. They don't look at us. I think they will get the shock of their lives, if they do. In Scotland, the general public can walk where they like, as there are apparently no laws of trespass. All the same, it is not often that you encounter the Prince of Wales and friends when you go for a ramble.

We set off on our genteel walk up through the forest of pines to the bright open light we see beyond us, where we reach the treeline and a kind of plateau. It is magical and I feel so privileged. We are stopping here, I am told, because it becomes a bit more remote after that. HRH guides us back down and, as we go, I ask about some orange netting above the ground.

'Oh that is for the capercaillie,' explains HRH.

I nod. What on earth is 'capercaillie'? Is it a rare plant, some herb perhaps? And why does the netting have to be orange, I wonder? Perhaps it is the cheapest?

'The capercaillie are driven through the wood, and when they come to the netting, they fly sufficently high for our guns to shoot them.'

Oh clever HRH.

'And you know what capercaillie means?' he asks.

No, darling HRH, I don't even know what capercaillie *is*.

'It is Gaelic for horse of the wood.'

I am now more bewildered than ever. Flying horses that

live in the woods! That can't be right. But, then again, perhaps centaurs really do exist. It seems a pity to shoot them, though.

'Yes,' he continues, 'they used to be found all over northern Europe. They are like grouse but much, much bigger.'

Ah, grouse! It is a big bird, then.

HRH seems to know everything there is to know about the countryside. And he is even trained in the art of being a ghillie! How many Royal or aristocratic landowners can claim *that* as an accomplishment?

During the stalking season, he personally guides his friends to stags. I can see him now, shuffling on his stomach along the heather in his tweeds to get within shooting distance of his quarry. If and when there is a kill, he 'grallochs' the stag himself, by which I mean he cuts it open from the throat downwards and empties its stomach onto the side of the mountain to be later devoured by ravens and the like.

How manly is that? No lily-livered wimp is he. If we are ever bombed back into the Stone Age, HRH would definitely be a man to be around. I would choose to live in his cave any day. Oh yes, you do not get a truer countryman than His Royal Highness.

October 1996

Following the divorce of the Boss and Bossette, there have been some huge changes in the office recently. It is enough to make even a Lady Clerk insecure!

Commander Richard Aylard has been fired as HRH's Private Secretary, which I think is terribly sad. It is probably all to do with the Jonathan Dimbleby book, which everyone still blames him for. Poor Richard, he worked so hard for the Boss that his marriage broke down. So now he is divorced *and* out of a job. Can't life deliver cruel blows? Stephen Lamport has been promoted to Private Secretary and Mark Bolland is the new deputy Private Secretary.

Now, Mark Bolland is an extraordinary appointment because he is not the type you would ever expect to find here at the Palace. Normally the candidates for the various posts of Private Secretary come from the Foreign Office or the Armed Forces. They are upper-middle-class Oxford or Cambridge types, or at the very least have had a smart Public School education. Mark, as he insists I call him, is from a modest background, having attended a comprehensive in Middlesbrough and York University. He is about two years older than me, smart, sophisticated and camp, and his boyfriend, Guy Black, is Secretary to the Head of the Press Complaints Commission. He is also *huge* fun.

Mark has taken me to lunch at Le Caprice. Everyone seems to know him and he is so trendy that even the club he also takes me to is named after him! He probably owns it. Yes, Mark's Club in Mayfair is very different from the gentlemen's clubs in St James's. It is not at all stuffy. Half the people there are celebrities. Mark and I get on famously. What a joy it is to work for him!

8

Goodbye, England's Rose

April 1997

It has been quiet so far this year. Earlier in January, I broke up with Eddie. The passion exhausted, we are now 'good friends'. Any romance in the offing? Let me tell you that I have been harbouring a crush on one of HRH's valets. For reasons of propriety, let us call him Sam. Sam is absolutely yummy. But there is one problem: he has a girlfriend. He is not married, though, so technically he is a free man. Well, in my book he is. I had spotted him about the Royal corridors these last twelve months and began, in my more idle moments, to develop certain fantasies about him which I won't regale as it is not that sort of book. They had started to become so lurid that at the last Christmas staff dance it was all I could do not to throw myself at him.

Then, this month, I was posted to Balmoral. Where was I to be billeted? Not Birkhall this time, but Tom-Na-Gaidh. I don't mind at all since the ghost of the mad woodcutter has yet to make an appearance. Also, I'm not alone, as Stephen Lamport, HRH's Private Secretary, is staying in the next room. Yesterday, HRH asked his guests to join him on a personal tour of the castle. Would I like to come, too, he solicitously asked? But of course. After all, I have never even seen the castle.

We arrive at the castle in our Discovery Land Rovers. What a dark and dingy place it looks, more suitable to the Addams family than the Royal Family. We go inside. The interior is festooned in tartan tapestries – on the floors and all over the walls. It is drafty and cold. No amount of whisky could get me through a stint working here.

HRH starts the tour. He shows us the rooms open to the public and then takes us to the private parts of the castle, surely the most fascinating. We enter his childhood nursery and he points out the little graffiti signatures on the table. Aha, so even Royal children are not immune to compulsions to vandalise.

Next, he takes us through to the bedroom that he slept in as a small child. He then bends his ear to the plughole in the basin. 'When I was bored, I used to listen to the sounds. I could hear everything in the next-door bedroom,' he says.

Hmm. That is interesting. A Royal housekeeper once warned me that if I ever had to stay at Balmoral and wanted some privacy, then I should put the plug into the sink at night. Apparently, listening in through the pipes is an established recreation for many of the Royal Family.

We eventually finish the tour downstairs, where a large statue of a kilted Scotsman stands. 'I will ask you all to guess whether he has anything under the kilt,' says HRH teasingly.

Just as the party leaves through the door, I cannot resist having a quick peek. I dip my head and look underneath. Suddenly, I blush. Out of the corner of my other eye, I spot a grinning HRH. He has popped his head round the door.

'Oh I thought you would do that, Sarah,' he says.

I am about to answer that, having asked us to guess the sculpted contents of the kilt, the least he could expect is for one amongst us to discover the answer. But I hardly feel this to be an appropriate response from a Lady Clerk to her future king. And it is not as if there was anything there anyway! I walk with the Boss, still blushing, out of the front door and back to the entourage of Land Rovers. HRH must think I am such a slapper.

We then drive back to our respective residences. At Tom-na-Gaidh this evening, there are three of us for dinner – Stephen Lamport, myself and, what excitement, Sam! I am aquiver with excitement, as he has remained my number one Palace crush these last six months.

At the end of dinner, Stephen pleads tiredness and announces that he is retiring to bed. Go Stephen, *go*! My heart is palpitating. Four minutes later, I am alone at last with Sam, this gorgeous man. But, damn it, he now says he has to drive back to Birkhall. Oh no you don't, my fine Valet, not if I have anything to do with it!

'Oh don't go just yet!' I say. 'Stay a bit longer and keep me company.'

'Oh all right,' Sam mumbles. 'I'll stay for a bit.'

We repair to the cottage's sitting room. The fire is still blazing, the lights are low and my body language is screaming for him to touch me.

We sidle next to each other on the sofa, then clink our glasses. We gaze into each other's eyes and are now lost for words. His lips move closer to mine.

Next thing, he kisses me. Am I complaining? I am now in his tight embrace. We slowly roll off the sofa onto the rug by the fire. The fire roars next to us, sending out primeval encouragement to consummate our passion. Sam's hands are all over me. What practiced hands you have, Sam. You dress the future monarch and now you undress his Lady Clerk. Continue, please. This is so naughty and yet so wonderful.

Suddenly, I remember! Stephen Lamport's room is directly above us! Oh my God, he can hear everything! Will he keep it secret? Maybe, but maybe not. What if HRH gets to hear about his Valet's fifteen-minute seduction of his Lady Clerk? That would be too awful! It is one thing for HRH to suspect I am a slapper; it is quite another for him to know it.

I suddenly sit up and start buttoning my blouse. Sam looks startled.

'No, Sam, not now! We will have to wait! Yes, you have to go, I am afraid! We have to exercise control!'

Poor Sam. The last of our limbs are now untangled. He looks so deflated and forlorn. He must think I am a terrible tease.

'So will I see you again?' he asks plaintively at the door.

I march up to him and kiss him hard. 'That is your answer,' I say. One hot and flustered Lady Clerk retires to bed.

June 1997

My news since April. I have taken up polo, HRH's favourite sport. Well, if it is good enough for him, it is good enough for me! Every weekend, I have been gallivanting round on polo ponies at the Ascot grounds of the amazing Grace sisters, who are all pretty and really popular. I even played in a few matches. Afterwards, there was a big party and we ate a South American roast lamb. I am not talking here of a leg or shoulder, but the entire creature. They roast it all on a fire and they call it *asada*. I am not yet sufficiently good to play in the

Boss's set, but who knows about the future?

Polo is not a cheap sport, so how can I afford it, you might ask? Good question. You see, Daddy sent me some money to put down as a deposit on a flat. Yes, yes, I know! But it wasn't just the polo – there were a few debts I seemed to have forgotten about and a new wardrobe that I just *had* to buy. After all, how will a girl find a husband if she doesn't keep up appearances?

So I have now spent the flat deposit, but I don't like to think I have squandered it. Who knows, maybe I will pick up my future husband on the polo field while wearing one of my new outfits? Polo lessons could turn out then to be a brilliant investment. Hasn't the witty Jilly Cooper dedicated a book to the sport of polo and the dashing figures who play it? Isn't the hero, Rupert, based on Andrew Parker-Bowles, no less? If I can't find a suitable swain for marriage on the polo field, where can I?

My feelings for Sam remain as strong as ever. In May, we passed each other in the Palace three times. The last time I told him to come to the kitchen. Checking no one else was around, we snogged passionately.

'Can I see you?' he asked breathlessly. 'Alone?'

We arranged a meeting, but the bastard cancelled at the last minute! We agreed on another meeting; then he cancelled again! What is the matter with this man, I ask you?

Maybe it is because he has a live-in girlfriend, answers inner nanny. Yes, I concede, I suppose that is true.

Then I brush into Sam again. I want to tell him to get lost, that obviously there is no future for us and that if he has such strong feelings for me then he should break up with his girlfriend. Then I think again – if he actually did that and it got serious, I would become the official girlfriend of a Valet for HRH. Is this what destiny has prepared me for – a Valet's girlfriend? I don't think so. It is better, is it not, that I remain a bit on Sam's side? So we agree to meet up after work the following week while his girlfriend is visiting her mother in the country.

The following Tuesday, I drive out with Sam in the late afternoon over the river. He takes me to his modest home, which is God knows where, but inner nanny tells me not to be such a snob. At least Sam is sensible enough to own his home. No sooner are we in the house than he leaps on me. Really! Can't a girl have a drink first to relax herself? He musters some self-control and pours me a stiff vodka. Soon after, I lose my control and Sam has his wicked way.

The weird thing is waking up in the early hours and seeing all her things in the bedroom around me. I am an interloper and I feel wretchedly guilty. I have never done this before and I am not entirely sure I want to do it again, at least not in her bedroom.

We drive back early, hardly speaking. It is definitely one of those relationships to be bracketed under 'lust only'. Sam is great. He is sexy. But for me, at least, he is a creature of the loins, not of the heart.

August 1997

I am up in Shropshire staying with Mummy and Daddy for the long August weekend. In the battle between Mummy and cancer, I fear cancer is winning. But she is being very English about the whole thing and tells me not to fuss. But I do fuss and the idea of Mummy suffering and then me losing her is just too horrible to contemplate. I try and park this feeling of creeping desolation into some other room in my mind. I notice I am drinking more than usual. If it wasn't for my rôle with the Royal Family and the stability and routine it provides, I might soon become a bit of a mess.

What news of my master and mistress, the Boss and the Bossette? While HRH seems happier following his divorce, Princess Diana, as we must now call her, seems to be getting out of control. After my little flingette with Sam, I am hardly in a position to make moral judgements; however, I cannot help but feel that the Princess is having her cake and eating it.

Put it like this: for a woman who complains about the sanctity of her marriage being destroyed by another woman (Camilla Parker-Bowles), which, in any case, is not true, the Bossette has little compunction about destroying, or trying to, the sanctity of other people's vows. I speak of two instances.

The first is the marriage of the suave fine-art dealer Oliver Hoare, whose wife is the daughter of HRH's friend Baroness Louise de Waldner. Apparently, the Bossette has been having an affair with Oliver Hoare. These things happen. You keep it discreet. But it is unfair, is it not, to try and disturb the balance of mind of your lover's wife by making mystery telephone calls, then putting down the receiver? The calls have actually been traced by the police, following a complaint by Mrs Hoare, to Kensington Palace, so there is no denying the Princess was responsible.

If you ask me, it smacks a bit of the kind of destructive behaviour displayed by Glenn Close's character in *Fatal Attraction*.

Then, of course, there is the England rugby hero Will Carling, with whom she cavorted on a few occasions in a Fulham fitness club. Again, if discretion had been exercised,

Will Carling's marriage to his lovely new bride, Julia, might have survived. But the Princess made sure that the whole world knew about her latest conquest. Front-page publicity in the national newspapers is a terrible way to wound your lover's wife. Result: divorce.

I am beginning to think the Princess is hooked on power – especially over men. When she sets her cap at some chap, she relishes the inevitable conquest. Mindy tells me, though I am sure it cannot be true, that the Bossette is not beyond practising the eye-popping leg-crossing move that made Sharon Stone so famous in *Basic Instinct*! Honestly, some people do make things up! Or do they?

The only man that I have heard of on Mindy's grapevine who has not succumbed to the Princess's lethal charms is the handsome football legend Gary Lineker. Our Gary met the Princess at the same function as Will Carling. She invited the stars of both the curved and the round ball back to Kensington Palace. The astute Gary Lineker was quickly alive, I hear, to the Bossette's game. And it was *not* the beautiful one! How well Mr Lineker deserves his pure and unsullied reputation.

But my complaint about the Princess is not really her double standards; what upsets me is her treatment of others, specifically my friend Victoria. She is devoted to the Princess, as you know. She has worked as her Lady Clerk for eight years now. In the last two years, the Bossette has taken her on her holidays. Jolly nice, too. However, out of the blue, in January, she presented Victoria with a bill for over £6,000!

'This is for your contribution to flights and hotels,' she declared.

Yes, £6,000. Imagine! Victoria was distraught. If she had been told she would have to pay, Victoria would never have gone. Quite simply, she could not afford it. The Princess lives in a palace and has a divorce settlement of £17 million. Victoria lives in a modest house in Essex with her parents and is paid peanuts.

In desperation, Victoria posted the bill to Tony, the Royal Accountant at St James's Palace, explaining her position. The bill was then sent back to Kensington Palace for settlement by the Bossette. The Princess went ballistic. She harangued poor Victoria, then fired her. On hearing what happened, HRH personally settled the extortionate amount on Victoria's behalf. Kind HRH.

Victoria may be heartbroken, betrayed and out of a job, but thanks to HRH she is at least not facing bankruptcy proceedings. The Princess may be to many people the 'Queen of Hearts' but, as far as I am concerned, her treatment of Victoria shows her to be the 'Queen of Mean'.

The Princess is now publicly cavorting in France with a wealthy Arab playboy, Mr Dodi Fayed, the son of the tycoon Mohamed al Fayed, who owns Harrods. Even the *Daily Mail*, which is normally so pro-Diana, has taken her to task for her lack of decorum. Perhaps, I wonder, the huge star-rating of the World's Number One Fashion Icon is starting to tumble?

Next morning, I am just waking up when there is a knock on the door and Mummy enters. This is strange because I normally just see her downstairs at breakfast.

'I have some startling news for you, darling. Brace yourself!'

What on earth can it be?

'Princess Diana has just been killed in a car accident in Paris.'

I am completely stunned. I check I am awake. This is not

some sort of bad dream, is it? I then get up and go downstairs to watch the terrible news unfold on television. Throughout the day, I see interviews with grief-stricken members of the public. The whole nation, it appears, is shocked.

What is my reaction? How tragic, and what a terrible waste of a good but very flawed woman. I sip some coffee. The idea of the Princess actually being dead is quite extraordinary. It is almost impossible to take in. Poor Princess, poor Dodi, poor chauffeur and poor Protection Officer. At least he might yet survive. All negative criticisms now banished, I remember her smile, her mesmerising laugh and her acts of generosity.

I think of the time she was stuffing trifle down herself by the fridge in Kensington Palace, and the other time she swept past me like a triumphant charioteer in the go-cart race in Clapham. And now my thoughts move to the two vulnerable young princes who must have been informed only a few hours ago that they have lost their mother. I have a picture of the two tearaways gleefully ambushing me from a hideout in Highgrove. How tragic to think that they have now lost her. I find myself sniffling and tears begin to roll down my cheeks.

By the end of the day, I am more focused on practicalities. Because Eddie and I remained such good friends after our break-up, we booked to go to Portugal together for a week's holiday and are due to leave next Friday. But is it disrespectful to go away when such a tragedy has befallen our office? Am I going to be needed? Should I cancel my trip?

On Tuesday morning, I am heading to the office when I hear on the radio that the Princess's body has been flown back from Paris and is now lying in a private chapel in central London. Where can that be, I ponder, as I swing round into the Mall. My God, there are thousands of people outside

Buckingham and St James's palaces. My car can barely move for the crush.

There are people wailing, some looking glum, many are carrying flowers. This is more than respectful grief; it is an hysterical emotional outpouring. It is extraordinary and also frightening. I manage to park the car, and as I am getting out I am suddenly hit by the realisation that the private chapel is here. Yes, the Princess is now lying in the Chapel Royal right in the centre of St James's Palace.

As I move towards the doors, I feel distinctly menaced. Everyone appears agitated and aggressive. I feel that if I do not look utterly grief-stricken, they will think I am not showing proper respect and, with this crowd, such a perception could trigger something nasty. To be safe, I think of imitating the wailers, but my hangdog expression appears to suffice.

The office is in pandemonium. We are being inundated with telephone calls and bunches of flowers, and handwritten letters are arriving in their thousands. So we immediately set up a special team of people to cope with the public grief. Extra staff are recruited by lunchtime. This operation is going to take months.

After lunch, I talk with David Baldwin, the Sergeant of the Vestry, which means he is second-in-charge of the Chapel Royal. Poor fellow, he is exhausted. He has been up all night organising the transfer of the Princess's body from the airport to the Chapel. David confides in me that he too finds this massive outpouring of emotion outside the Palace scary.

David says that not since the Glorious Revolution in 1688 has St James's Palace been a fixture of such raw human feeling. But the emotion then was jubilation; this is something else, with dark undertones.

We both agree that the Royal Family have to play Diana's death very sensitively, or who knows what could happen. A stolid German response might do for them privately, but publicly what the people want is a display of emotion to match their own.

By this time, we have set up the first Book of Condolences, which we place in one of the Palace annexes that is accessed from a public entrance in Marlborough Street. We next arrange for the police to set up a semicircular barrier of railings outside the chapel window. This has two crucial purposes. First, it is to be used as a skeleton for the erection and display of the bouquets of flowers. Second, by creating this floral shrine outside the window of the chapel, a screen is created to keep the public at bay and obscure the view of the Princess's coffin inside. The last thing we want is the mourners to see the coffin, break the window and invade the Chapel. With the mood of the people here, such an eventuality is distinctly possible.

The next day, the Mall is even more tightly packed and the mood more ugly. Why, in heaven's name, is the flag not flying at half-mast? Can't Her Majesty make even a simple gesture to demonstrate respect, if not grief? And where is the Royal Family, for goodness sake? Why aren't they here? Why are they still up in Scotland? Don't they realise what is being said in the papers? Don't they realise their inaction could trigger a republican revolt?

In the meantime, we carry on answering the telephone calls. By this time, we have more recruits. The Princess's former Private Secretary, Patrick Jephson, and her former Lady-in-Waiting, Anne Beckwick-Smith, have volunteered to come and help with compiling the guest list for the funeral. How wonderful of them to rally round in this time of need. The problem is that in the last year the Princess had dumped most of her old and real friends. Who will they invite?

At 4 p.m., David Baldwin asks if any of us wish to pay our respects to the Princess, and so we take it in turns to go into the Chapel. I go to the front pew with my fellow Lady Clerks, kneel and pray. The Princess is just two feet away from me. I could, if I like, touch her coffin. But my hands remain clasped to my forehead.

Farewell, you strange and contradictory creature, the World's Number One Fashion Icon, frozen now at the height of your beauty and fame to become as much a legend in death as you were in life.

I cross myself and leave.

The next day, Her Majesty, thank goodness, comes down to London to make her address. Phew. The nation is pacified and the mood of the crowd moves to one of pure sorrow. The office is by now humming efficiently and I am told by a Private Secretary to take my holiday, as everything is now 'under control'.

Two days later, I am in Portugal in my rented villa with Eddie. We switch on the satellite television. The audience for the funeral, I learn, is hundreds of millions all across the globe. The pageant unfolds.

We see the procession from Kensington Palace move towards Westminster Abbey. Emotion overwhelms the crowd. It overwhelms Eddie and me. The television cameras swing onto the members of the congregation inside the Abbey. I find myself gulping. Amongst the celebrities, Ministers of State and members of the Royal Family, I notice Victoria, Patrick

Jephson, Ken Wharfe, Geoff Crawford and many others who had resigned or been sacked.

How utterly and unbelievably moving. A funeral is the time, if any, to bury recrimination. Darling Bossette, there were the good times as well as the bad. I promise you this much: none of us will forget you, neither those of us who knew you nor those of us who just read about you. You touched all of us.

Elton John comes on to play his adaptation of his famous song 'Candle in the Wind'. I raise a glass and wipe a tear.

Goodbye, England's rose.

9

Ahoy, the Empire

November 1997

An array of metal boxes stands outside St James's Palace, studiously guarded by the Travelling Yeoman, Ron Lewis. Three of these have my name tags on them. Yes, I am off with HRH and his party on a Royal tour. To where? Swaziland, Lesotho and South Africa.

We are picked up in a minibus and set off to Heathrow. HRH is travelling to the airport separately, so no motorcade and outriders, which is a shame since I so enjoyed that memorable sense of grandeur the time I went with him as his Lady Clerk to Seville. We arrive and are whisked into the VIP lounge. A glass of pink champagne, madam? Yes, that will do nicely.

My goodness, HRH has arrived with Prince Harry. Is the young Prince here to see his father off? No, it appears he is joining the tour. Well, they kept that very hush-hush.

We board the plane. We are flying first class and I am sitting just two seats behind HRH and Prince Harry. The seat in front is occupied by the Boss's Valet, my very own Sam. Sam, I am sorry to report, is not best pleased with me because I let slip to another member of the Royal Household about our night of passion. Yes, yes, I know he has a girlfriend, and I know I should have been discreet, but you know what it is like when you are starting an affair, you just have to share the excitement of it by telling *someone*, don't you? Well, if you are a woman, you do.

Anyway, word has got back to the girlfriend and she has been giving him hell, he says, and I am to blame. Oh dear. We have only done it that once but I was hoping for more rumpy-pumpy with sexy Sam, this time under African stars. This prospect looks doomed now. But, who knows, Sam might relent? Here's hoping.

The plane lands in Johannesburg. We are then whisked away by a smaller plane courtesy of South African Airways to Swaziland. There we are met by a colourful parade and much exuberant whooping. How wonderful. Our party is put up in Swaziland's Royal Guest Palace. Just like in Seville, none of us actually leaves our accommodation and during the day we never get to see HRH. So what do we do? We sensibly re-energise ourselves by resting by the pool, where Ron insists we try out a succession of his cocktails – Bloody Marys and a couple of rum concoctions: Light and Stormies, and Dark and Stormies!

The next day, we are driven to the airport. Our destination: Lesotho, another small kingdom within South Africa, where HRH is to attend the King's Coronation. Apparently, he is a very fine man with many wives.

On our way back to South Africa, the British press corps is settled at the back of the plane. HRH takes great delight in pulling back the curtains to greet 'the pack of wolves', as he calls them.

Our party is stationed at the residence of the British High

Commissioner for the day while HRH does his duties. On route to Johannesburg, everything seems to be running smoothly. Goodness, this is wonderful. We have twenty minutes before we land. Suddenly, I notice Juliet, my Lady Clerk colleague. Something is amiss. She looks distressed. What's happening? She catches my eye and waves frantically, beckoning me over. I get out of my seat and crouch beside her.

'What's wrong?'

'HRH needs his briefing for the first event!'

'So?'

'It's in the diplomatic box.'

'That's right.'

'I can't find the key!'

'Oh my God.'

We rummage round the seats. The key has gone. There is only one thing for it. In a whisper, we pass the problem to HRH's Equerry, Commander John Lavery. The beautifully white-clad Naval Commander assesses the situation. Next thing, he pulls out a letter opener, takes off his shoe and bangs its heel hard against the sharp object, which is now poised over the lock of the diplomatic box. Nothing happens. The Commander methodically whips his heel down again. Bang! The lock breaks. Phew! It was with such ingenuity, was it not, that we British built and maintained an Empire?

Just two seats away, HRH is happily oblivious to the commotion behind him. Juliet presents him with his brief.

We land. HRH is whisked off to his first appointment while we are driven to set up office and home at the Presidential Guest House in Pretoria. Jacaranda trees, with their beautiful mauve flowers and fernlike leaves line the roads. We arrive. The Guest House is a large, white building. Scores of mop-capped African ladies greet us. I feel transported back a hundred years to the reign of Queen Victoria.

Soon we have set up office in a large room downstairs. What to do next? HRH won't return till late in the evening. Check out the swimming pool, of course! The next thing I know, Juliet and I have changed into our bikinis and we are down by the pool performing cartwheels and handstands on the lawn and gymnastics off the diving board, to the great amusement of Ron, who has set up a cocktail bar. We remain there all day. It is a tough and responsible job being a travelling Lady Clerk for the Prince of Wales, but someone has to do it.

The next evening, as part of our official duties, we are to attend a Spice Girls concert in the main stadium in Johannesburg with HRH, Prince Harry and President Nelson Mandela. Before the tour, Juliet and I were given £300 each for our tour wardrobe. What shall I wear? I have two jackets, a skirt and a dress that I purchased with my clothes allowance.

Yes, the dress it is – a black sequinned number from Monsoon. That will do.

We arrive at the concert and the Spice Girls do their stuff. The roar from the crowd is so loud that, from then on, it's difficult to know what these pop ambassadors from Britain are playing. Who cares? Do you want, do you want, do you really, really want? Yes, girls, we want! The atmosphere is fantastic.

Afterwards, we are invited to a celebrity post-concert party. I shake hands with the stars of the evening and stand just four feet from President Mandela, basking in his aura of greatness. I feel giddy with exhilaration. This is a long way from rural Shropshire.

Suddenly, HRH is beside me with Prince Harry. Ginger and Scary let out a great whoop and kiss HRH, who looks absolutely delighted. Wouldn't any middle-aged man, indeed *any* man, be thrilled? What of his son and second heir? I look at Prince Harry. He is a cartoon of lust. His eyes are out on stalks and his jaw is bouncing on the floor as he surveys Ginger's wobbling breasts just two feet away from him. I then watch him slowly look up and down Ginger's shimmering Union Jack minidress. Young man, control yourself!

His eyes then swing to Scary, Posh, Baby and Sporty. He is like a deprived child who has been given the keys to Willy Wonka's chocolate factory. There is no doubting young Harry's proclivities. Oh no. The young Prince is pure heterosexual testosterone, and lots of it. There will be trouble ahead with this young man. Mark my words!

Suddenly, His Godliness, President Mandela, comes over and a group photograph just has to be taken. As I think the thought, light bulbs pop all around me. Imagine, the natural King of Africa, the future King of England, his second son, Prince Harry, and five queens of British rock immortalised together for posterity. Amazing.

Later on, I am back at the Guest House bashing out some thank-you letters for the hospitality and gifts kindly given to HRH. There is, of course, reciprocity. We send back a framed signed photograph of HRH and a leather wallet with the Prince of Wales's feathers. Ron has a stack of these for distribution.

It is way past midnight and we have finished the letters and the present list, which will be distributed tomorrow by the British Embassy. Ron suggests that Juliet and I need a nightcap before we hit the pillow. Good idea, Ron. What's it to be? A Dark and Stormy? That'll do nicely.

Juliet and I are slowly imbibing his killer cocktail when Ron tells a joke. It's so funny that my hands shake and, oh my God, half of the Dark and Stormy is spilt into my laptop! No, I can't believe this is happening. The laptop makes a peculiar noise and suddenly there is an ominous phut. I desperately press the buttons and adjust the leads . . . but to no avail. The computer is kaput. It is a goner.

I can't believe this! The same thing happened on my first Royal tour, but at least it wasn't *my* fault that time. How am I going to explain a computer sabotaged by a Dark and Stormy? What are we going to do tomorrow? We are flying to Durban first thing. There are a huge amount of letters we have to write. Now my computer is out of action because I drowned it in a cocktail. I am going to cry or explode or both.

Juliet and Ron comfort me. Don't worry, they say. I remain frozen in a state of paralysis as Juliet wakes up the British Consul in Durban with a telephone call to explain that we need an IT expert on our arrival, as 'one of our computers has mysteriously crashed'.

The next morning, we board the plane and fly south. I am holding the laptop, which is making peculiar gurgling noises every time it is nudged or jolted. Imagine, I have a drunk computer! We get to the hotel and the IT wizard is there, ready and waiting. Well done, Foreign Office! Within a minute, he has begun the surely impossible task of mending my laptop. Juliet, Ron and I watch with rapt interest as he starts to dismantle it.

'I think I have ascertained the problem,' he says in a thick South African accent, peering into the bottom of the laptop carcase. 'How did *thees* get in here?'

He points to a pool of Dark and Stormy floating at the bottom of the machine and looks at the three of us questioningly. We all adopt an air of innocence. How indeed? How extraordinary! We all look bemused and shrug.

Our IT expert then proceeds to pour Ron's Dark and Stormy out of the bowels of the laptop and into the basin. What a waste. I could do with one of Ron's specials right now, to steady my nerves. Mr IT then gets out some special cleaning fluid and a cloth. Ten minutes later, lights flash and the computer whirrs! My God, I am overjoyed! The man is not an expert, he is a wizard! I think I am going to kiss him. I have a sudden flashback to Manuel in Seville and manage to restrain myself, just.

The rest of the tour proceeds without incident. Sam continues to spurn me, but a girl can't always have everything she wants when she wants it. Even Princess Diana discovered that with Mr Lineker.

The trip to South Africa, I learn from reading the newspapers, has marked a turn in HRH's fortunes. Suddenly, the British press are no longer being so beastly to him. HRH has even been getting some *positive* reports. Was it the fortunate picture of HRH with the sexy Spice Girls and Nelson Mandela? Have they woken up to the fact that the Prince is a nice man in a difficult job he inherited and is just trying to do his best? Or is it that the Bossette is old news now, so there is no mileage in continuing to attack him on her behalf?

I suspect it is the latter. Am I wrong or is this world we inhabit not just strange but sometimes a little sick?

January 1998

I am feeling particularly delicate now. I am up at Birkhall
helping out HRH while Mummy is in hospital. I fear she may
not be long for this earth. I trust I will get back in time. At
least I have one consolation during this difficult moment,
which is that my status seems to have risen yet further with
the Boss. Bernie the butler told me that, unless HRH says
anything to the contrary, I am to join in with all lunches and
dinners. It is good to be part of the family when you're maybe
about to lose your mother.

Yesterday I helped organise a picnic and I chatted almost
exclusively to Daniel Chatto, a cousin-in-law of HRH
through his wife Sarah. Besides the Chattos, there was the
Queen Mother's retired ghillie Willie Potts and Sarah
Keswick, whose nearby estate covers 70,000 acres, dwarfing
even Balmoral.

I am just doing some correspondence when Bernie comes
into my office.

'It is your brother,' he says. 'He wants you to call him.'

I ring Toby. He tells me the news I really had not wanted to
hear. I put down the telephone. Though I knew that her death
was inevitable, I find myself shocked to the core that it is now
so close.

I enter HRH's office to tell him I have to leave immediately
and apologise to him for the inconvenience. HRH looks
utterly bewildered. He stands up, embraces me and then says,
'But why did they send you up? Surely they must have known
about the state of your poor mother? They must have known
this could happen.'

I don't confess to him that I never told the office that
Mummy was so sick, so the blame is entirely mine. A week

before, I had told Mummy that I was going to stay with her to the end. She affected to be horrified.

'The last thing I want is you moping by my bedside. It will make me much happier knowing you are up at Balmoral. I know you love it up there. You won't do any good hanging round here.'

Those were the last words she said to me.

Seven hours later, I am by her bedside, holding her hand. She slipped into unconsciousness in the early part of the day. Two hours later, she dies. Tears are streaming down my face.

Days later

My family are all quite strong and we are holding each other together. We all knew the end was coming, but however much you brace yourself for it, death is still a shock. My lovely new boyfriend Alastair, who is Australian and the cousin of a famous movie actress whose name I cannot mention, is being wonderfully supportive. Another reason I am coping so well, I think, is my job. Having a boss to whom I am dedicated helps me enormously. Amongst the bouquets of flowers we have received, the biggest was from HRH. It was actually a huge basket. The local florist was astounded at the order.

This morning, I have also received a private handwritten letter on his personal blue-crested notepaper. I quote from one particular passage:

> My biggest concern is whether you got there in time.
> I do hope so. I should also tell you the entire party up
> at Birkhall want to express their profound sorrow and
> I also want to tell you that you were much missed by
> everyone when you had to leave so suddenly.

I find the letter so moving that, if you don't mind, I am going to put down my pen and go upstairs to compose myself. I loved Mummy so much, and it is so wonderful I have not just a strong family where we can all give each other mutual support, but a boss who is sensitive enough to give emotional support too.

June 1998

I am totally broke again! How do I get through so much money? Where does it all go? And it is not as if I have anything to show for it. So, in what is now becoming an annual ritual, I grovel to my father. 'All right,' he sighs and writes out a check for £2,000.

Phew! The problem is that it is coming out of the wedding fund he established for me. Initially, it was substantial. Eight years ago, I could have had a cathedral service in St Paul's, a champagne reception at the Ritz, and a dinner and dance at Annabel's. Unless I get hitched soon, my wedding will be a quiet family do in the Registry Office followed by beer, sandwiches and a knees-up in the local pub.

I hear the whole time of yuppies making a fortune in property and the City. In the old days, such people were called *nouveau riche*. I am *nouveau pauvre*.

But I have decided to do something about my financial situation. To supplement my Palace wages, which have incrementally risen to £287 per week before tax, I have signed up with a company called Azur.

Azur is run by an enterprising woman called Fiona Aitken (now the Countess of Carnarvon) and I am selling her range of well-designed clothes to my friends. Network Marketing is all the rage these days. There is nothing to be embarrassed about at all. Oh yes, there are Lords and Ladies who are selling all kinds of stuff from jewellery and water-filter systems through to bathroom products. Imagine, they give parties in their drawing rooms to sell you toothpaste and shampoo, and they sign you up to do the same! Selling clothes is, I think, slightly more upmarket, and I really need not be ashamed of it. All the same, I wouldn't want HRH or my colleagues to hear about it.

On this particular day, I have driven down the M4 to Somerset to see a surrogate aunt called Lynette who has helped organise a charity drive for the local hospice in the grounds of Binden House, a lovely hotel. In the back are my Azur samples for my stall. Ten per cent of anything I sell goes to the hospice. Twenty per cent goes to me. I am also bringing down a book signed and donated by HRH about his Highgrove garden. It will be the first prize in the raffle.

Lynette tells me that, because of my employment at the Palace, it has been decided that I am going to draw the raffle! *Quelle honneur.*

I arrive at the hotel to be greeted by Lynette. We have a coffee and catch up on the gossip, then I set up my stall. As I do so, I notice some people who are setting up theirs looking at me and whispering to each other. One or two even point at me. What's going on? I feel paranoid. Is it my haircut? Do my shoes not go with my dress? I go back to Lynette to ask her if there is something wrong with my appearance.

'Of course not,' she says.

'Well, why are people pointing and whispering?' I ask.

'It's your Royal connections, dear.'

Goodness, in the absence of a real Royal, I suppose that a Lady Clerk at the Palace is the next best thing.

Flushed and inflated with a sense of my importance, I return to my stall and smile regally at the people around me. Yes, I could get quite used to this. Banished now are my miserable downwardly mobile neuroses. Yes, being part of the Palace definitely raises self-esteem.

I think back over the last ten years and recall how certain people have seemed in awe of me because of my job at the Palace. Of course, it is not just awe. They know you have influence, too. I remember one particularly nice breakfast I was treated to in the East India Club by a distant cousin of HRH who pleaded with me to get the Prince to sign a copy of this same Highgrove book. He wasn't close enough to HRH to ask himself, so he was asking me to do so on his behalf. Imagine that!

Has it affected me? I suppose it must have done. But I am just a Lady Clerk. What on earth must it be like, then, for a real Royal? What a peculiar thing to have everyone around you bobbing and bowing the entire time. Who will ever tell you off for being a prat? All of us can be prats sometimes, even, if like me, we don't care to admit it. Who is there to tell off a Royal?

I think how difficult it must be for HRH because everyone close to him defers and some blatantly suck up. I certainly do. So he must be astonished when journalists disrespectfully attack or mock him in the papers. No wonder he hates the media.

Psychologists say our childhood is the key to problems as adults. It doesn't take brains to work out the source of HRH's adult anxieties. His acute sensitivity to personal attack would have been inevitably seeded at his Scottish boarding school, Gordonstoun, which was incidentally Prince Philip's old school.

Gordonstoun in HRH's day was not just remote – it was tough. Or so a friend told me. It was physical and philistine. Weakness was stamped on. After all, it was started by a man who originally espoused fascist ideals.

While it was, then, a testing place for all the boys, it was particularly brutal for the Boss. Because of his position as heir to the throne, he was socially isolated. Any boy who went up to him to be pleasant was hissed at by the others, so it was a brave fellow pupil who stuck his neck out even to be cordial to him. Imagine being in 'Coventry' the whole time.

Then, of course, there were the field games. What malicious delight those schoolboys took in tackling a Royal limb extra hard. What a thing to boast about – that you 'chopped' the heir to the throne! This, of course, is something Princes William and Harry must suffer, too. Still, they are at Eton. Eton is a better school for the young princes. A school with so many aristocrats can happily accommodate two Royal princes. And, of course, HRH, as I have seen personally, is a loving father, which must be a great source of comfort to his sons.

Do you think HRH had much emotional support in his teenage years? From the tone of the letters I have seen him receive from his parents, I don't think warmth is a word one would pick. I don't think, however, Her Majesty and Prince Philip are personally to blame. It was the way they were brought up themselves. Cuddles are not part of their culture. They knew no better. Imagine having a father who says he would like to be reincarnated as a 'deadly virus', to sort out the world's population problem.

Prince Philip has many qualities, but I challenge his most

loyal supporters to say that empathy is one of them. So, emotionally, HRH's formative teenage years might just as well have been spent in a borstal. And this was a boy who played the cello and loved to paint. They say a tough and beastly childhood is character-making. I think it is more likely to be character-breaking.

Then, in his early 30s, HRH is pressured into marrying a respectable 'virgin' bride only to wake up to a marriage from hell. No wonder he has been so depressed so often.

Ah, I have some interest in my stall. There are clothes to be sold and some money to be made.

Now, four hours later, I am driving back down the motorway. What a great day. We raised £800 for the hospice and I made £92 for myself. Moreover, when I was invited up onto the stand to draw the raffle, I was applauded. I can tell you, I felt very grand indeed!

Not that it ever would, of course, but I can see how this kind of unqualified admiration might go to one's head!

10

Red-Carpet Fever

October 1998

I am up in Scotland again, staying with Phyllida at Tom-na-Gaidh. Phyllida is fantastic and has been most supportive over my grief at the death of Mummy. Besides our secretarial duties, we have both been given the task of Keepers of the Royal Pets. We are both aware of how important pets are to the Royal Family. Inner Palace circles say it was at the Bossette's insistence that HRH got rid of his Labrador, Harvey, to whom he was utterly devoted. Apparently, this did as much to kill his feelings for Diana as her tantrums.

I am charged with looking after Tigger while Phyllida looks after Widgeon, a beautiful highly strung black Labrador adored by Prince William. Tigger is a roly-poly animal and easy to manage; Widgeon is a nightmare. Yesterday, while walking him, he suddenly belted off into the distance and poor Phyllida trekked for hours calling out for him before coming back to the cottage distraught.

'I built a cairn to mark where I last saw him,' she said.

Quite how creating a mound of rocks would help bring back Widgeon, I wasn't sure, but I suppose it was a gesture of a kind. We sat in the kitchen getting increasingly gloomy over the prospect of never seeing the missing Labrador ever again. Then, as the light was fading, Phyllida went out into the lane to call out his name one last time. Joy of joys, two cagoule-clad hikers were coming up to the cottage with Widgeon at their side.

'He attached himself to us,' they explained. 'He is a lovely dog, but we felt he ought to be returned to his rightful owner. Yours was the only home for miles, so we guessed he just had to be yours.'

We never told them the owner's true identity. It is a pity. They should have received some kind of recognition. They saved a young Prince from heartbreak and Phyllida from a nervous breakdown.

The Queen Mother is currently in residence at Birkhall and the old girl – she is ninety-eight – still loves to party. The parties at Birkhall are legendary. The Queen Mother is always escorted by her Equerry. She has a different one every eighteen months.

Traditionally, her Equerry is always young and very, very yummy. Why not? If I was a queen, I would do the same. If I could get away with it, I would have two Equerries and change them on a whim. The Queen Mum also loves to play after-dinner games. Besides charades, her favourite is *Twister*. Would you believe it?

Usually, those of us who stay over at Tom-na-Gaidh never get invited to these hoolies. Out of sight, out of mind, I suppose. But not tonight: We have been summoned to the Ghillies Ball. The Queen Mother will be there with HRH and all his pals.

Phyllida and I are so excited. It is Cinderella all over again.

We arrive at the village-hall building in the grounds of Birkhall. Are there any friends of HRH that I recognise? Oh yes, there is Charlie Palmer-Tomkinson, father of the two celebrated beauties and girls about town, Santa and Tara. There are also many fit young men who have been clambering the Balmoral hills during this stag-shooting season. How sexy these tough physical specimens of Scottish manhood look in their kilts and sporrans.

The band strikes up and the dancing begins. Now, I am not remotely fazed by Scottish dancing, but I am being introduced to a new dance that I have never encountered. Perhaps it is known only to the occupants of Royal palaces? We all stand in a circle holding hands, then dance round to the side like ring-a-ring o' roses. What happens next?

The handsome young ghillie on my right now turns to me and waltzes me round and round, rotating as he does so. Next, he places me between the two men on my left. What fun. Suddenly, I see Charlie Palmer-Tomkinson out of the corner of my eye. He has decided to break the chain and go solo. He is now dancing around with an imaginary woman. Suddenly HRH notices him, too.

'Oh Charlie, you damned fool!' he exclaims.

The disgraced Charlie gets back into line, literally, and the dance continues. I see the Queen Mother being whisked round and round. My God, she is a superstar. Ninety-eight years old! Imagine. Then another handsome, muscular ghillie swings me round into the arms of a familiar face.

My goodness, I have waited for this for more than ten years now! Yes, I am dancing all of a sudden with His Gorgeousness himself, darling HRH! I gaze at him demurely. He looks *so* dashing in his green velvet hunting jacket and his

Lord of the Isles tartan kilt, his crotch accentuated by the Celtic fig leaf of a large, white-fur sporran.

'Oh it's you,' he says cheerfully. 'Still not married yet?'

No, my Lord of the Smiles! Should I ask the same of you? I do have a rather wonderful boyfriend, though. Round and round we go. Let me relish this moment. Posterity, please note that, at this moment, the future King of our dominion is holding me in his strong regal hands. To be anatomically precise, they are on my waist and shoulder. HRH and I waltz and then he rotates. I catch a whiff of exotic aftershave.

This is wonderful. The heir to the throne and I are locked for these brief few seconds in an age-old courting ritual that is the basis, of course, for all Scottish dancing. He now spins me off to the next man. Farewell HRH, until we dance again. If ever. Sigh.

I sit down and savour the moment. Yes, at last, I can truthfully claim I have danced with the Prince of Wales! And think of it, now all my boyfriends can say: I have danced with a girl who has danced with the Prince of Wales, just like in that old song!

November 1998

I am here, just inside the red-carpeted entrance to Buckingham Palace. The occasion is the official 50th birthday party of HRH. My task is to hand out a programme of events to the three hundred guests. I am wearing my 'safe' long black skirt and black lace blouse with a necklace, which has beautiful green stones, given to me by my godmother.

'Wear it with white, dear,' she told me.

Alas, I have no white outfits. Is it wrong to wear it with black, I wonder? Surely the occasion of the Prince of Wales's

50th surmounts such aesthetic objections.

Because there is still some official *froideur* over the role of Camilla in recent Royal upsets, my friend, the Royal mistress, is not making an appearance. Instead, she and HRH's influential Valet, Michael Fawcett, are arranging another party for him at Highgrove.

To my mind, the guest list for HRH's Buckingham Palace party is the weirdest you can imagine. The Boss has instructed his office that the Chairmen or Chairwomen of all his charities, and of any organisation which has helped him or one of his charities, is to be invited – but they cannot bring their spouse or partner. The principle has even been extended to the showbiz guests, though one or two must have stuck their necks out, protested and got their way because I see the likes of Mr and Mrs Ben Elton on the list.

I can imagine the rows the invitation must have created in households around the country when one spouse had to tell his other half they were not invited! To put it crudely, therefore, HRH's 50th is a singles party. Well, as a helper who will doubtless have to mingle, that suits me just fine. After all, I am single and pretty. All those detached men should have an unattached woman to talk to.

As the visitors stream through, I spot clusters of celebrities, famed stars of television and film. It feels like a night at the oscars. And I am part of it all. How thrilling! Rowan Atkinson, Emma Thompson, Ben Elton, Lenny Henry, Stephen Fry, Dawn French and Ben Kingsley all stream past me, all within touching distance.

I suddenly see that hilarious impersonator I watch on television, whenever I can, who takes off all today's politicians. I don't understand all of his jokes, but those I do are *so* funny. This is my chance to make contact with a major TV icon. I bustle forward and fix him with a flashing smile.

'Sir, would you care for a programme?'

'Thank you,' he says.

'I *love* your show,' I say, batting my eyelids slightly flirtatiously.

He smiles at me slightly bemused, nods and carries on upstairs. All that talent, I sigh. How modest he is, I think. Then suddenly I blush. Oh my God. What an idiot I am! I have mistaken the former Prime Minister John Major for Rory Bremner, the impersonator!

The guests filter upstairs and I can now hear the party in full swing. So, up I go. What else am I supposed to do? Go home? There must be something I can assist with. I must go upstairs and do what I can.

What an amazing sight to behold. In each of the gilt-and-mirrored State Rooms there are quartets and musical ensembles playing classical music. Footmen in full regalia – black tail jackets with red and gold edging – ply the assembled throng with champagne. Jugglers and conjurers wander round performing their stunts.

I gaze around and recognise the towering figure of the great boxer and pantomime performer Frank Bruno. Good for you, Frank, and good for HRH for inviting you, though what the two of you might have in common is hard to fathom.

Another incongruous guest is Alex Ferguson, the red-faced football manager of Manchester United, the most successful football team in England right now. Whenever I see him on television, he always looks as if he is about to explode. He is wearing the same expression right now. Perhaps he only has this one expression? Still, the angry expression must be useful for keeping his prima donna footballers in line. I can imagine that handsome Mr Beckham can be quite a handful at times, especially now he is boosted with extra confidence from having the gorgeous Posh of Spice Girls fame as his girlfriend!

Then I see one of my heroines, the *Absolutely Fabulous* actress Joanna Lumley. Now, there is 'posh' for you. How old is she? Who knows? Who cares? What a combination of style and beauty! And I read that she is really clever, too. Yes, she is definitely one of nature's princesses. Now, if HRH wanted to marry again and become truly popular with the public, Joanna would be the girl! Oh yes.

Next to her is the Prime Minister Tony Blair. At least I think it is – if it is not, it must be Rory Bremner. I am getting confused. And not far from him is the Leader of the Opposition, William Hague.

I remember being told that politicians are usually brought down either by a money or sex scandal: Tony Blair has said that none of that will happen in *his* government. That is all very well, but human nature is what it is. There is bound to be *some* politician in his Cabinet getting into trouble.

Oh and there is John Prescott talking to David Blunkett, the blind but highly able Minister of something or other. His famous dog, Lucy, is beside him. Mr Blunkett is from Sheffield, I read somewhere, and his rise to national prominence has been inspiring, especially given his blindness. At least, I think, with his unfortunate disability we can be confident there isn't any chance of *him* getting into any trouble for naughtiness, is there?

Having scanned the list of guests in the programme, I am aware there are lots of media types in the party as well, including people from what are known as the 'red tops', whose coverage of HRH's personal life often makes him upset and sometimes incandescent with rage. It seems jolly odd to me that HRH should warmly welcome such people at his 50th birthday. You are supposed only to have friends at such a milestone, not your critical enemies.

But I suppose that is the influence of HRH's artful spin master Mark Bolland, who is here with his boyfriend Guy Black. Mark knows all about these things. I suppose he is calculating one or two will start to be nice to HRH, now he has invited them to his birthday. All the same, it must be hard for the Boss to swallow.

Suddenly, there is a tap on my shoulder. I swing round. It is 'Mr T-J', as we fondly know him in Shropshire. He is here because of his big connection with the Ironbridge Gorge Museum Trust. He introduces me to two friends from his days at Cambridge University. Caught up in the festive atmosphere, we are soon laughing and swapping stories.

Suddenly, HRH is amongst us. He looks at me slightly surprised. 'What are you doing here, Sarah?'

All at once, I feel terribly embarrassed. Here I am technically working, and yet to his eyes I am having a good time joining in the party. Can I help it if I personally know one of his guests? What am I supposed to do? Shun him? Does he not know I was asked to help? Was I really supposed to go home after handing out the programmes? Why did no one tell me? Is my status here at Buckingham Palace different to that at Balmoral, where I am made part of the family?

HRH moves along.

I feel crushed. The joy has flown. Perhaps I should go home now. I then play back in my mind what HRH said. No, his tone wasn't hostile or critical. It was matter-of-fact. Perhaps I am being oversensitive to the point of paranoia; nonetheless, I can't help feeling strangely wounded. I suppose that I remain in a gray zone, a no-man's-land between staff and friend.

Mr T-J and his pals sense something is amiss. One of them puts his arm around me. They are determined, it appears, that I am not going to be deflated. Mr T-J's pal now takes off his gold-and-burgundy striped tie and presents it to me to make me an Honourary Member of the Hawk Club from his Cambridge days.

Hell, I might as well make the most of it. So I party through to 11.30, the tie wrapped round me. Ever the perfect gentleman, Mr T-J drops me off at Moylan Road in his chauffeur-driven limousine. Anyway, I have given HRH for his birthday a modest but, I hope, thoughtful present of my favourite book, William Boyd's *An Ice-Cream War.*

Three days later, a beautifully composed handwritten letter arrives. It is from HRH! He writes to say how touched he is by my present and how much it helped make his day. That's wonderful, I think. And then another thought strikes me. The poor fellow must have had to write hundreds of such letters. I find myself greatly moved that he has bothered to make mine a priority. I read it three or four times, dab my eyes, then carefully put it away in my drawer.

March 1999

It is 10.30 in the morning and I am inside Buckingham Palace standing in red-carpeted line outside the Throne Room. Inside are seated five hundred guests waiting to see their friend or relatives receiving an honour. A military band serenades everyone from the minstrels' gallery. No, this time I am not helping out!

Let me go back ten weeks to the Christmas break. I am in Cornwall, staying in the family cottage, when my brother Toby comes through with the *Daily Telegraph*. He cannot believe it, and frankly neither can I. His sister (me!) is in the New Year's Honours List!

Can you believe it? I am to receive an MVO!

What is an MVO, you might ask? Let me tell you. MVO stands for Member of the Victorian Order, and it is traditionally awarded to Officials who have given more than ten years of service to the Royal Household. In rank, MVO stands above an OBE and MBE. Now, mathematically, I am in line to receive an MVO, but all too often many members of staff have to wait fifteen years. I have received mine on the nail. Clearly, I have friends in high places.

Who else is being honoured with me this year? The names I recognise are all from the world of showbiz: Lenny Henry, Dusty Springfield, Roger Moore, Nigel Hawthorne and Robert Carlyle. I realise that Robert Carlyle is an excellent actor, but I can't help wondering if the Honours Committee might have been slightly influenced by the fact that *The Full Monty*, in which he stars (albeit magnificently), is one of HRH's absolutely favourite movies?

Within days of the announcement, I receive a telegram and a letter from HRH congratulating me, though whether he has had anything to do with the swiftness of the honour, I am not sure. I receive thirty other letters of congratulation. I am giddy with the huge thrill of it all.

Every year, twenty-two Investitures are held: One at the Palace of Holyroodhouse in Edinburgh, one at Cardiff Castle and twenty at Buckingham Palace. Up to one hundred and fifty recipients attend each Investiture. I am going to one at BP. For the ceremony, you are allowed to invite up to three people. I go for the full quota and have invited Daddy, my brother Toby and my hunky boyfriend Alastair.

For this most important day, Daddy has generously opened up his chequebook and I am consequently wearing a pale powder-blue Louis Feraud skirt and jacket, and a matching hat from Fortnum and Mason. I have followed the Investiture instructions and have placed a hook on the lapel so the medal can be slipped on, which saves Her Majesty the trouble of pinning it on. However, today Her Majesty is not officiating due to a clash in her diary; instead, she has been replaced by HRH! Yes, it will be His Gorgeousness who pins on my medal. Swoon!

I have read the booklet they give us all, so I can tell you in advance how the ceremony proceeds. It goes like this: HRH enters the ballroom attended by two Gurkha Orderly Officers – a tradition started by Queen Victoria in 1876. On duty on the dais, the technical name for the Throne's platform, are five members of the Queen's Body Guard of the Yeoman of the Guard. They were created in 1485 by King Henry VII after his victory at the Battle of Bosworth Field.

I remember that battle because it was the start of a new Royal Family, the Tudors, who did for the last of the Plantagenets in the person of Richard III, supposedly a baddie who murdered the two young princes in the Tower. There have been quite a few Royal families since. Her Majesty's family, I learned at school, originated in Germany, which my history master said disturbed more than a few thoughtful people when we were fighting the Germans to the death in the last two world wars.

But I digress. Back to the ceremony. Four Gentlemen Ushers are on duty to look after the recipients and their guests. Today, these are Lord Camoys, Major General Sir Simon Cooper, Lieutenant Commander Lavery and Lieutenant Colonel Anthony Mather.

All the recipients are lined up outside in a long corridor while the four hundred-odd guests watch the proceedings in the Throne Room. The ceremony is in senior order, starting with the Most Honourable Order of the Bath, the recipient of which receives a Knighthood and is made a Knight Commander. All of us hear the National Anthem, which is being played by the Orchestra of the Scots Guards. So we know the Investiture is about to begin.

Through the National Anthem we all stand to attention. Never have any of us, I think, stood more proudly and patriotically. After all, we are about to be anointed as 'Members of the Establishment'.

The orchestra continues to play its way through its repertoire. Right now, they have moved on to *'El Capitan'*, a march by Sousa. The first recipient enters: Vice-Admiral Ian Garnett. On the dais is HRH, standing next to the Lord Chamberlain (Lord Camoys). I then hear the Lord Chamberlain's voice calling out his name and his achievement.

The Admiral proceeds to kneel on the velvet Investiture stool. Then, with the sword that HRH's grandfather, George VI, used when Duke of York as Colonel of the Scots Guards, HRH taps the Admiral lightly on the left shoulder. Arise Vice-Admiral *Sir* Ian Garnett. The Admiral then receives a badge on a sash and a star, which HRH takes from a velvet cushion held by the Master of the Household, Sir Simon Cooper. I try to imagine how the Admiral feels. Elation and pride. Will I feel the same?

Two Knights from the Foreign office then follow. Next is Diana Collins, soon to be Dame Diana Collins, whom I read has done great work in South Africa for human rights. Another three Knights go through to be honoured: a musician, a pharmacologist and a molecular biologist.

Next follow Companions then Commanders of the British Empire. Cripes, it is me soon! I see my name on the program along with the charismatic Emmanuel Amadi, a leading light of the Prince's Trust, who stands behind me. Today, he and I are being made Members of the Royal Victorian Order! I still can't believe it: a girl from Shropshire who, by pure fluke, landed this job of Lady Clerk for HRH through Bernadette of Bond Street. I have to pinch myself to remind myself this is not a dream.

As the line shortens, I read more of the achievements and dedication of my fellow recipients. I begin to feel awed and chastened. Ahead and behind me stand some of the finest citizens in the United Kingdom. I feel especially humbled by those who have devoted their lives to helping the unfortunates in society – the disabled, the mentally afflicted and the sick – those whom the gods have given a rotten hand in the poker game of life. As the Orchestra of the Scots Guards strikes up Purcell's *Abdelazar*, my mood becomes introspective and self-examining.

Here, amidst 'the Great and the Good', I cannot help but feel a bit of an impostor. After all, I am certainly not great, and do I really qualify as being good? My work is undemanding, I get invited everywhere because of my Palace status, and I make no personal sacrifices. While I get the job done, my timekeeping is not what it should be. Sexually, I might be considered wanton, and I am developing a cunning bordering on the deceitful.

Example: I wangled it with a friend in the office that I attend this ceremony rather than the one to which I was originally designated, where Her Majesty would hand out the honours. Her Majesty is a fine and indeed remarkable woman. She is the nation's sovereign, but she is not 'the Boss', not mine, anyway. Yes, I naughtily pulled strings in order to attend one of the few honours ceremonies where HRH is doing the 'decorating', the Palace term for putting on a medal.

To say I am not good is perhaps, on reflection, being a bit harsh on myself. Yes, my timekeeping *is* bad, but I unfailingly carry out all my tasks. As for enjoying sex, which I do, that is neither good nor bad. Morals don't enter into it. It is more about getting lucky or unlucky. Office cunning doesn't make me bad either, but over these last ten years I have certainly shed much of my original innocence. Yes, I am not good through and through, but I am good enough.

My turn comes and I enter the Throne Room, my heart beating hard. The minuet I recognised by Mozart has finished. The orchestra then breaks into the next piece. I cannot believe it. It is the score for *Gigi*, one of my absolute favourite movies, where Maurice Chevalier sings 'Zank evern for leetal girls'. It is the story, in case you don't know, of an enchanting, innocent schoolgirl in Paris who is destined, through lack of money and the plotting of her aunts, to become a high-class tart. Happily, Gigi ends up marrying a society prince. I can't help but be slightly unnerved that *Gigi*'s theme tune is being played at the very moment the Royal Prince bestows a medal on me. I trust this is not one of HRH's little jokes.

As I walk slowly towards the dais, I briefly scan the sea of faces. But, with so many, it is impossible to pick out my supportive little band. Drat. Never mind. I approach HRH. Damn it, the emotion in me is overwhelming. I fear I may cry. Get a grip, Sarah, growls my inner nanny.

I take a deep breath. Now before me is His Magnificence. He is in full dress uniform, in dark blue with gold braid and ropes. Darling HRH, how magically handsome you look as Colonel of the Welsh Guards. I catch his eye, bend my knee and curtsey.

In a ritual handed down through the centuries, the Lord Chamberlain now speaks. The voice of the holder of this historic and ancient post bellows in this great Throne Room of Buckingham Palace: 'Miss Sarah Goodall, for services to the Household of His Royal Highness the Prince of Wales to be a Member of the Royal Victorian Order!'

Everyone in the room applauds. I am about to choke. But in my mind's eye is inner nanny. She is telling me to be steady.

HRH, my future King, then takes from the burgundy-red velvet cushion proffered him by Sir Simon Cooper the brass four-inch cross with blue, white and red ribbons. He studiously proceeds to place the cross on the hook of my lapel, an inch above my palpitating heart. My eyes at this very moment are moist with emotion. I look into his beautiful blue eyes, which, as ever, are twinkling. He opens his mouth and speaks.

'Oh Sarah, I can't believe it. You've been with me now ten years!'

I find myself giggling inadvertently. 'Thank you so *much*,

Your Royal Highness. I couldn't have managed to stay so long if I wasn't working for someone so great as you!'

I want to burble on that I am devoted to him and want to remain in his service for ever. But inner nanny stops me, thank goodness. An emotional declaration like that would undoubtedly be embarrassing.

So, summoning all my self-control, I smile demurely and move on. I then reflect on HRH's smile. It is difficult to interpret sometimes. If I was being at all paranoid, I might just imagine that it reflected a sense of resigned irritation. After all, few Lady Clerks stay as long as *ten* years! Was there a touch of sarcasm in his observation about my length of service?

Inner nanny cuts in. Stop all this neurotic nonsense! This is your moment of triumph. You don't want to mar it with any self-critical introspection. Relish the moment, girl. This day you are a queen!

The path is cleared for the next recipient, Emmanuel Amadi. Emmanuel, old chum, this is *your* moment and you have truly earned it. Enjoy!

I find my band of men and sit with them for the remaining ninety minutes of the ceremony. We all listen to *'Born Free'*, two excerpts from Tchaikovsky's *6th Symphony, Fiddler on the Roof* and *'O Sole Mio'*. It is wonderful music and enhances my state of joy.

How do I describe what I feel? Elated is the word I should use, but the feeling soaring through me is levels *above* elated. Elated is inadequate. Elated is when you score a goal in hockey, or score with a man you fancy. But I have scored an honour, I realise, for life. My head is not in the clouds but the stratosphere. I am not just with the stars; I am now one of them.

The ceremony is completed while the orchestra concludes with a favourite of mine, and not just because it evokes naughty images: a Highland Fling called *'Swing o' the Kilt'*.

All of us, decorated recipients and friends and family, now troop out. The Goodall party then jumps into a taxi and heads off to the Cavalry and Guards Club in Piccadilly. Daddy has booked the Balaclava Room. There are thirty of us for lunch and I sit at the head of the table. There is Karen, Eddie the Entrepreneur, my friends Tony and Pam from the Palace, and, of course, Alastair and Toby.

Having had this amazing honour ceremoniously bestowed on me just hours before, I fear that I and one or two of the party celebrate with an unfettered exuberance that is not entirely in keeping with my newly exalted position of Sarah Lucy Georgina Goodall MVO. Personally, I blame the port.

We stumble from the club hours later. Alastair is so plastered he ends up horizontal on the taxi floor for the journey back home, with the flowers from the lunch table strewn all around him. Toby and I are barely less disgraceful. We have to drag Alastair up the stairs to bed.

Yes, I know. It is shameful behavior but, to be fair, it is not every day that you have a medal pinned on you by your future King.

May 1999

A love quandary: for the last six weeks, things have been going wrong with Alastair. I appreciate his qualities, but we are not connecting properly any more. Moreover, I have met another man, whom I find mesmerising. He is called Carlo. He is Italian. Where Alastair is large, Carlo is small. It is odd.

I never go for in between. With me it is either the gorilla or the ferret. Right now, I am moving into ferret mode.

The problem is that, at this moment, I am with my gorilla. I think Alastair has been sensing these last few weeks that he is about to lose me, so he has gone to enormous lengths to win me over with an extravagant gesture. At this very minute, we are drinking champagne together in a fabulous suite in The Ritz in Paris. How generous of him is that? And it is no expense spared. A vase stands before me with red roses in full bloom. The bed is a four-poster and the furnishings are delicate and feminine. Moreover, we are in the very rooms reserved for Dodi Fayed and Princess Diana on the night of their terrible deaths – at least that's what one of the porters told us. Having this suite is so romantic. But another part of me thinks it is pretty spooky, too. It is eerie to think that this is where the Bossette spent her last day and early evening.

I send that morbid thought to mental Siberia and attempt to enjoy the moment in hand. But I am finding it hard. Come on, Sarah, act the part and you will soon get into it. Remember, you are staying in a top suite in one of the best hotels in the most romantic city in the world. Your suitor is clearly in love and right now is telling you that you are the most beautiful woman in the world.

I sip more champagne. Perhaps alcohol will help. Alastair comes over to the bed and places his hand on my lap. Oh dear. A month ago, even a week, I would have been delighted, rewarding him with more physical action than a can-can dancer on Spanish Fly.

What is it? Something has changed. My love for him seems to have evaporated like so much springtime mist. Is it the lure of the Italian ferret? Is it the mournful ghosts of Dodi and Di?

Or have I realised that our time together has come to an end? What should I do? He tries to kiss me. I find myself pushing him back.

'Later, darling, later!'

I feel such a fraud. I take another gulp of champagne. Poor Alastair. He thinks I am doing this on purpose to make the moment when it happens all the more explosive. The way I am feeling, however, is that there will be no moment. I am the girl who is not going to deliver. How did I get myself into this situation? How the hell am I going to get myself out of it?

Alastair is trying to kiss me once more. Again, I turn my head to the side. He pours more champagne into my glass. I get up and move to the window.

'What a fantastic view!' I say dramatically, staring out intently.

'Yes,' he repeats, coming alongside me. 'Fantastic!'

We are like two sad poseurs acting out some hackneyed clip from a movie. Fantastic views are the furthest thing from our minds right now. In truth, Alastair is thinking of every stratagem to get me out of my clothes and into bed, and I am thinking of every trick to stay in my clothes and out of bed.

Last night when we arrived, it was easy.

'Darling, I am so tired right now' and 'Sweetheart, we have all day tomorrow!'

That was sufficient to put him off. The morning was fine too. I was up and dressed before he had even woken. So, after breakfast, we went for a walk through the beautiful streets of this romantic city. We stop and have a leisurely lunch in a lovely brasserie. How to kill the afternoon? How better than a visit to the Bond Street of Paris, Rue du Faubourg Saint-Honoré? Heaven.

We peer into the exquisite emporiums of high fashion. I cannot resist it. I just have to go into Gucci to ogle their latest offerings. Suddenly, I see it! It is the bag I have been dreaming of for months – the Gucci classic and currently all the rage: padded black leather with a gold chain. I look at it yearningly. Don't be stupid, Sarah. It costs £700 and, remember, you are on Palace wages! The next thing I know is that Alastair has pulled out his credit card.

'Oh, Alastair, you shouldn't. Please don't. You are too kind.'

There is no stopping him. It appears to give him so much pleasure. Who am I to deny him his joy? So there I am, holding the bag of my dreams. It is mine!

Now we are back in the suite and Alastair understandably wants his oats. My gorilla's arms are around me. Come on, girl, just act it out! Get it over and done with. He has been your lover for over a year now. What's one more time? I swing round to kiss him but, instead, I instinctively avoid his mouth, bury my face in his shoulders and cuddle him. Hell, this is really, really difficult!

I disengage from his enveloping arms, then walk purposefully to the television. Well, I have done the view, haven't I? What else is there left? I switch it on. Next thing I know, he is cuddling me from behind.

Oh no! He is trying to undress me. I find myself wriggling unhelpfully. Come on, Sarah. He has bought you a Gucci bag, for goodness sake! Just think of a little carnal sacrifice as a 'thank you'! What's the matter with you?

By now, Alastair has arrived at the same conclusion.

'Sarah, what's the matter with you?'

I turn round. He looks baffled and angry. I feel so sorry for him. But I just can't do it.

'I am sorry, Alastair, but I can't!'

'What the hell do you mean, you *can't*!'

'I can't. That's all.'

There is a five-second pause. Alastair stands there looking shocked. I cannot bear this any longer.

'I am going to pack my bag and leave right now.'

'What?'

'Please don't try and stop me, Alastair. I don't want any fuss.'

'Any fuss?'

As I pull out my clothes from the wardrobe, Alastair stands there and shakes.

'Well, I think you can at least give me back my signet ring,' he says.

I look down at his sweet gift of the beautiful signet ring engraved with his family coat of arms. It is pure gold and probably the closest thing I have had to an engagement ring. I twist it off my finger and hand it to him. Silently, he takes it. He then walks to the open window and flings it out into the night air. What a silly gesture! What a waste!

'The bag, please.'

Fair enough. I felt a fraud taking it anyway. I empty out the contents onto the bed. Thank goodness I didn't throw my old bag out. I hand the iconic Gucci handbag back to him, saying nothing. He slowly places it carefully in the cupboard then looks down at the carpet. Phew. At least he doesn't throw *that* from the window.

Within an hour, my flight booking has been moved forward. It is now approaching dawn. The stately streets of Paris are deserted and I am on my way by taxi to Charles de

Gaulle airport, alone, leaving the wretched Alastair at the Ritz in Diana and Dodi's suite to try and make sense of what has happened.

In my broken French, I tell my driver to drive very, very slowly though the car tunnels.

June 1999

What a life! I am standing right now on a boat that is cruising down the Thames. It is a warm and sunny day. We have just gone under Putney Bridge and I catch sight of the lovely Mall of Chiswick to my right. HRH is right next to me. With us are the assembled loonies of the Architectural and Planning Group. I point out to HRH the famous Dove Pub.

How interesting, I think. He has probably not drunk with friends in a pub since his student days at Cambridge. And he can't really, can he? By dint of his position, he can't do the kind of normal things the rest of us take for granted. Imagine, he only has to say or do one unusual thing and he will suffer for it the next day with some lurid headline and unkind commentary. He learnt that early on in his life, at just fourteen. His Protection Officer took him for a discreet drink in a pub in the Scottish Highlands while boarding at Gordonstoun.

'What will you have to drink?' asked the barman.

'A cherry brandy,' replied our future King, enjoying this brief respite from the rigours of his boarding school.

The next day it was all over the newspapers. The Cherry Brandy Scandal! The heir to the throne consuming alcohol illegally! The Protection Officer took the rap for the misdemeanour and was fired. But the Protection Officer was more than HRH's bodyguard. He was the young Prince's friend, and a comfort at that unpleasant stage of his life. It is said the Boss has never quite forgiven those responsible for the decision to sack him.

But these are happier days. I watch him gaze contentedly at the river view. Then I see him joining in conversation with the lovely Candida Lycett-Green, who helped write the book on the garden at Highgrove that has been such a success. HRH does enjoy his cultured company.

I reflect for a while on my own activities. I am not really a cultured girl at all. I like parties and I like sport. Because I work at the Palace, I get invited to all sorts of openings and events. Naturally, I go to everything in which the Prince's Trust is involved, like movie premieres and concerts. One of my fondest memories is of a concert where HRH sat in the Royal Box at the Odeon in Leicester Square. He tried to affect an air of hip cool, tapping his hand uncomfortably on his knee as Robbie Williams gyrated on stage, clutching his groin and thrusting his pelvis. It didn't work. Royalty and rock don't go together. But, hey, HRH tried, bless him.

But my favourite events are the grand shop openings. I virtually live off the goody bags that are so generously donated to their A-List invitees. Oh yes, to those who have much, *more* will be given! Somehow I don't think that is really right. Doesn't the Bible say the opposite should be the case? But it is the way the world is right now. And though I appear to be solvent, the truth, as we know, is very different.

The other day, I did some calculations. How very depressing. It seems that I have to give up hunting, which is such fun in the winter months. The fact that I have yet to be out on a hunt where a fox has been caught is beside the point. The pursuit is such a thrill. But a day's hunting costs, all told, about £315, and that is doing it on the cheap. I will also now have to watch polo matches, rather than play in them, to save money.

Thank goodness I still have tennis, sailing and skiing. For the first, I have the lovely Christopher Cole, who organises tennis matches at The Queen's Club, and for the other two I have as my Patron the Hoist King Fred Vonck, who keeps a yacht on the south coast and a flat in Verbier.

But these are not the only sports I have tried. The other day while up at Balmoral I was invited by a friend, who lives near Ullapool, to go stalking with him on his family estate.

Would I care to try my hand at shooting a stag? Oh dear. Like every other girl my age, I was brought up in the cinematic world of Walt Disney inhabited by sweet animals with human emotions who can talk. Now is the moment of truth. Could I kill Bambi? One of the party then explains that there are too many stags right now and some *have* to be shot. So why don't you do it, he says. It is like killing a cow, he adds. The meat is there to be eaten.

So, with trepidation, I join him for the stalking. Up the hills we climb. The views are breathtaking. A herd is spotted and we drop to our stomachs, then wriggle through the heather. And there I see the stag that the keeper has singled out for me. It has a switch antler, which I am told is very dangerous. The rifle is handed to me. I take careful aim at his heart and fire. Bang! His legs give way and he drops.

Soon my friend, the keeper and I are standing over the dead stag. I am heartily congratulated for my clean shot. The gralloch is performed while I stand there in a state of shock, gazing at this creature whose life I have just taken. Think of the venison, I keep telling myself. Think of the meals this beast will provide.

All of a sudden, the keeper comes up to me and puts his blood-soaked hands on my face. I jump back a foot. What on earth does he think he is doing?

'It's the ritual for the first kill,' says my friend.

Well, I mustn't be churlish. This is a Highland tradition and I must respect it. All the same, a girl of my background usually expects her face to be covered by Estée Lauder, not stag blood.

Later that afternoon, I drive back to Birkhall. The thing is that although HRH and Willy Potts are creatures of the country, a lot of the staff, including some of the Lady Clerks, are quite sniffy and disapproving about stalking and shooting. Why on earth does HRH employ people with such sensibilities, I ask myself? So, though I feel excited about my first kill, I tell myself to be quiet about it. Not just modest but silent as well.

I park the car and enter the house. A butler and one of the Lady Clerks stop dead in their tracks.

'My God, are you all right!'

What on earth is wrong with them?

'I am fine. What's the matter?'

'It looks like you are covered in blood!'

Oh no! I have forgotten to wash it off. How do I get myself out of this one?

'Oh you know how it is,'I say breezily. 'It's just one of those Highland traditions.' I leave the two of them open-mouthed while I head to the bathroom to scrub off the last vestiges of my slaughtered stag.

Someone calls out and I am broken out of my reverie. We have arrived at Twickenham. Our boat pulls up at a jetty and HRH, his retinue of loonies and I step out to be greeted by a local councillor. We have come for a special guided tour of Strawberry Hill, a fantasy Gothic castle created by Horace Walpole, youngest son of former prime minister Robert Walpole. The building was completed in 1792 and is now regarded as an architectural treasure.

The Councillor proceeds with the tour. Sometimes, though, he has to stop because certain members of the APG take a lingering interest in some of the rooms and fall behind. I am instructed to find them and bring them back. Really, it is worse than taking out a party of ill-disciplined children.

Fondant Fancy has come up with the idea of strawberries and cream at the end of the tour of Strawberry Hill. And strawberries and cream are nothing without champagne, are they? So we have half a case, at least, of chilled bubbly. The APG does love its booze.

So, at the end of this delightful afternoon, we are tucking into the strawberries and swilling back the champagne. HRH fills my glass, again. I see his eyes twinkle. I understand now. My mind goes back to the early days at Sandringham, where he poured me lethal gin and tonics. One of the Prince's little delights is seeing others getting tiddly.

Very well, HRH, I shall not disappoint you; but if I end up with a serious drink problem, I shall blame you as the one who set me on that path.

The cars have now arrived to take us back. The day is done. The heir to the throne has enjoyed himself. So, by the looks of it, has the APG. And so, most certainly, have I.

Hic.

August 1999

I am sitting at my desk in St James's Palace, having just returned from Balmoral. Camilla was there this time, and on one of the walks she had a bit of trouble keeping up with HRH, who was chatting to me about architecture. Possibly it is all those cigarettes she smokes. I still have an image of her panting fifteen paces behind us. It is a real bore because they have moved me out of my secluded basement haven and I am up with the other Lady Clerks, some of whom are right harpies, though there are other new recruits. The beautiful, black-clad Belinda Harley was one of them, though she left recently, which is a pity because she was fun, theatrical and great to have around.

As one of just two Lady Clerks with an MVO, I definitely feel I am one of the top girls round here, and if one or two of the new girls think I am a bit grand, they can lump it. I have done my ten years of Royal service and, stuff the T-shirt, I have the medal to prove it!

Before Geraldine left, she warned me to 'beware of red-carpet fever'. Red-carpet fever is an affliction caused by working at the Palace so long that you think you are a bit Royal yourself. I certainly don't think I am at all Royal, but I really do think that, given my seniority and my MVO, one or two people round here could be slightly more respectful.

I am helping to break-in new recruit Elaine Day. Like Mark Bolland, her appointment here is breaking the mould. We have had girls from Essex like Victoria working here, and we have had a cockney receptionist, but Elaine is only the second coloured girl – or, to use the correct phrase, 'only the second girl from an ethnic background' – to work here in the office. Personally, the liberal in me is delighted. Everyone should have the opportunity to rise wherever their talent naturally takes them. Isn't that what the Prince's Business Trust promotes, helping especially those from poorer backgrounds?

Elaine is methodical, if sometimes a bit slow. Sometimes I do get exasperated, having to explain everything in detail to her, as I am used to working super-fast. But, all credit to the girl, she is learning the ropes and I take many tasks here for granted. I just wonder, though, how she will fit in. This is a fun office, or at any rate it is supposed to be, and while I have had one or two giggles with Elaine when we have gone out to lunch with the waspish Mark, she does seem a bit solemn – politically very correct. I am therefore always scared of saying the wrong thing in front of her. The first coloured girl who worked here was the delightful Lizzy Norris, who went on to marry an Equerry of the Queen Mother. In spite of her occasional temper, she fit in well because she was so relaxed as well as amusing.

Talking of lunch with Mark, I must confess to feeling a little foolish the other day when I learned that Mark's Club, the discreet members' restaurant off Berkeley Square, is not named after my boss Mr Bolland but Mark Birley. Mark, for those who don't know, is a grand man of society who named his famous nightclub Annabel's after his former wife, the daughter of the 8th Marquess of Londonderry. Annabel left him for the sexually irresistible tycoon Sir Jimmy Goldsmith, and we all know what they say about him in Palace circles!

I am currently finishing off some correspondence about the Elfin Oak. The Elfin Oak is a tree stump in Kensington Gardens on which someone, ages ago, carved images of elves that inspired J.M. Barrie in his writing of *Peter Pan*. More recently, it was defaced by some disrespectful yobs who probably did not know about the story of this fabled stump and would not, I venture, have given a hoot even if they had.

Two years ago, while I was taking notes on the APG, 'any other business' loomed on the agenda and one of the committee members produced a letter from the great humourist and author Spike Milligan about the plight of this vandalised magical stump. HRH worships Spike. He famously took Irish citizenship because he refused to take the oath of allegiance. HRH remonstrated, reasonably pointing out that even *he* had to take the oath of allegiance, urging Spike to think again.

'Yes,'replied Spike, 'but it's *your* mother, isn't it? You don't get board and lodging at Buckingham Palace if you don't swear an oath.' He once replied, when asked to describe his fondest memories, 'When I look back, it is not really *The Goons*. It is of a girl called Julia with enormous breasts.' Wistfully I wonder if my boobs might ever inspire such devotion.

Anyway, Spike's letter was seized upon and HRH swung into action. Frankly, it is very much to the Boss's credit that his affection for Spike is so unqualified. Five years ago, Spike was on television receiving a reward in front of an audience of millions when a letter of tribute from HRH was read out. All of a sudden, Spike interrupted, loudly, calling HRH a 'little grovelling bastard'! The newspapers were full of it.

Publicly, HRH put on a staunch show of not caring in the slightest. Privately, I can tell you, he was rather hurt. Who of us wouldn't be? None of us could quite believe it in the Palace when a fax came through the next morning from Spike, which read: 'I suppose a knighthood is out of the question now?'

Two years after Spike's clarion call to save the stump from

further vandalism, a group of us attended an unveiling ceremony in Kensington Gardens. A beautiful wrought-iron cupola, like some birdcage, had been created over the Elfin oak, thereby protecting the precious carved fairies for eternity.

Who was there at the occasion? There were a few of the architectural loonies, Mark Bolland, Spike, HRH and myself. All of a sudden, a huge limousine drew up and out stepped the billionaire recluse and philanthropist John Paul Getty. He unsteadily hobbled towards us with the aid of a walking stick and a beautifully coiffured, glamourous wife (I think). I later learned that Mr Getty had put up the money at HRH's request.

And there the three of them stood, the richest man in Britain, the funniest and the grandest, solemnly looking in appreciation at a tree stump they had joined forces to preserve. It is a picture I won't forget.

What I also won't forget is the wonderful, forthright response I received from HRH to one of my memos on the benighted oak stump. His Gorgeousness scribbled that what was really needed was a corrective thwack to be delivered to the posteriors of the vandals who desecrated it! Quite right! How obvious! How wise!

And how terribly sad that if he ever ventured such an opinion publicly the politically correct brigade would come storming out in high dudgeon fulminating against him for advocating sadistic corporal punishment. The truth is that I don't know a single sensible soul who doesn't in their heart agree with him. At such times, I feel a communion with the Boss. I long to tell the world how wonderful he is and what a great future King it is that awaits us. But, frankly, who would listen to me?

Suddenly, I am called into my boss Mark's office. I bring in my notepad and pen, assuming that he wants to dictate a letter.

'Sit down,' he says to me in a level tone, like a headmaster about to address an errant pupil.

This is odd. Mark has never spoken to me like this before. Oh dear. Has he something dreadful to report? He must have. Probably because I am such a senior Lady Clerk, he wants to break it to me first. I do hope that no one in the Royal Family has died or anything. I brace myself for the worst.

'I am sorry to report to you, Sarah, that I have had word from Balmoral. The opinion is that your behaviour on your recent visit was too familiar. That's all. You can go now.'

I walk out of the office. To say I am in a state of shock is an understatement. I feel completely numb. What on earth does he mean that I was 'too familiar'? How was my behaviour at Balmoral on my last visit any different to my visits before?

What terrible *faux pas* have I committed? Did I get drunk and do something unspeakable about which I have completely forgotten? Did I make a pass at HRH or one of his guests? Did I speak out of turn? Did I fail to be deferential at any time? And what does this mean for my future? Am I to take it that I have now moved from Royal favour to Royal *dis*favour? Is my position secure? Will my MVO give me any protection? Or have I tumbled from Royal grace, never to be redeemed?

I feel as if my whole world is suddenly inverted. To be told in the Royal Household that you are 'too familiar' is tantamount to utter disgrace. I feel as if I am about to cry.

Steady, Sarah, says my inner nanny. You are Deputy Head Girl round here, remember. You have the MVO! Your dignity is at stake. You do not cry, at least not in front of your colleagues.

So I stand up and head to the bathroom. I lock myself in the lavatory cubicle and let myself go for a few minutes. Then I brace myself. Honestly, Sarah, what would your mother say? I wipe away the tears, pull my shoulders back and march into the office a model of composure and resolution.

When everyone is out at lunch, I put in a call to Bernie at Balmoral.

'Bernie, can I talk to you for a minute?'

'Certainly, Sarah.'

'I have just been reprimanded.'

'I am sorry to hear that, Sarah. Why?'

'I was told that my behaviour during this last stay was too familiar.'

There is silence.

'Bernie, are you there?'

'Yes.'

'You were with me and HRH the entire time. Please tell me how my behaviour was any different to how it normally is.'

'I have been thinking and I am puzzled. Your behaviour was the same.'

'I didn't get drunk or say something I shouldn't have that I have completely forgotten about?'

'No, Sarah.'

'Do you promise me that, Bernie?'

'Yes, I honestly do.'

'Thank you so much, Bernie. Goodbye.'

On the one hand, I am relieved. On the other, I am getting completely paranoid. What is going on? I am completely baffled. What should I do when I next encounter HRH?

Grovel? Abase myself? How should my behaviour change? Should I never look him in the eye again? Should I creep about? What am I supposed to do?

Two nights later, I have a drink with a work colleague. In terms of rank, he is far higher up on the Palace ladder than me, a mere Lady Clerk. I tell him what has happened.

'Yes, I got to hear about it.'

I groan. Oh no. That means other staff got to hear, including, no doubt, some of my rival Lady Clerks. How one or two must be gloating now.

'The terrible thing is that I don't know what I did.'

'Perhaps you didn't do anything,' he says.

'But if I didn't do anything, then why am I being reprimanded?'

'Perhaps you should be thinking less *why* and more *who*.'

This is absurd. What possible enemies can I have up at Balmoral or Birkhall? Why would anyone want to hurt me? After all, I am virtually family there. I am a little Lady Clerk, for goodness sake. This is not Cawdor Castle in the days of Lady Macbeth; this is Balmoral in the twentieth century. I look at my friend. 'You know something, don't you?

He nods. 'Well?'

'I have just one word.'

This is driving me mad. 'What?'

'Camilla.'

'Camilla?' I exclaim. 'That can't be right. She is my friend! I talked to her at length about her mother and she couldn't have been sweeter about mine.'

'Camilla,' he laconically repeats.

What on earth have I ever done to Camilla? I think she is wonderful. Surely she knows that? I think hard and replay the last week's stay up at Birkhall. Suddenly, I have a picture in my mind's eye of Camilla trudging behind me and HRH. My God, that's it! She's jealous! She has it in mind that I am some sort of a rival! This is too absurd for words. It is laughable. Then I ponder slowly. Perhaps it is not laughable, not at least from Camilla's perspective. After all, we are from similar country backgrounds. We both like hunting. We are both quite jolly. In the looks department, are we that different? No. More than that, I am fifteen years younger. Yes, and I suppose the other day it was with me that HRH chose to discuss architecture on the walk after the picnic. But that is only because I am familiar with what's going on with the APG. This whole thing is mad. HRH has never made a pass at me and, though I adore him, I have never thought of him like *that*!

'Is there anything else I should know?' I ask.

'All right, but you better steel yourself.'

I take a deep breath. 'I am ready.'

'Her words were: "That girl has to go."'

I am frozen to the spot. My God, my career at the Palace has finished. This is like something out of a medieval court intrigue. Well, it actually *is* a court intrigue. And I am in the centre of it. It is terrifying.

'So I am finished here,' I say weakly, gazing into the abyss of inevitable destruction.

'Not necessarily. You have done ten years' service and you have your MVO. They cannot get rid of you on any old pretext. It would make the Palace look bad. Besides, HRH, as everyone knows, is fond of you. He won't be pressing for your dismissal even if Camilla has her guns aimed at you. My advice is to keep your head down. Camilla's displeasure may pass and Camilla herself might pass.'

'Pass away?'

He laughs. 'Certainly there are a few here at St James's Palace, and even more at BP, who would be delighted if Camilla passed away. Rightly or wrongly, she is being blamed for many of the Royal woes right now. It would make lots of people extremely happy if HRH moved on to someone else.'

Phew. This is a bit much to take in.

'So I just have to keep my head down?'

'That's right. A low profile.'

December 1999

In difficult times, when life is not going so well, good friends become truly valued, don't they? One of my greatest friends is the wonderful stalwart Christopher Cole. Christopher's family once supplied block printed wallpaper to Royal palaces and the stately homes of the world before the business was bought out by Walker Greenbank, a large conglomerate quoted on the stock exchange.

Something about supplying grand people with their wallpaper must have rubbed off on Christopher, because he is a gentleman of the old school. He talks to not just anybody but *everybody*. His magnanimity and exquisite manners extend way beyond conventional social courtesies. A two-minute walk down the street takes him half an hour because he says hello to everyone, be they dustmen, old ladies, tramps or dukes. One of nature's gentlemen, Christopher treats all with equal civility. Boundlessly curious, even when a street is empty he will often pause to make comment to his walking companion on a passing squirrel, a shrub in a neighbour's garden or a fluttering butterfly.

I once took Christopher as my companion to a Buckingham Palace Staff Dance. I was in between boyfriends, so I needed a 'walker'. Now, walkers are often thought of as gay; not so Christopher but, as he is old enough to be my uncle, I felt safe from any 'pouncing'.

Ever the gentleman, Christopher picked me up from home and complimented me on my ball gown. He, in turn, looked absolutely superb in his black tie. How proud I was to have this elegant blade on my arm. So, happy Cinderella and her walker arrive at BP. Would there be a Prince Charming awaiting me, I wondered?

Soon, however, this Cinderella started to get frustrated: Christopher was so enraptured by the surroundings he stopped to peer intently at every picture on the way to the ballroom and make studious comment.

Half an hour later, I am in the assembled throng with a glass of Her Majesty's infamous paint stripper in my hand. Christopher, meanwhile, was now happily engaged in conversation with a bemused Footman, whom I could see was trying to work out whether my walker is gay. Fortunately that is not the kind of attention Christopher himself would ever notice.

I left them to it and proceeded to chat to some of my office chums. Suddenly, there was a murmur through the crowd. Yes, the Royal Family had arrived. We, the guests, part before them. Slowly, they walk through the room, as ever in the Royal pecking order, with Her Majesty at the front, Prince Phillip behind, and so forth. Christopher and the Footman had by now parted and I could see him peering intently at yet another painting.

My goodness, I then see Christopher stride in amongst the

Royals, craning his head this way and that, presumably searching for me and Phylidda. He was clearly oblivious to the fact he had gatecrashed the Royal procession. On one side of him stood Prince Edward; on the other, Prince Philip, looking completely baffled. The surrounding staff, meanwhile, bowed and curtsied, clearly accepting Christopher as some obscure Royal cousin.

Eventually, Christopher spotted me and came over. He could not understand why it took me ten minutes to stop laughing.

Christopher has also been a tennis companion at Buckingham Palace. I remember once we had planned doubles, then one of our party failed to turn up, so it was just the three of us – Christopher, me and Christopher Buxton, a famous and ingenious re-designer of large country houses. Walking through the garden, Christopher Buxton suddenly pulled out his pocket camera. Before I knew it, he was snapping at some Royal architectural feature. Then something audibly rustled in a nearby rhododendron bush. Was it a fox? To our amazement, out jumped an aggressive armed policeman.

'Hand over the camera, sir!' He barked.

I had quite forgotten to tell our little party that photographs were strictly forbidden. Whoops!

'Would you care to join us for a set?' Christopher promptly enquired. His solicitous invitation had an immediate disarming effect on the warrior before us. After looking at us bemused, he politely declined. Calmed now by this considerate invitation to swing a racket with us, the policeman generously conceded the camera could be kept after exposing the film to daylight. Phew!

On another occasion, Christopher and I were walking to the tennis courts when suddenly we were charged by seven of her Majesty's yapping corgis. Corgis are often thought of as 'little' dogs; they are not. They are medium sized with short legs. Short-tempered and temperamental, they often bite. Instinctively, Christopher and I felt like running for it, but I told him not to move.

As a child, I had a corgi myself called Blodwyn, so I know quite a bit about Her Majesty's preferred species of pet. You have to stand your ground with a corgi, and so we stood there as they furiously yapped around our ankles. Eventually, they lost interest and trotted back to the flustered liveried Footman who had been walking them.

Tonight I am taking Christopher as my companion to a Royal Banquet at Buckingham Palace in honour of His Excellency President Jiang of China. Of course, Christopher and I are not actually going to attend the Banquet ourselves, though he would doubtless be a perfect guest of Her Majesty. No, we are going to be spectators.

Before every Banquet, officials at the Palace can apply for tickets to watch the proceedings. The tickets are picked through ballot, and this time I succeeded. Excellent! I deserve something good this year.

After a light dinner in the Royal Official's Dining Hall, we, the lucky twenty, are ushered into a room overlooking the Banquet below. We all take our seats.

This Banquet is particularly interesting because HRH has flatly refused to attend. HRH dislikes the Chinese government, particularly because of its treatment of that nice Dalai Lama and his people, the peaceful Tibetans. I could tell you *precisely* what he says of the Chinese leaders but that could get me into trouble. But I will report that Mark has been briefing all his media chums that the heir to the throne has marked down President Jiang and his entourage pretty much as stinkers.

'Officially', of course, this is not the case: he could not attend the Banquet because of a prior engagement. But 'officially', I am beginning to learn, is just a euphemism for lying.

As we are ushered into the room overlooking the Banquet, we are specifically instructed by a solemn official *not* to talk. But, oh dear, can you instruct a dog not to bark? Christopher, bless him, proceeds to pass non-stop comment throughout the proceedings: on the food, the table decorations, the Royals and their illustrious guests. Darling Christopher does not whisper either. Is it my imagination or does Prince Phillip twice glare up angrily at the gold-painted trellis concealing us as Christopher gives me the benefit of his observations?

Well, what do I care? Out of favour as I am with my Royal masters, Christopher, my good friend, can continue to chirrup as long as he wishes.

One thing that strikes all of us is the spectacle of the interpreters who kneel during the entire meal between the chairs of the English hosts and Chinese guests. I suppose this is a time-honoured way of dealing with an otherwise unbreachable language barrier. But hitting the millennium, as we are, it does seem a bit demeaning on the interpreters to have them in this state of physical discomfort. At least in medieval times interpreters would have been chucked the odd victual from the Banquet before them.

October 2000

Well, a whole year has passed since my reprimand. There are no signs of Camilla's star waning. Rather, it is in the ascent. However much Her Majesty's Household at Buckingham Palace may wish for the demise of her son and Camilla's relationship, it is getting stronger, not weaker.

More than that, there is a force here at St James's Palace in the person of Mark Bolland that is achieving what was until recently unthinkable: *positive* media coverage for Camilla. It was only eight years ago that she became the most hated woman in Britain, *'the Rottweiler'* to the now sainted Diana, the alleged breaker of the Royal marriage. Now, if you please, Mrs Parker-Bowles is a gracious and supportive Royal Consort, combining glamour with her work for charity.

How does Mark do it? I'll tell you how. He trades stories and exclusives as if they were mere commercial commodities, which I suppose, when you think of it, they are. The antics of HRH and Camilla, and the photo opportunities that arise, are now items to be bartered to the press for favours.

The 'old guard' at BP are horrified by these dark and wily manipulative practices, especially as they strongly suspect some of the stories that are traded are at the direct expense of other members of the Royal Family. Aptly, young Prince William, a future Royal star, has wittily nicknamed Mark 'Lord Blackadder'. Inevitably, it has stuck.

Another thing that makes the old guard at BP particularly angry is that they know that, with continuing positive spin, Camilla will eventually become palatable to most of the public. And if Camilla becomes sufficiently likeable, then who knows, HRH could even *marry* her!

As for me, I have not received even one invitation to any

of the Royal palaces to help out the Boss. Indeed, I have had no communication with him at all. The chill of Royal disfavour hangs on me like an old, wet coat. How do I feel? Dreadful. It is like being dumped by someone you love and trust. The hurt remains because you still love even if you no longer trust. I feel alternately discarded, sad, demoralised, abandoned, empty and furious.

I feel particularly angry at the moment because I am getting written warnings. I have office colleagues who I could once count as friends spying on me, reporting me for taking calls on my mobile phone in the corridor. So I take a call in the corridor. Goodness, what a sin!

My timekeeping is also being scrupulously recorded by my treacherous, beady-eyed colleagues. So I was fifteen minutes late back for lunch, was I? Oh dear. How appalling. The machinery of St James's Palace will collapse, no doubt. The fact that I work at twice the speed of nearly every other Lady Clerk appears to make no difference. Neither does my seniority, nor my MVO.

To add insult to injury, I am now instructed to report to Elaine Day, my former protégée! Of course, I ignore her. When she asks me to do something, I simply pretend I haven't heard. Is that *me* you are addressing, Elaine? No, it can't be. It is funny, Elaine, how you become invisible and inaudible when you are addressing me. Strange, isn't it? La, la, la, la. Elaine now exists in another dimension.

I have always liked a drink or two over lunch, but now it is three or four. Yes, yes, I know, I am digging my own grave here, but as far as I can see it has been dug for me anyway. Do I fall into the aforesaid pit now or later? Unimpeachable conduct is frankly not going to change the inevitable, is it?

Earlier this year, I consulted the new overall boss, Sir Michael Peat, who was particularly charming to me at the Royal Garden Party this summer.

'Contact me any time,' he said.

So I did.

Our meeting was hush-hush. Very off the record, if you know what I mean. I poured out my heart to the great man and I cannot tell you how sympathetic he was. He sat there, smiling non-stop, nodding as I told him of my troubles. Goodness, I must have made a spectacle of myself!

So what was the outcome? Well, obviously I felt happy to have offloaded a lot of my worries. But did it work? Has it helped? I really don't know. He is like the Cheshire cat. There is the fixed, knowing grin, but what's behind it all? There was a display of sympathy and huge understanding, but is there sincerity?

The other day, one of my colleagues said Sir Michael was 'omniscient', which I had to look up and which means something like greatly knowing. Well, that helps, I thought. Speaking to him, then, is a bit like imploring God. But at the end of it, I remind myself, he is not God. He is just head of our Royal Household and he answers to HRH. And if HRH is now answering to Camilla, I am finished.

November 2000

This is so humiliating. I am in a pawnbroker's in Victoria, 400 yards south of Buckingham Palace. And just to think that, until yesterday, I did not realise what a pawnbroker really was! In truth, I thought it was someone who sold naughty magazines and videos and the like. Well, there is such a slight difference between 'pawn' and 'porn'. However, now I know pawnbrokers are where poor people go to raise some cash.

Poor! *Moi*? Oh yes! Absolutely broke and terrified. So why don't I go to the bank for a loan? They seem to rather have had it with what they term as my 'excessive' overdraft. And, in the final battle between your creditors and ruin, those in the know resort to pawnbrokers. Bless them, they are the last line of defense.

Unfortunately, you have to give them something valuable in return as 'security'. In other words, if you run away and never pay them back, they have something to sell. You only get your valuables back when you have handed back the loan plus interest. What is interest, I asked my friend, feeling a bit stupid? Interest is regular payments to support aforesaid loan, says my patient friend. Ah, so that's why my overdraft always seemed to grow.

The interest at a pawnbroker, I have been warned by darling Karen who once visited one, is steep enough to make Shylock blush. Gosh, again I felt an idiot. Shylock who? I asked. Shylock, I was reminded, is a controversial character from Shakespeare's *Merchant of Venice*, who demanded excessive terms for a loan. It is not like getting credit from a building society, she told me, you pay through the nose. That is all very well, but in dire straits what's a girl to do?

So I am inside this pawnbroker's shop about to hand over my jewellery. My main anxiety is whether anyone has seen me come in here. Of course, I don't mean just *anyone*; I mean colleagues from the Palace. Talk about compounding the humility! That would be too awful. It would be worse than being observed entering a betting shop, though I understand both Her Majesty and her darling party-loving mother revel in a regular flutter on the horses!

Mind you, they place their bets through emissaries or over the telephone. I don't think either of Their Majesties has, of yet, been personally spotted entering the premises of a 'turf accountant', the quaint name for betting shops. I must admit, for ages I thought turf accountants sold lawns.

So what do I need a loan for? To pay a gas and electricity bill, of all things! For my 'security', I am reduced right now to handing over some pieces of my jewellery. First are my diamond and sapphire earrings. Next is a gold signet ring. And finally there is my beloved golden teddy bear, which has enamel paws and diamond eyes, given to me ten years ago by my beloved darling Andy. Oh Andy, wherever you are, *please* forgive me. I calculate that I am not desperate enough yet to pawn my medal for the Royal Victorian Order or the brooch I wore at HRH's 50th birthday party.

What is the world coming to? I would have thought being an exalted Lady Clerk at St James's Palace, with an MVO no less, would protect me from such indignities.

The pawnbroker proceeds to examine my baubles with something that must be a magnifying glass. Goodness, he is taking a long time over it. Get on with it, I think, fretting and looking nervously through his shop window to the world outside. It is bad enough being in here in the first place. This studious examination is, frankly, rubbing salt into the wound.

Inner nanny cuts in. Don't be silly. He has to see that you are not proffering him some old tat from down the market.

As ever, she is right. Yes, Mr Pawnbroker. Examine away, though I am sure you will agree that these beautiful jewels are real quality! Oh yes, I bet you don't often see items like this, do you? What are they worth, I wonder? At a modest guess, I would say they have to be worth £2,000 at the very least.

He smiles at me. 'I will have to weigh them,' he says. He then pulls up some scales.

Whatever for, I wonder? He seems to read my mind.

'The value that we place on your jewellery is based solely on the gold content, though we do make allowances for the stones,' he says.

How interesting. So, reduced to mere bullion, what will I manage to raise from my beautiful baubles? £1,200? Perhaps that is a bit high. What about £800 then? Yes, that would do nicely. I might be able to have my highlights done next week with that cash injection.

'£50, madam!'

'I'm sorry?' I find myself spluttering.

'£50,' he repeats.

I slowly absorb the information. The light bulb illuminates. He is talking about the first quarter's interest, surely? Let me speak to him plainly. Finance has never been a strong subject of mine. I can only work on the basics.

'How much are you giving me and what are my monthly payments?'

He looks back smiling.

'We give you £50 and you pay us £20 a month interest.'

I look at him aghast. Whoever you are, Shylock, I can understand why you might now be blushing. I am not sophisticated about these things, but I know a rip-off when I see one.

'This is outrageous!'

He shrugs. 'Those are our terms.'

My head slumps. Meekly, I take the notes and leave.

December 2000

I come into the office after a particularly heavy session with Carlo, my little Italian stallion. Whoops, a few minutes late!

Dear, oh dear. That's right, girls, you better record it. Won't our employers be keen to know that? I go to the kitchen, make myself a coffee, shut my eyes, then dream I am back in the arms of Carlo.

He was thrilled to come as my partner to the staff party at Highgrove the other night. The affair was quite surreal. It was a fancy-dress party with the theme of eighteenth-century Royal England. Being a staff event, HRH was not in attendance. It was hosted instead by Michael Fawcett, whose position appears unassailable. His arrogance to other staff is the stuff of open gossip now, but he is pleasant enough to me.

What is it, I wonder, with Michael? Two years ago some Royal staff members made a joint complaint about his bullying manner. He resigned but was later re-employed. Meanwhile, all the complaining staff members resigned instead.

So close is Michael to the Prince that he personally squeezes the toothpaste onto the Royal toothbrush. He even famously once held a container for HRH to pee into for a urine sample. Admittedly HRH had a broken arm at the time, so one understands he needed assistance; nonetheless, the incident elevated more than a few eyebrows, I can tell you.

What a rise in the ranks! In 1981, he was just a mere footman at Buckingham Palace. Posted over to Kensington Palace, he became one of HRH's valets and developed the trust of both the Boss *and* the Bossette which, during their civil war, is some feat, I can tell you. But unlike other staff, he did not take the line that he knew his place. He started to develop airs and graces, even adding 'Buxton' to his name.

'Hello, I am Michael Buxton-Fawcett.' You can imagine how this went down with other members of the Royal Household, which is nothing if not heirarchical and snobbish. Sniggering, some started called him 'Sir' Michael behind his back. Michael got the message and 'Buxton' was duly dropped. But perhaps his mockers were being accidentally prescient. Michael is now HRH's indispensable major-domo. Who could now say a knighthood is out of the question. Arise, Sir Michael!

To give him his due, Michael Fawcett knows how to throw a party. Everyone, save a few dweebs like me and Carlo, had gone to huge effort, wearing breeches and frock coats and so forth. It was held in the Orchard Room, an annex that HRH had built ten years ago. Michael directed everyone to the buffet, then commanded us all to look at the stage.

My goodness, they have laid on a pantomime for us. What fun! It is Cinderella. One of the best performers is Bernie the Butler, who plays one of the ugly sisters. It is all the more poignant because, for reasons of which you are all too aware, I have not seen him now for a year and a half.

The panto finishes and the discotheque strikes up. We are all boogying away when on comes that striptease song from HRH's favourite movie *The Full Monty*. Suddenly, I see Michael Fawcett really getting into the spirit of it. And I *really* mean the spirit! To everyone's astonishment, he starts to strip! And, to give the monster credit, he does it well.

Go, Michael, go! Bare that barrel chest! Not a bad torso, though I say so myself. Are you going to drop your trousers, Mr Fawcett? Ah, you are restraining yourself. Ah well, it is a Half Monty, then.

The next thing I know, we have all formed a conga-line and are being led round the dance floor led by the half-naked Michael Fawcett as the head of the snake. It is hilarious. We are doing the hokey-cokey and we are shaking it all about! No, this is not Buckingham Palace. It is not Windsor Castle or Sandringham. Nor is it Balmoral. It is Butlins at Highgrove. Yippee! Frankly, we can all do with a bit of Butlins in our life.

And we can all do with the occasional break. I am actually taking a week off right now before Christmas. It seems a mad time to holiday, I know, but these continuous reprimands are getting me down. Naturally, I want Carlo attending to me and I have chosen the perfect place, miles from anywhere – Tom-na-Gaidh!

Yes, I have booked it for a token sum of just £15. How great is that? It is not just that it is cheap but also that I just adore Balmoral, and I love it at the cottage. I haven't been up there for over a year now. Will I see Willy Potts? I do hope so. And perhaps, who knows, I might bump into HRH and Camilla. I will then have an opportunity to abase myself so they might look on me fondly once again.

I go to my desk and switch on the computer. Now, what work do I have on today? I start to open up the correspondence. Will Elaine Day try coming over to my desk today? I do hope not. She must know by now that I have an acute hearing problem every time she addresses me.

I am now invited into Mark Bolland's office. That's better. I am ever attentive to my Noble Lord Blackadder. What is he going to give me? What is the bet it is a reprimand about arriving six nanoseconds too late this morning? Or will it, I venture, be yet another warning about the one-minute mobile telephone conversation I was spotted having yesterday afternoon in the corridor? As I walk to his room, I tell myself not to be such a pessimist; it is probably dictation or some instructions on a new project.

I sit down and Lord Blackadder looks at me in a sad, apologetic way. That's not like Lord Blackadder. Perhaps he has had a row with his boyfriend? I smile in a neutral fashion. Then he tells me.

I am fired.

He proceeds to trot out the details of my poor timekeeping, mobile telephone calls, insubordination to Elaine, blah, blah, blah, etc. I put up no protest. What's the point? That's it. My twelve years as a Lady Clerk for His Royal Highness the Prince of Wales are over.

Yes, I knew this was coming, but, all the same, I am gripped by that numbness, which, I am told, always comes with shock. I feel as if I am detaching myself from reality right now, that this somehow is a dream. I am now ordered to give back my security pass. My security pass! Why does this instruction make me feel sick all of a sudden? I go to my desk, on which it is sitting, then hand it over. I feel like I am surrendering my identity.

Everything takes on a strange, dream-like quality. I feel oddly detached, as if I am cruising on automatic. What do I do next? Come on, Sarah, says inner nanny. Don't make any fuss. Keep your dignity. It is very hard, I reply, because I think I am going to start crying. No! her voice commands me. Whatever you do, do *not* make a spectacle of yourself by crying! You are Sarah Lucy Georgina Goodall MVO. And don't you forget it. Members of the Royal Victorian Order do not start blubbing at one of life's mere setbacks.

I go quietly to my desk and sweep all my belongings into a

bag. None of my colleagues look at me. Their heads are all down as they pretend to be engrossed in their work.

I am escorted downstairs. Do they honestly think I am a security risk? That I am going to grab a Canaletto as a memento and run off down the street with it? I walk out into Colour Court, then gaze round one last time at the Palace walls I know so well.

St James's Palace has been the home to Kings, Queens, princes and princesses throughout the centuries. Great events have unfolded here. But it has also, for twelve years, been not just my place of work but also, in a way, my home too. My escort walks me through the gates and then, in a final touch that is both graceless and gratuitous, he instructs the policeman before me that I must not be allowed to re-enter.

So it is official, then. I am banned from the Palace.

I walk up St James's and on to Piccadilly. I then catch the bus back to my flat. The numbness remains. After ten minutes, I go to the fridge and pour myself some wine. I find myself trembling. Then the tears start rolling down my cheeks. I can't help myself. Let it go, girl! I start to cry.

Five minutes later, I stand up, go to the bathroom, dab my eyes and tell myself to stop being a big girl's blouse. You don't need the Palace any more, Sarah, inner nanny reassures me. You are done with it.

Suddenly, I remember my booked holiday up at Tom-na-Gaidh. Can I still go there? Will I be welcome? Another two glasses of Chardonnay later, I summon the courage to pick up the phone. I hope I don't sound drunk. I call the Palace number I know so well. I am put through to personnel. A minute later, I put it down. The holiday booking has been automatically cancelled with my employment.

EPILOGUE

Beyond the Royals

April 2008

Seven years have gone by. HRH is now married to Camilla. She is now Her Royal Highness the Duchess of Cornwall. And I stand by what I said at the beginning of my memoirs: 'forgive and forget'. No one ever completely gets over being dismissed from a job they not only love but which has shaped and defined them. But, with the help of inner nanny, I have come to terms with it. As someone who still adores HRH, I want the best for him, and Camilla gives him unqualified love and a happiness, I suspect, that he has missed much of his life.

I ought to tell you that I *did* actually see HRH again, and no, it wasn't a chance meeting. I rang Stephen Lamport, his Private Secretary, and he kindly arranged a twenty-minute meeting between HRH and myself at the Boss's private apartment within St James's Palace two months afterwards. HRH's diary was packed. I was flattered he could actually see me so soon.

I will take you through what happened.

It is a cold February morning. I arrive early and the policeman who was instructed never to let me through again nods at me as I enter. Do I detect a half-smile playing on his lips? I am let into the York House apartment by HRH's other butler Tony, and then sit on a seat in the corridor and try hard to compose myself while I attempt to read a newspaper. All I can think of, though, is the impending moment with HRH. However hard I try to concentrate, the stories are all a jumble. Some fifteen minutes later, I am summoned.

My heart is beating fast again as I enter the Drawing Room. There I behold HRH, wearing a charcoal suit with a cream cotton Turnbull & Asser shirt and a woven indigo silk tie. He looks as marvellous as ever. He fixes me with that restrained smile I know so well. I curtsey.

'Oh, hello, Sarah.'

'Good morning, Your Royal Highness.'

He waves a hand to a large green sofa. I sit down. The Drawing Room is cluttered and full of books. I glance around. There is nothing here that shows the light touch of a woman. How different, I think, to Kensington Palace in the days of the Bossette. Then it was all flowers, potpourri and framed family photographs. Kensington Palace was feminine. This apartment is the epitome of masculinity.

Though we have not spoken now for over a year and a half, I feel the same gush of worship for him that overwhelmed me when I first sat next to him at the staff Christmas lunch, a worship that has remained with me since. I feel so close to him – literally. I could reach out and touch him. The cramped medieval proportions are helping to accentuate our physical proximity.

But my role has changed; I am now an outsider. Though by kindly giving me this audience, HRH is ensuring I no longer need feel like a *disgraced* outsider. He proceeds to ask me about my family and my plans for the future. My family?

Fine. My plans for the future? Er. Future? In truth, I couldn't then see a future, just a blur. But I mumble something about hoping to become a personal assistant to a chairman of a company in the City. He wishes me all the 'absolute best' with the final interview.

But there is a terrible tension inside me. I am like a volcano ready to erupt. It is a 'Don't mention the war' situation but, for me, it is 'Don't mention the sacking!' I keep biting my lip to stop myself. I feel this momentous struggle between two internal tectonic forces. The one that wants to gush out and the other that wants to keep the lid on it. Do I manage to control myself? I think you know me well enough by now. Of course I don't.

'You do realise that I am rather upset, Sir!' I suddenly find myself blurting, tears brimming.

HRH looks startled, as if I have just jumped up and bit him, which, conversationally, I suppose I have. He then looks down and appears to take a studious interest in the carpet. I notice he is now twisting his signet ring.

'Yes,' he says. 'It *is* a bit sad.'

There is a pause and we are both now studying the intriguing weave of Wilton. I pull a handkerchief from my bag and dab my eyes. Goodness, what a fool I am! Oh why couldn't I have restrained myself, just this once? Where do we go from here?

HRH then looks up and turns to me. I gaze into his blue eyes once again. He furrows his brow, then shakes his head.

'This foot and mouth! *Frightful* business!'

My goodness, he is reprimanding me! He is rebuking me for putting my foot in my mouth! I cannot believe it! He is right, though. It is indeed a frightful business. I feel crushed.

Goodness, I have really messed this up, haven't I? This is yet another moment when I wish the earth would swallow me up.

'Yes, sir,' I say, looking down at the carpet once more, ready now to burst into tears.

'I mean, it's all over the country. It's hitting farms *everywhere.*'

What is he talking about? Suddenly, a light bulb comes on in my head. Oh, Sarah, you idiot. He wasn't rebuking you. Don't you watch television? Don't you read the news? He is talking about the disease in cattle!

Relieved, I look up at HRH, who, for the next ten minutes, proceeds to give me the benefit of his thoughts on the ruinous epidemic. Clearly, HRH is very passionate about 'foot and mouth', so I sit there on the sofa and nod at him earnestly, keeping steady eye contact and not taking in a single word he is saying. It is strange not to have a notepad in my hand. I feel I should be taking dictation.

My angry emotions then start to get the better of me. What is this speech for? Does he, I wonder, think that, because I am from rural Shropshire, I am particularly interested in foot and mouth? Does His Magnificence think that is really what I sought a last audience with him for, to hear his views on an agricultural blight?

Don't be stupid, says my inner nanny. You were never his wife or girlfriend. You cannot, in all seriousness, expect him to address the issue of your feelings! What are you expecting? A one-on-one psychotherapy session? You should be flattered he is bothering to give you, an *ex*-employee, his precious time.

The future King has a hectic schedule and he has more serious duties with which to occupy himself than soothing a former Lady Clerk. And while Camilla may have initiated your fall from favour, you hardly helped your cause with your timekeeping and attitude! What other employer would frankly bother?

Inner nanny, as always, is right. All credit to darling HRH for this audience. The allotted time I have with my future King now draws to a close. I gaze around his apartment for one last time and start to head to the door. Suddenly, HRH stops me.

'Don't go just yet,' he says.

Oh my God! Has he changed his mind? Am I now back in favour? Will he now re-employ me? He then walks to his desk, opens a drawer and pulls out a blue leather wallet with his initials on it. He hands it to me.

'Oh thank you, Sir.'

He next picks up a signed and framed photograph, and presents that to me as well. I look at it and feel a surge of affection coursing through me. The picture is of HRH in happier days as a younger man, leaning against his walled garden gate at Highgrove, long before his troubles started in earnest with the Bossette.

'Thank you so much, Sir,' I blurt out, repeating myself.

My eyes brim with tears, again. Sometimes I am so pathetic! Why can't I be restrained and sophisticated? I desperately want to hug him and say something like, 'Thank you for twelve fantastic years.' But the words remain unspoken, which is probably just as well. It would be so un-English. We would have both been highly embarrassed.

I take his proffered hand and shake it. Does he realise how much I adore him, I wonder? Perhaps he can see that from my eyes, which are brimming with tears of emotion.

'Goodbye, Sir.'

I slowly turn round and take four paces to the door. As I turn the handle, I look back furtively to take one last glimpse of His Gorgeousness, the heir to the throne. He is now picking up some papers to read. Sigh.

I close the door quietly but firmly behind me this one last time. Tony, his butler, then shows me out of the apartment. I walk from the Palace as slowly and regally, I hope, as any princess, with HRH's wallet and signed picture pressed closely to my bosom.

Adieu.

So what has been my news since?

Since the first publication of *The Palace Diaries* two years ago in Britain I have forged a whole new career as a Royal Expert. And because I appear on television so often now, I have even been called a 'media personality' - would you believe it? Accident-prone, self-doubting little me sitting on the couches of stars like Sharon Osbourne - keeping the world informed on Royal developments such as would Prince William's girlfriend be a suitable Princess. To think!

But is it as much fun as being a Senior Lady Clerk to His Gorgeousness, the Prince of Wales? Let's put it this way: Green Rooms have their compensations but, to my way of thinking, nothing can beat the ornate rooms of Buckingham Palace, St James's Palace, Balmoral or Highgrove!

I have followed the fortunes of many of my former friends and colleagues from the Palace, and some of the characters I met in the course of my Royal duties. In spite of his comment about his admirer, the Prince, being a 'little grovelling bastard', Spike Milligan received a knighthood soon after I left. Well done, 'Sir' Spike. I salute you. Also HRH for your magnanimity.

Sir Robert Fellowes, former Head of the Royal Household at Buckingham Palace, and brother-in-law of the Princess of Wales, has been elevated to the Lords. Given that he was at the helm during some of the most tempestuous years in recent Royal history, a peerage is the least Bobby Bellows deserves.

A few years back, I visited the incomparable Sarge – the Travelling Yeoman himself, Ron Lewis – in hospital before cancer took him. Wherever you are, I hope you are knocking back the Dark and Stormies, Ron!

Ken Wharfe received his MVO after being posted as Protection Officer to the Duke of Kent. He has since written a book about his observations and experiences while looking after the Bossette and the young princes. The Palace was infuriated at the publication of his book.

Tony Burrows, whom Ron drunkenly toasted at the Christmas lunch at Simpson's, has retired as the St James's Palace accountant and is living on the Norfolk broads. His colleague Pam, also a friend, now has her MVO and continues her work as Mistress of the Payroll.

What of the butlers I met? Bernie and Tony are (I think) still there, doing their sterling work. Then there are Paul Burrell and Harold Brown. I watched with horror the run-up to their trial for the alleged theft of the Bossette's belongings. The intervention of Her Majesty was timely. But the prospect of disgrace, prison and ruin must have been terrifying for them both.

Harold, I have learned, has now retired to Tunbridge Wells.

As for Paul Burrell, I am happy that he is now financially secure, having faced ruin, but, my goodness, he does over-egg his special relationship with the Bossette. 'She called me her rock'! The Princess had more rocks than the white cliffs of Dover. As for his decree on the lecture circuit that HRH is not fit to be King! Really! Continuing the Bossette's marital vendetta is uncalled for and tawdry. Reports of him wrenching a ring off her finger before her funeral paint an unattractive picture. I wonder if he really did?

Following the collapse of the Burrell trial in 2002, HRH ordered an inquiry into the conduct of his Household by Sir Michael Peat, his Personal Secretary. On publication of the report, Michael Fawcett left the Prince's service only to be reemployed immediately as a freelance personal consultant. He now reportedly has a guaranteed income of more than £125,000 ($250,000) a year.

Those members of HRH's staff who complained about Fawcett's bullying back in 1998 have all since left. These include Tiggy Legge-Bourke, Phyllida, Simon Solari and Sandy Henney. As of now, Michael Fawcett continues to reign supreme. It baffles and distresses many close to HRH. 'I cannot live without Michael,' the Prince allegedly remarked. Reliable sources tell me that Her Majesty is not amused by Fawcett's continuing power over her son. How is this Michael Fawcett matter going to end? Unless there is a skillful and diplomatic resolution, I think his eventual parting from the Royal Household could be seriously damaging. He knows all HRH's secrets.

What of my superiors? Dreamy Dave Wright has been knighted. Sir David is Vice-Chairman of Barclays Capital, having been Ambassador to Japan for three and a half years. He is also a Governor of the Royal Shakespeare Company.

Stephen Lamport, now Sir Stephen Lamport, is a Director

of the Royal Bank of Scotland.

Peter Westmacott is currently 'our man' in Turkey. He was in post when al-Qaeda blew up an outbuilding of the Embassy. The Bossette's former Lady-in-Waiting, Anne Beckwith-Smith, who was there with both of us in Seville, recently joined Peter for a charity drive for the victims and their families.

Richard Aylard is now a Senior Director at Thames Water. Come on, Honours Committee, you cannot lay the blame on the Commander for Jonathan Dimbleby's biography of HRH. His devotion to his boss cost him his marriage. Give him a knighthood, too!

My boss, Mark Bolland, fell into Royal disfavour within months of sacking me. He was fired. For his extraordinary achievement in helping to make Camilla acceptable to the public, Mr Bolland deserves a peerage at least. Arise, Lord Blackadder! He did not even get his MVO. He is now a PR consultant and freelance writer.

Tiggy Legge-Bourke is married, has two children and lives in the country. I remain a fan of the redoubtable Tiggy, who remains irritated that she was ever referred to by the media as a Royal nanny. She tells friends, 'I never was the Royal nanny, I was the Royal gopher.' Historians, please note.

My friend Victoria Mendham lives in Fulham and works in the West End. Elaine Day attempted to sue a Palace colleague for sexual harassment and lost her case. The case cost her more than a year's worth of Palace wages. In hindsight, I should not have been so difficult with her; my *froideur* could not have been pleasant. It certainly wasn't a racial issue. I had just become too proud to answer to those of my colleagues whom I saw as my juniors. Yes, I admit it. By the end of my

Royal employment, I had succumbed to a bad case of red-carpet fever.

When I am on the Internet, I occasionally search out Brian Hanson, my former boss at the APG. I have found he is still writing wonderful critical essays on architectural controversies. It is a pity I still can't understand most of what he is going on about, but I continue to share his penchant for fondant fancies.

The other day, I found myself walking into Candida Lycett-Green on Bond Street. You can never be sure how people in Royal circles will react to you after you have left, but she was charm and grace personified. And her charm and grace, may I say, are reflected in the many articles and books she writes.

Occasionally, I bump into His Massiveness, Nicholas Soames, at parties. He is always polite and solicitous, but I suspect that, though he knows he has met me somewhere, he can't quite place me. I giggle at the wonderful stories I continue to hear about him.

I have even glimpsed from time to time Mr Sexy Woodentop, the Duke of Westminster. He certainly doesn't remember me. Sometimes I wonder whether the attraction I still feel for this aloof and alluring aristocrat is also perhaps due to the fact that he owns a large chunk of London.

Sir Jimmy Savile OBE has retired – his curious sartorial legacy secured for posterity by American rap stars. As to his counselling efforts, all credit to you, Sir Jimmy, you tried your best! Shame about the finger-licking.

I stay in contact with my former boyfriends. Andy and George are both happily married with children. Eddie the entrepreneur is still doing his deals, and Carlo is still belting around on his polo ponies. Alastair has found love and is still as dashing as ever.

I have since met the much-maligned James Hewitt and he has confirmed the story I heard from Mindy that I have repeated here: Yes, he did see Camilla across the street in the nude. I would also like to state categorically that he could not have been the father of Prince Harry. The Princess met him three years after Harry was born! James is capable of driving tanks into victorious battle and making women swoon, but his attributes do not extend to time travel. Scandalmongers might be irritated, but unless a new skeleton comes tumbling out of the Royal closet, HRH is undoubtedly the father of *both* the Royal princes.

Not many people know it, but if ever a member of the Royal Family is proven not to be from, ahem, the official Royal bloodline it makes not a jot of difference. Once the Heralds have declared a baby to be a Royal prince or princess, Royal they remain, whatever. Nor would it affect their position in the line of succession. So, in effect, a cuckoo in the nest could start a whole new biological Royal Family.

Some might think I have been tough on the Bossette. That is not my intention. I just want to be realistic. What, you might ask, about all those love affairs that Mindy mentioned? Are they for real? What do you think? In 1993, Juan Carlos, the King of Spain, was witnessed giggling with his retinue at the Zarzuela Palace on reading the excerpt about himself and the Princess in the Spanish edition of Lady Colin Campbell's book, *Diana in Private*.

Ken Wharfe has also corroborated many of those on the roll call of Diana's lovers in his account of the Royal marriage. Indeed, he was actually with the Princess of Wales for much of the time during her affairs, even sleeping in James Hewitt's mother's cottage in the West Country while the Bossette slept with the Captain upstairs.

As to the speculation about Princess Diana's parentage, does it matter whether or not there is any truth in Sir Jimmy Goldsmith possibly being her father? I think it does, if only to provide some clues as to what made her tick. If she had even a suspicion that he was her true father, it would surely have compounded the insecurities that took root when her parents divorced. Ultimately, either the knowledge or just the suspicion of a different father could be an 'unconscious driver', as psychologists say, for her erratic behaviour. Wouldn't it affect any of us?

For all her many good points, the Bossette had bad ones, so forgive me if I believe the sugary worship so many uncritically accord her is misplaced. At the risk of offending the Dianaphiles, can I suggest that instead of going to a Diana shrine on 31 August, the anniversary of her death, those selfsame sentiments be redirected closer to home? What about tending the grave of a lost relative or friend instead? I bet if the Bossette could speak from the grave, she would agree.

I am constantly asked about the conspiracy theories concerning the Bossette's death in the Paris tunnel. I don't believe for one moment in the conspiracy theory espoused by Dodi's father, Mohamed al Fayed, that Prince Philip with 200 other members of the British Establishment did her in, and neither did the Coroner at her 2008 Inquest.

However, other things continue to disturb me. The first is the claim that the driver, Henri Paul, was completely drunk. I cannot believe it. Why? There is CCTV footage of him at the

Ritz taken minutes before he took off in the Mercedes with Diana, Dodi and the bodyguard. It shows him deftly dropping to his knees and tying his shoelaces. I am sorry, but a drunk would have keeled over.

Does anyone seriously believe he necked a bottle of spirits in the car in the hundred seconds before he drove his passengers into the tunnel to their ultimate doom while attempting to escape their hunters, the paparazzi?

Another bothersome matter: a former station chief with British intelligence tried to provide evidence for the Official Inquiry by showing a blueprint for an assassination attempt on Slobodan Milosevic, leader of the Serbs during the Balkan War. According to the agent, the plan was to murder the tyrant in a car tunnel and make it look like an accident. So do we have a startling coincidence? Other people crash cars in tunnels. Are these all assassinations? Of course not. It probably is just a strange coincidence. Any way his evidence was discredited at the Inquest. Let us hear, however, what the former station chief has to say. But no, he has been prevented from giving evidence. He was apparently beaten up in his hotel bedroom, rendering him physically incapable of doing so. Presuming what he says is true, such 'discouragement' could, of course, simply have been carried out to make sure secret service plans remained secret.

But such devious intervention confuses the picture further. Moreover, it is cack-handed. Dirty tricks of this kind make people believe that the authorities have something to hide. The official verdict of 'accident' is all very well; but until all the hard questions are answered to reasonable satisfaction, the unofficial verdict for many will remain 'assassination'.

The recent Inquest into Diana's death has supposedly laid

all the facts on the table so to speak. But I can reveal one that was not. In August 1997, the month of Princess Diana's death, the Military Attaché in post at the British Embassy in Paris was Brigadier Charles Ritchie. The Brigadier separately had close connections to the Royal Family. His wife was once Lady-in-Waiting to Diana's former sister-in-law, the Princess Royal, Princess Anne. In 2004 the Brigadier mentioned in conversation at the New Club in Edinburgh, Scotland that he and a colleague had been in the tunnel the day of the crash.

During the recent Inquest the Brigadier was questioned about his movements on the day of the crash. Did he say that he had been in the tunnel? No. Why not? After all, it was surely just a macabre coincidence. So why not mention it?

To be fair, though, the Brigadier was never asked the question directly. You can make of this what you will.

Personally, I am inclined to believe it was an accident. But what do I know? Someone in the future might produce evidence that would prove the Coroner and me wrong. All I can say is that, even if some sinister characters did manage to plot and pull off such an outrageous murder, it is absurd to think HRH would ever condone it, least of all have anything to do with it – kill the mother of his children? He would be as outraged as any of us.

Writing these memoirs has led me to reflect long and hard on the Royal Family and its relationship with us, ordinary citizens. It really cannot be easy for any of the Royals to be perpetually under the spotlight, but I think that media interest inevitably comes with the territory. You can't have a Royal Family without everyone being fascinated; it is something they have to bear – but who among us could cope with such scrutiny and critical comment the entire time?

It is not surprising, then, that the result is paranoia, making it difficult for members of the Royal Family to distinguish between accurate reporting and fabrications, fair comment and malice.

The job they are born into, it has to be said, is really weird. Imagine yourself as a Royal, your diary brimming with openings, ceremonies, visits and glad-handing. It never stops. And it is not something you can give up either. The Royals are chained to their duties. Think of *Groundhog Day* . . . in a Palace.

Then there is the psychological effect of everyone around them bobbing and bowing and generally grovelling to you. I was only a little Lady Clerk, but even I caught red-carpet fever .

So should we continue to bob and bow to them? Is this the natural order of our relationship with the Royals? It was a friend who read history who put forward an alternative theory, one that was adopted by leaders of the Whig Party some two hundred years ago. Members of the Royal Family, it was mooted, were creatures of convenience, not objects of reverence. Yes, we should bob and bow, but we shouldn't take the Royal Family too seriously, even if some of them take themselves seriously. It is not their fault. They are shaped by the world in which they live. So there you have it. The Royals serve a purpose, but reverence is for gods, not people. Unless, like me, you can't help yourself worshipping Prince Charles.

Author's Note

The experience of relaying my stories to my co-author Nicholas Monson has been wonderfully therapeutic. Creating this record of experience makes me feel that I have saved a piece of history. Of course, I cannot imagine that the neurotic blatherings of a Bridget Jones at the Palace will be of any interest to solemn historians. But I hope it has given you, my patient reader, an insight into life amongst the Royals during this most extraordinary period of their history. And I hope you have enjoyed sharing the unalloyed pleasure it gave an astonished girl from rural Shropshire.

I have disguised a few of the characters and one or two are amalgams of different people – Geraldine and Esther, for instance. I could hardly reveal the true names of those colleagues who once so brilliantly instructed me in the art of a good BJ, now, could I? Anyway, I hope the lesson from St James's Palace is as instructive for some of you girls out there as it was for me.

Equally, I have changed the names of my two Palace lovers. I believe one remains in Royal service. I have also changed the name of three of my lovers outside the Palace – Eddie the entrepreneur, Alastair my lovely Australian and Carlo the Italian stallion. You know who you are, boys!

As far as the Royal gossip contained herein goes, apart from the stories which happened to me personally or personally to someone who related it to me directly, I have only included those names that have already been printed in other Royal books, in particular *The Real Diana* by Lady Colin Campbell. I have excluded those not already published. Lady Colin Campbell is remarkably well connected and her research is thorough. The sources she quotes are impeccable. Though derided and pilloried for her initial revelations about the Princess of Wales back in 1992, virtually all of her Royal revelations have since been proven to be true.

For those who are seeking a further perspective on this extraordinary recent period of Royal history, I recommend you also read the Royal books by Gyles Brandreth, Jonathan Dimbleby, Penny Junor and Christopher Wilson. Christopher was particularly encouraging with this book, and I thank him wholeheartedly. Those who want Princess Diana's personal perspective on her marriage should look no further than the book by Andrew Morton.

Sarah
Goodall
May 2008